Navigate

A Professional Aviator's Notebook

James Albright

Navigate

A Professional Aviator's Notebook

James Albright

Acknowledgements

Thanks to the thousands of readers at Code7700.com for their part in this notebook through their many inputs. Thanks especially to my partners at the site, Steven Foltz and Ivan Luciani. Without them, this book would never have happened.

Also by James Albright

Aviate: A Professional Pilot's Notebook

Equity Airlines

International Operations

Flight Lessons 1: Basic Flight

Flight Lessons 2: Advanced Flight

Flight Lessons 3: Experience

Flight Lessons 4: Leadership

Flight Lessons 5: People

Fly By Wired

The Brothers Bellum

An Introduction to a Professional Aviator's Notebook

With the help of over 30,000 professional pilots visiting and commenting on the contents of www.code7700.com, I've amassed hundreds of procedures, techniques, and "hacks" to make flying easier and safer. As I approach retirement, the question I keep getting asked is what will happen to this reservoir of knowledge? The answer is this series of books:

1. Aviate – a collection of procedures and techniques for keeping the airplane flying in the middle of the air, avoiding the edges of the air. The edges are defined as the ground, the ocean, obstacles, and extraterrestrial space.
2. Navigate – a collection of procedures and techniques for keeping the airplane headed to where it needs to be, flying from Point A to Point B. Point B doesn't have to be the intended destination. Ideally it will be a suitable runway, but it could be someplace to set the airplane down so everyone on board can walk (or swim) away safely.
3. Communicate – a collection of procedures and techniques for letting everyone else know what you are doing and what you need and collecting information to help you do what you need to do.
4. Relate – a collection of procedures and techniques to make sure everyone is working together as a team, how to lead the team, and how to understand and preserve the physiology and psychology of everyone on the team.
5. International Ops – a capstone of the previous volumes, focusing on the procedures and techniques dealing with international operations.

Each book is intended not only as a reference, but an introduction to the topic with a mixture of technical and practical explanations. As reference, the topics are presented alphabetically, but you don't need to start at the beginning, each chapter stands alone.

The usual caveats and disclaimers

Please note: Any aircraft mentioned in this book have no affiliation or connection whatsoever with this book, and the manufacturers do not review, endorse, or approve any of the content. As a result, they are not responsible or liable for your use of any materials or information obtained in this book.

Always remember that I am just a pilot. I try to give you the facts from the source materials but maybe I got it wrong or maybe I'm out of date. You should always follow your primary guidance (aircraft manuals, government regulations, etc.) before listening to me.

Table of Contents

Coordinates

Why is a better understanding of coordinates important to modern aviators when not too long ago it was only needed by international travelers? GPS. If you navigate by GPS, you should understand what exactly makes up a coordinate.

The History of Lines of Latitude and Longitude

Lines of latitude and longitude began crisscrossing our world view in ancient times, at least three centuries before the birth of Christ. By A.D. 150, the cartographer and astronomer Ptolemy had plotted them on the twenty-seven maps of his first world atlas.

The Equator marked the zero-degree parallel of latitude for Ptolemy. He did not choose it arbitrarily but took it on higher authority from his predecessors, who had derived it from nature while observing the motions of the heavenly bodies. The sun, moon, and planets pass almost directly overhead at the Equator. Likewise, the Tropic of Cancer and the Tropic of Capricorn, two other famous parallels, assume their positions at the sun's command. They mark the northern and southern boundaries of the sun's apparent motion over the course of the year.

Ptolemy was free, however, to lay his prime meridian, the zero-degree longitude line, wherever he liked. He chose to run it through the Fortunate Islands (now called the Canary & Madeira Islands) off the northwest coast of Africa. As the world turns, any line drawn from pole to pole may serve as well as any other for a starting line of reference. The placement of the prime meridian is a purely political decision.

Source: Sobel, p. 2

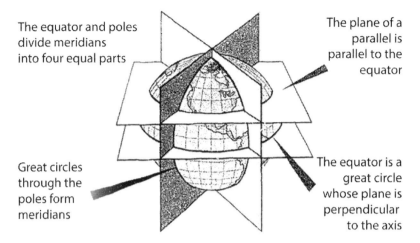

The equator and poles divide meridians into four equal parts

The plane of a parallel is parallel to the equator

Great circles through the poles form meridians

The equator is a great circle whose plane is perpendicular to the axis

Figure: Planes of the Earth, from AFM 51-40, figure 2-3.

Great Circles

For most navigational purposes, the earth is assumed to be a perfect sphere, although in reality it is not. Measured at the equator, the earth is approximately 6,887.91 nautical miles in diameter, while the polar diameter is approximately 6,864.57 nautical miles, and this difference may be used to express the ellipticity of the earth.

A great circle is defined as a circle on the surface of a sphere whose center and radius are those of the sphere itself. The arc of a great circle is the shortest distance between two points on a sphere, just as a straight line is the shortest distance between two points on a plane.

Circles on the surface of the sphere other than great circles may be defined as small circles. A small circle is a circle on the surface of the earth whose center and/or radius are not that of the sphere. A special set of small circles, called latitude, is discussed later.

Source: AFM 51-40, pp. 2-1 to 2-2

From a pilot's perspective, a great circle is simply the shortest route between two points on the globe.

Latitude

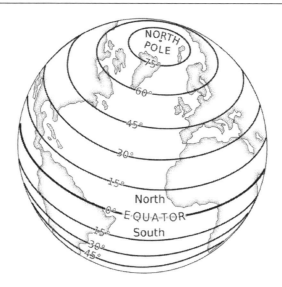

Figure: Latitude lines, from Wikimedia Commons, Pearson Scott Foresman.

The zero degree parallel of latitude is fixed by the laws of nature.

Any sailor worth his salt can gauge his latitude well enough by the length of the day, or by the height of the sun or known guide stars above the horizon. Christopher Columbus followed a straight path across the Atlantic when he "sailed the parallel" on his 1492 journey, and the technique would doubtless have carried him to the Indies had not the Americas intervened.

Source: Sobel, p. 2

Once a day, the earth rotates on its north-south axis which is terminated by the two poles. The equator is constructed at the midpoint of this axis at right angles to it. A great circle drawn through the poles is called a meridian, and an infinite number of great circles may be constructed in this manner. Each meridian is divided into four quadrants by the equator and the poles. Since a circle is arbitrarily divided into 360 degrees, each of those quadrants therefore contains 90 degrees.

Take a point on one of these meridians 30 degrees north of the equator. Through this point pass a plane perpendicular to the north-south axis of rotation. This plane will be parallel to the plane of the equator as shown [in the figure] and will intersect the earth in a small circle called a parallel or parallel of latitude. The particular parallel of latitude chosen is 30° N, and every point on this parallel will be at 30° N. In the same way, other parallels can be constructed at any desired latitude, such as 10 degrees, 40 degrees, etc.

Source: AFM 51-40, p. 2-3

Longitude

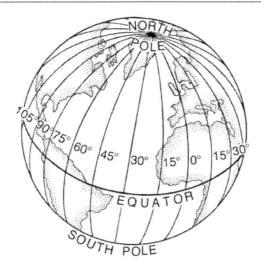

Figure: Longitude lines, from Wikimedia Commons, Pearson Scott Foresman.

To learn one's longitude at sea, one needs to know what time it is aboard ship and also the time at the home port or another place of known longitude. Since the earth takes 24 hours to complete one full revolution of three hundred sixty degrees, one hour marks one twenty-fourth of a spin, or fifteen degrees. And so each hour's time difference between the ship and the starting point marks a progress of fifteen degrees of longitude to the east or west. Every day at sea, when the navigator resets his ship's clock to local noon when the sun reaches its highest point in the sky, and then consults the home-port clock, every hour's discrepancy between them translates into another fifteen degrees of longitude.

Those same fifteen degrees of longitude also correspond to a distance traveled. At the Equator, where the girth of the Earth is greatest, fifteen degrees stretch fully one thousand miles. North or south of that line, however, the mileage value of each degree decreases.

Source: Sobel, p. 2

The latitude of a point can be shown as 20° N or 20° S of the equator, but there is no way of knowing whether one point is east or west or another. This difficulty is resolved by the use of the other component of the coordinate system, longitude, which is the measurement of this east-west distance.

There is not, as with latitude, a natural starting point for numbering, such as the equator. The solution has been to select an arbitrary starting point. A great many places have been used, but when the English speaking people began to make charts, they chose the meridian through their principal observatory in Greenwich, England, as the origin for counting longitude, and this point has now been accepted by most other countries of the world. This Greenwich meridian is sometimes called the prime or first meridian, though actually it is the zero meridian. Longitude is counted east and west from this meridian, through 180 degrees.

Source: AFM 51-40, p. 2-4

References

Air Force Manual (AFM) 51-40, Air Navigation, Flying Training, 1 July 1973

Sobel, Dava, "Longitude: The true story of a long genius who solved the greatest scientific problem of his time," Thomas Allen & Sons Canada Limited, Markham, Ontario, 1995

Course Reversal Techniques

In the United States it is common practice to use holding pattern procedures when flying a procedure turn, what is more properly called a course reversal under ICAO. The U.S. procedures will not always work in other parts of the world. You can use those same procedures in the United States now, just keep in mind you have to limit your entry speeds to 200 knots and you may not be able to fly as fast during some of the maneuvering.

You may have flown internationally for years not knowing the difference between a U.S. procedure turn and an ICAO course reversal. You probably got away with it too, since we hardly ever fly full procedures. And even when you do, chances are you can get away with using U.S. FAA procedures. But not always. An Air Force crew was violated for entering the 45°/180° course reversal shown here just as they had been taught, using U.S. FAA procedures. They were cleared direct to the NDB and for the approach. They hit the NDB and turned right. And they were violated. What would you have done?

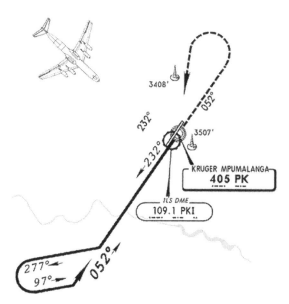

Kruger Course Reversal Example

45°/180° Procedure Turn

45°/180° procedure turn starts at a facility or fix and consists of:

1. a straight leg with track guidance. This straight leg may be timed or may be limited by a radial or DME distance;

2. a 45° turn;

3. a straight leg without track guidance. This straight leg is timed. It is:

a. 1 minute from the start of the turn for Category A and B aircraft; and

b. 1 minute 15 seconds from the start of the turn for Category C, D and E aircraft; and

4. a 180° turn in the opposite direction to intercept the inbound track.

The 45°/180° procedure turn is an alternative to the 80°/260° procedure turn [b] below] unless specifically excluded.

Source: ICAO Document 8168, Vol 1 §5, ¶3.2.2.3 a

Unlike the U.S. FAA Standard Procedure Turn, also known as the 45°/180° Procedure Turn, the straight leg without track guidance is timed under ICAO procedures. The timing is mandatory unless a DME limit is given.

In the Agana, Guam (PGUM) example, the procedure begins with course 242° and executing the left turn so as to remain with 10 nm of the VOR. Unlike U.S. procedures, the 45° leg is timed.

45°/180° procedure turn, from ICAO Document 8168, Vol 1 Figure II-5-3-1.A.

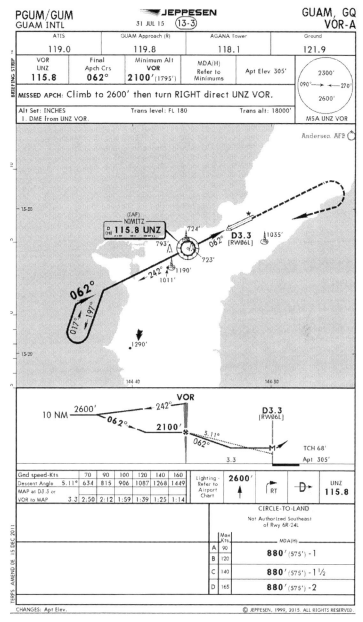

Figure: Agana VOR-A, from Jeppesen Airway Manual, page PGUM 13-3, 31 Jul
2015. Reproduced with permission of Jeppesen Sanderson, Inc.

80°/260° Procedure Turn

> 80°/260° procedure turn starts at a facility or fix and consists of:
>
> 1. a straight leg with track guidance. This straight leg may be timed or may be limited by a radial or DME distance;
>
> 2. an 80° turn;
>
> 3. a 260° turn in the opposite direction to intercept the inbound track.
>
> The 80°/260° procedure turn is an alternative to the 45°/180° procedure turn [a) above] unless specifically excluded.
>
> Source: ICAO Document 8168, Vol 1 §5, ¶3.2.2.3 b

The only advantage of the 80°/260 over the 45°/180° is that it gets you pointed back to the runway more quickly. But there is a big disadvantage: adjusting for wind, the only correction available to you is bank angle. If the wind is strong enough, you could find yourself blown onto the non-protected side before completing your turn inbound. The ICAO says you can use a 45°/180° procedure turn as an alternative to the 80°/260° procedure turn unless specifically excluded. You would be wise to do that if there is any kind of wind.

I've never seen a published 80°/260° Procedure Turn in the United States and most places that had them long ago changed to racetrack, base turn, or standard procedure turns.

80°/260° procedure turn, ICAO Document 8168, Vol 1 Figure II-5-3-1.B.

In the example shown you should avail yourself of the full 3 minutes outbound allowed to give yourself enough time to intercept the course inbound. If the winds are from the south the 80°/260° should work well. If the winds are from the north, the 45°/180° may be a better choice.

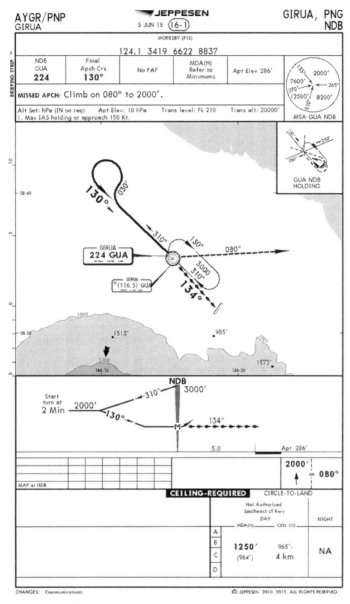

Base Turn

Base turn consists of:

1. a specified outbound track and timing or DME distance from a facility; followed by

2. a turn to intercept the inbound track.

The outbound track and/or the timing may be different for the various categories of aircraft. Where this is done, separate procedures are published.

Source: ICAO Document 8168, Vol 1 §5, ¶3.2.2.3 c

I asked to fly the entire procedure, just to say I did, but they wouldn't have any of that and we ended up with vectors to final. Notice the alternative procedure, in this case, allows you to enter from the holding pattern.

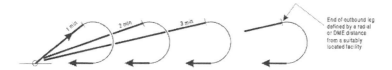

Base turn, from ICAO Document 8168, Vol 1 Figure II-5-3-1.C.

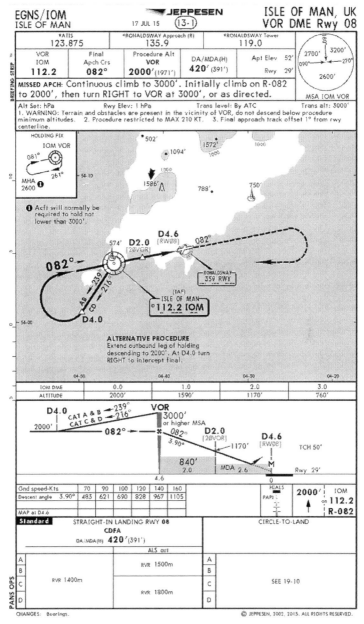

Isle of Man VOR/DME Rwy 08, from Jeppesen Airway Manual, Page EGNS 13-1, 17 Jul 2015. Reproduced with permission of Jeppesen Sanderson, Inc.

Racetrack

A racetrack procedure consists of:

1. a turn from the inbound track through 180° from overhead the facility or fix on to the outbound track, for 1, 2 or 3 minutes; followed by

2. a 180° turn in the same direction to return to the inbound track.

As an alternative to timing, the outbound leg may be limited by a DME distance or intersecting radial/bearing.

Source: ICAO Document 8168, Vol 1 §5, ¶3.2.3

The ground track is flown as depicted.

Of the various course reversals, this one may seem the easiest to execute and it probably is. But take care with the entry, it could get you in trouble. More about that right now . . .

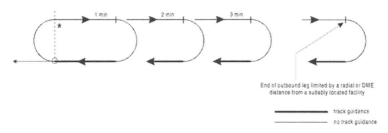

End of outbound leg limited by a radial or DME distance from a suitably located facility

——————— track guidance
- - - - - - - - - no track guidance

Racetrack, from ICAO Document 8168, Vol 1 Figure II-4-3-1.D.

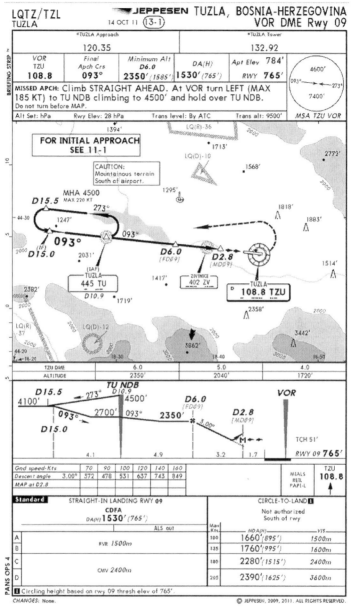

Tuzla VOR/DME Rwy 09. Reproduced with permission of Jeppesen Sanderson, Inc.

Entry Procedures

Course Reversal entry procedures are not the same as in the United States; the difference can get you into trouble. You need to understand the 30° entry sector, the base turn exception to the 30° entry sector, and racetrack entry procedures.

45°/180°, 80°/260°, and base turn entry procedures

Unless the procedure specifies particular entry restrictions, reversal procedures shall be entered from a track within ±30° of the outbound track of the reversal procedure. However, for base turns, where the ±30° direct entry sector does not include the reciprocal of the inbound track, the entry sector is expanded to include it.

Source: ICAO Document 8168, Vol 1 §5, ¶3.3.1

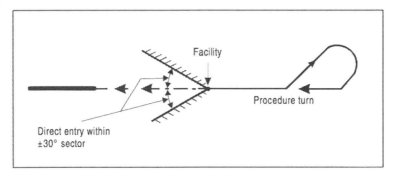

Direct entry to procedure turn, ICAO Document 8168, Vol 1, figure I-5-3-2.

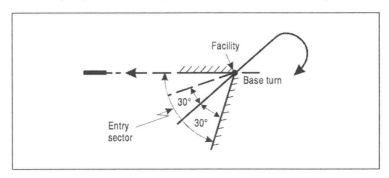

Direct entry to base turn, ICAO Document 8168, Vol 1, figure I-5-3-3.

You've got to be within these entry sectors to be permitted to begin the 45°/180°, 80°/260°, or base turn procedure. What if you aren't?

Most of these procedures have a holding pattern nearby and ICAO Document 8168, Vol 1, figure I-4-3-4, states "arrivals from this sector must enter the holding prior to the reversal procedure." What if there isn't a holding pattern depicted? I would request "maneuvering airspace" opposite the course reversal so that I could maneuver the aircraft into the entry sector. That's what the C-141 crew mentioned earlier should have done.

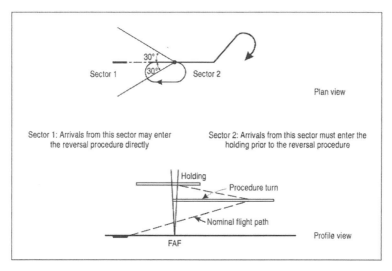

Omnidirectional arrival holding associated with reversal procedure, ICAO Document 8168, Vol 1, figure I-5-3-4.

Racetrack entry procedures

Normally a racetrack procedure is used when aircraft arrive overhead the fix from various directions. In these cases, aircraft are expected to enter the procedure in a manner similar to that prescribed for a holding procedure entry with the following considerations:

a. offset entry from Sector 2 shall limit the time on the 30° offset track to 1 min 30 s, after which the pilot is expected to turn to a heading parallel to the outbound track for the remainder of the outbound time. If the outbound time is only 1 min, the time on the 30° offset track shall be 1 min also;

b. parallel entry shall not return directly to the facility without first intercepting the inbound track when proceeding to the final segment of the approach procedure; and

c. all manoeuvring shall be done in so far as possible on the manoeuvring side of the inbound track.

Source: ICAO Document 8168, Vol 1 §5, ¶3.2.3.2

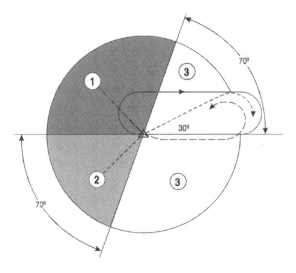

Entry Sectors, from ICAO Document 8168, Vol 1 Figure I-6-1-2.

References

ICAO Doc 8168 - Aircraft Operations - Vol I - Flight Procedures, Procedures for Air Navigation Services, International Civil Aviation Organization, Sixth Edition, 2018

Jeppesen Airway Manual

Departure Obstacle Avoidance Techniques

What does departure obstacle avoidance have to do with navigation? While it seems the primary task is to outclimb the obstacles – a performance problem – the only way of avoiding some obstacles is to fly around them – a navigation problem.

There are at least three strategies for dealing with airport departure obstacles, each valid in its own way but each with limitations that must be understood to maximize existing safety margins. And therein lies the problem: the rules are spread across at least seven FARs, two ICAO documents, a U.S. Advisory Circular and the United States Standard for Terminal Instrument Procedures (TERPS), also known as Federal Aviation Administration Order 8260.3B. But once you understand the competing regulatory issues you can dispassionately sift through the strategies and pick one that works for you. That process begins with looking at how the performance coming out of your airplane gets reported to you in your Airplane Flight Manual (AFM).

Airplane Takeoff Climb Performance

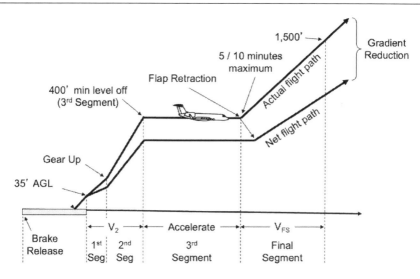

Net versus actual flight path

The takeoff performance data in your AFM may not be designed as you might think.

First off, the takeoff path of the airplane must assume the loss of the critical engine. The U.S. rules for transport category aircraft are covered by 14 CFR 25, Section 25.111. Internationally, these rules are covered by ICAO Annex 8, Part IIIA, Paragraph 2.2.3.

Secondly, the "net" takeoff flight path reflected by AFM performance data represents the actual takeoff flight path reduced at each point by a gradient of climb equal to 0.8 percent for two-engine airplanes, 0.9 percent for three-engine airplanes, and 1.0 percent for four-engine airplanes.

These reductions are found in 14 CFR 25.115. ICAO Annex 6 requires a net takeoff path be used. In either case, these numbers reflect a margin of safety. A margin of 0.8 percent for a two-engine aircraft doesn't sound like much and it isn't: just $(0.008)(6076) = 48.6$ ft/nm. There is, however, another margin to consider.

Obstacle Departure Procedures are Based on All Engines Operating (AEO)

Unlike aircraft takeoff performance data, obstacle departure procedures are designed assuming AEO. The U.S. rules are given in TERPS, Volume 1, paragraph 201: "criteria are predicated on normal aircraft operations for considering obstacle clearance requirements." The International Civil Aviation Organization (ICAO) has a similar provision in Document 8168, Volume II.

Both ICAO and TERPS specify a minimum climb gradient for all departure procedures. The ICAO calls this the minimum Procedure Design Gradient (PDG) and says it can never be less than 3.3 percent. TERPS calls this the minimum Climb Gradient (CG) and says it can never be less than 200 ft/nm. These values are about the same, since $(200/6076) = 0.033$ and that is another way of writing 3.3 percent.

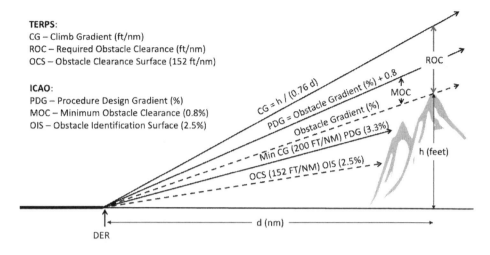

ICAO and TERPS climb gradient comparison

ICAO and TERPS also specify a surface below the aircraft's path that identifies a zone where obstacles cannot penetrate without having to change the climb gradient. (There is an exception for low, close-in obstacles, but more on that later.) The ICAO Obstacle Identification Surface (OIS) starts at the Departure End of Runway (DER) and inclines upward by 2.5 percent. The TERPS Obstacle Clearance Surface (OCS) also starts at the DER and inclines upward by 152 ft/nm. The values are about the same, since (152/6076) = 0.025 and that is another way of writing 2.5 percent.

If you take the minimum climb gradient and subtract the obstacle surface you get the safety margin between the two. Under ICAO the Minimum Obstacle Clearance (MOC) is 3.3 - 2.5 = 0.8 percent. Mathematically, MOC = (0.008 x d), where d is the distance from the DER expressed in feet. Note that this value does not change with the climb gradient. MOC is (0.008 x 6076 ft/nm) = 48.6 ft/nm, no matter how steep your climb gradient is.

Under TERPS the Required Obstacle Clearance (ROC) is 24 percent of the Climb Gradient. Mathematically, ROC = (0.24 x CG). For the minimum climb gradient of 200 ft/nm, you have an ROC of (0.24 x

200) = 48 ft/nm. But as you steepen your climb, you also increase your ROC.

If an obstacle, other than a low, close-in obstacle (more on that later) penetrates the OIS / OCS, the procedure's climb gradient must be raised to preserve the MOC or ROC. Under ICAO, the 0.8 percent MOC is added to the gradient created by the obstacle. If, for example, a line from the DER to the obstacle is 5 percent, the Procedure Design Gradient is raised to 5.8 percent.

Under TERPS, the Climb Gradient is adjusted to the following formula: CG = h / (0.76 x d) where h is the height of the obstacle in feet and d is the distance from the DER in nautical miles.

Let's say, for example, we have an obstacle that is 1500 feet above and 5 nm (30,380 feet) away from the DER. The obstacle has a gradient of (1500/30380) = 0.0494, or 4.94 percent. The ICAO MOC is always 0.8 percent so our PDG is 4.94 + 0.8 = 5.74 percent. Our height above the obstacle would be (0.0574 x 30380) - 1500 = 244 feet. Under TERPS, the climb gradient is h / (0.76 d), or 1500 / (0.76 x 5) = 395 feet per nm. (That's 6.5 percent, much higher than the ICAO PDG.) So our ROC = (0.24 x 395) = 95 ft/nm. At 5 nm, our height above the obstacle will be (5 x 95) = 475 feet, almost double the ICAO margin.

Low, Close-In Obstacles

U.S. TERPS, not too long ago, completely ignored "low, close-in" obstacles, but has become more specific. As of the 2024 version of TERPS (FAA Order 8260.3G):

> d. Takeoff obstacle(s). These include low close-in and takeoff minimums obstacles as applicable. Both low close-in and takeoff obstacles must be within the ICA.

> (1) Obstacles are considered "low, close-in obstacles" when they require a CG greater than standard to an altitude of 200 feet or less above DER elevation. These obstacles are allowed to

penetrate the 40:1 OCS provided they are identified as described in paragraph 13-2-2 (legacy, see Order 8260.46).

(2) Obstacles are considered "Takeoff minimums obstacles" when they require a CG greater than standard to an altitude greater than 200 feet above the DER elevation. These obstacles are allowed to penetrate the 40:1 OCS when they are identified as described in paragraph 13-2-2.

Source: FAA Order 8260.3G, para. 13-1-1

ICA is "Initial Climb Area." FAA Order 3260.36 allows for "Legacy" procedures when applied to "a previous standard."

(2) Legacy: When takeoff obstacle notes are required using paragraph 13-2-2, a DER crossing height will not be evaluated and apply Order 8260.46 for documentation.

Source: FAA Order 8260.3G, para. 13-2-2

It appears that if you are going to have a "low, close-in" obstacle, it will be accounted for in the climb gradient or there has to be a note about it.

In either case, a note is published to help us identify and plan to avoid these obstacles, but these are rarely written well enough to help the pilot.

Consider, for example, the note associated with Runway 33 at Bob Hope Airport, Burbank, California (KBUR). There are "multiple trees, poles, terrain, buildings, road beginning 33' from DER, 30' right of centerline, up to 100' AGL." For anyone who has used that runway, finding a 100' AGL target 33' from DER would seem an easy task, except that it doesn't exist. The poorly worded sentence provides the pilot with very little useful information.

BURBANK, CA
BOB HOPE (BUR)
TAKEOFF MINIMUMS AND (OBSTACLE) DEPARTURE PROCEDURES
AMDT 5 28JUL11 (11209) (FAA)
TAKEOFF MINIMUMS:
Rwy 8, std. w/min. climb of 410' per NM to 5000.
Rwy 15, std. w/min. climb of 335' per NM to 5000.
Rwy 26, std. w/min. climb of 325' per NM to 5000.
Rwy 33, std. w/min. climb of 550' per NM to 5000' or 600-2¼ w/min. climb of 300' per NM to 5000.
DEPARTURE PROCEDURE:
Rwys 8, 15, climbing right turn direct VNY VOR/DME.
Rwy 26, climb direct VNY VOR/DME.
Rwy 33, Climbing left turn direct VNY VOR/DME.
All aircraft continue climb in VNY holding pattern (SE, left turns, 295° inbound) to cross VNY VOR/DME at or above 5100,
then westbound on V326 to GINNA or eastbound on V186 to DARTS.
TAKEOFF OBSTACLE NOTES:
Rwy 8, multiple trees, poles, and buildings beginning 124' from DER, 42' right of centerline, up to 65' AGL/745' MSL.
Multiple trees, buildings and poles beginning 278' from DER, 73' left of centerline, up to 56' AGL/746' MSL.
Rwy 15, multiple trees, buildings, poles, and blast fence beginning 50' from DER, 2' right of centerline, up to 65' AGL/762'
MSL.
Multiple trees, buildings, poles, blast fence beginning 185' from DER, 53' left of centerline, up to 108' AGL/777' MSL.
Rwy 26, multiple trees, poles, transmission towers, buildings, and roads, and terrain beginning 26' from DER, 4' right of
centerline, up to 145' AGL/731' MSL.
Multiple trees, poles, transmission towers, railroad, and buildings beginning 302' from DER, 437' left of centerline, up to 117'
AGL/846' MSL.
Rwy 33, multiple trees, poles, terrain, buildings, road beginning 33' from DER, 30' right of centerline, up to 100' AGL/1333'
MSL.
Multiple trees, poles, buildings, antenna, railroad, and blast fence beginning 97' from DER, 11' left of centerline, up to 50'
AGL/878' MSL.

KBUR Takeoff Minimums and Obstacle Departure Procedures, FAA SW3TO, 3 Oct 2024

The FAA offers a digital obstacle file for the United States at http://www.faa.gov/air_traffic/flight_info/aeronav/digital_products /dof/ but these are very large, cumbersome, and take a good computer to really digest. If you wanted to try, you would see that the file covering KBUR is 790 pages long and includes these two gems:

06-030661 O US CA BURBANK 34 12 56.17N 118 21 50.28W POLE 1 00050 00846 R 2 C U A 2013106

06-001786 O US CA BURBANK 34 12 52.00N 118 21 41.00W POLE 1 00048 00831 L 1 A U C 2014152

So if you were able to find these two obstacles out of the thousands given, and if you plotted them, you would see exactly where two of your low, close-in obstacles are. The most critical appears to be 53 feet above and 812 feet from the DER, almost on centerline.

TERPS Vol 4 Para 1.6
Initial Climb Area
500' of centerline at DER
15° splay to 2 nm

DOF 06-030661
1580' from DER
68' above DER
16' above 200 ft/nm
28' above OCS

DOF 06-001786
812' from DER
53' above DER
26' above 200 ft/nm
33' above OCS

Two low, close-in obstacles at KBUR (Google earth image)

Is this a problem? Let's say it is raining, the weather is above standard and you are permitted to leave with the minimum climb gradient of 300 ft/nm to 5,000 feet. That comes to 300/6076 = 0.0494, or 4.94 percent. If the maximum weight for this climb gradient requires a ground run following an engine failure that equals the runway available, you can expect to cross the DER at 15 feet (for aircraft that have wet runway performance data). A 4.94 percent gradient across a distance of 812 feet results in a climb of (0.0494) (812) = 40 feet. If you cross the DER at 15 feet that means you are at 40 + 15 = 55 feet when you cross the pole marked as DOF 06-001786, which is 53 feet above the DER. You have a clearance of only 2 feet. A call to the airport manager might be useful but without a very good database of terrain and obstacles, the only way to guarantee low, close-in obstacle clearance is to cross the DER at or above 200 feet.

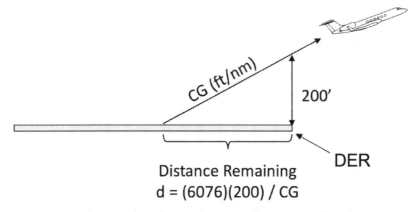

Distance Remaining

$$d = (6076)(200) / CG$$

Low, close-in Obstacle Avoidance, the "Brute Force" method

If, for example, your planned weight at Burbank produces an engine-out climb gradient of 600 feet/nm, you will need to have at least (6076 x 200) / 600 = 2025 feet beyond your planned takeoff run to guarantee you clear any low, close-in obstacles.

Of course, giving up such a large chunk of runway can be unnecessarily prohibitive if the low, close-in obstacles aren't really that close in. A sound strategy for dealing with departure obstacles must consider all obstacles, even those TERPS and the ICAO Procedures for Air Navigation Services (PAN OPS) choose to ignore with nothing more than a nebulous note. Unfortunately, most strategies are blind to the issue.

Strategy: OEI Performance for AEO Procedures

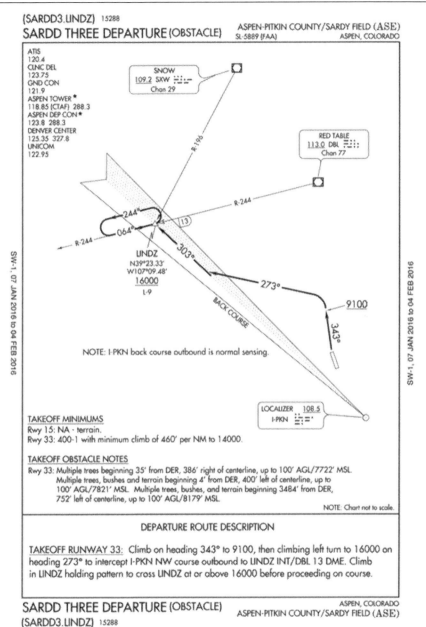

(SARDD3.LINDZ) 15288

SARDD THREE DEPARTURE (OBSTACLE)

ASPEN-PITKIN COUNTY/SARDY FIELD (ASE)
SL-5889 (FAA)   ASPEN, COLORADO

ATIS 120.4
CLNC DEL 123.75
GND CON 121.9
ASPEN TOWER * 118.85 (CTAF) 288.3
ASPEN DEP CON * 123.8 288.3
DENVER CENTER 125.35 327.8
UNICOM 122.95

SNOW
109.2 SXW
Chan 29

RED TABLE
113.0 DBL
Chan 77

R·196

R·244

244°

064°

R·244

13

LINDZ
N39°23.33'
W107°09.48'
16000
L-9

303°

273°

9100

343°

BACK COURSE

NOTE: I-PKN back course outbound is normal sensing.

LOCALIZER 108.5
I-PKN

TAKEOFF MINIMUMS
Rwy 15: NA - terrain.
Rwy 33: 400-1 with minimum climb of 460' per NM to 14000.

TAKEOFF OBSTACLE NOTES
Rwy 33: Multiple trees beginning 35' from DER, 386' right of centerline, up to 100' AGL/7722' MSL.
Multiple trees, bushes and terrain beginning 4' from DER, 400' left of centerline, up to
100' AGL/7821' MSL. Multiple trees, bushes, and terrain beginning 3484' from DER,
752' left of centerline, up to 100' AGL/8179' MSL.

NOTE: Chart not to scale.

DEPARTURE ROUTE DESCRIPTION

TAKEOFF RUNWAY 33: Climb on heading 343° to 9100, then climbing left turn to 16000 on
heading 273° to intercept I-PKN NW course outbound to LINDZ INT/DBL 13 DME. Climb
in LINDZ holding pattern to cross LINDZ at or above 16000 before proceeding on course.

SARDD THREE DEPARTURE (OBSTACLE)
(SARDD3.LINDZ) 15288

ASPEN, COLORADO
ASPEN-PITKIN COUNTY/SARDY FIELD (ASE)

SW-1, 07 JAN 2016 to 04 FEB 2016

SW-1, 07 JAN 2016 to 04 FEB 2016

Aspen-Pitkin County/Sardy Field SARDD THREE Departure, FAA SL-5889
NOT FOR NAVIGATION USE © Jeppesen Sanderson, Inc. 2016

Not too many years ago most pilots would tell you that the only way to legally and safely depart a mountainous airport was to use your aircraft's OEI performance charts to meet the AEO departure procedure's gradient.

In the Gulfstream G450, for example, the AFM restricts us to only 47,000 lbs gross weight when leaving Aspen on the SARDD THREE Departure at 20°C and 7,000 feet pressure altitude, just barely enough to fly for an hour but without any kind of safe fuel reserve. Armed with that information, the pilot would be forced to wait out the weather.

This strategy grounds the aircraft for obstacles that are miles away laterally and perhaps gives too generous a vertical margin as well. While they are maximizing their distant obstacle clearance, the published obstacle departure procedures do not consider low, close-in obstacles when establishing weather minimums or minimum climb gradients.

Strategy: Reduce Vertical Margins

Another technique is to keep the net takeoff path safety margin (between 0.8% and 1.0%, depending on number of engines) and remove the TERPS 24% ROC or the ICAO 0.8% MOC.

In our Aspen example, the required climb gradient is 460 ft/nm. You can remove the ROC by multiplying the CG by (1 – 0.24), which means you only need to climb at (460 x 0.76) = 350 ft/nm. An ICAO departure will also be given in ft/nm but should also have the value given as a percentage. If not, divide the ft/nm by 6,076 feet to get a percentage. An ICAO departure with a 460 ft/nm example becomes (460/6076) = 7.6 percent. To remove the MOC, subtract 0.8. Your new climb gradient target is 7.6 – 0.8 = 6.8%.

Using this strategy can be problematic because there is math involved and the principles can be confusing. Commercially available programs can automate the process but these too, in my opinion, can be confusing. When entering the obstacle departure procedure gradient in one such program, you are asked to note if the procedure is designed under ICAO or TERPS. If you select ICAO, the program subtracts the 0.8 percent MOC from what it calls the "Gross Gradient" to produce a "Net Gradient." Likewise, if you select TERPS, the program multiplies the "Gross Gradient" by (1 - 0.24) to produce a "Net Gradient." Selecting TERPS in our Aspen example yields a takeoff gross weight of 55,720 lbs, an increase of over 8,000 lbs.

Pilots may be misled into thinking they are only giving up their Part 25 net takeoff path and still have the more generous TERPS ROC. This isn't the case. TERPS and ICAO Doc 8168 do not use the terms "Gross Gradient" and "Net Gradient" to describe ROC and MOC. Using this program your climb gradient ends up being equal to the obstacle height plus only the net takeoff flight path factor. (For a two-engine airplane that comes to only 48.6 feet for every nautical mile traveled.)

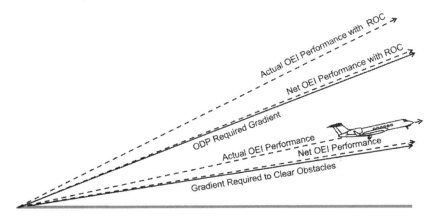

The impact of removing Required Obstacle Clearance from performance computations

Let's say we are dealing with an obstacle right at the maximum allowed without having to increase the climb gradient, which comes to 152 ft/nm. So we could conceivably have an obstacle at 5 miles that is (5)(152) = 760 feet higher than the DER. Loading the airplane to achieve the required climb gradient of 200 ft/nm means we will be at (5)(200) = 1,000 feet plus the net flight path difference of (5)(0.008)(6076) = 243 feet. We would clear the obstacle by (1000 + 243) – 760 = 483 feet. If we elect to load our aircraft with more fuel and passengers so as to achieve only the 152 ft/nm climb gradient, our margin is cut in half.

This strategy also leaves untouched low, close-in obstacles and ignores one more factor in the departure obstacle avoidance problem. We often think of obstacles vertically: we have to out-climb what is directly beneath us. But we must also consider the lateral dimension.

Strategy: Airport Obstacle Analysis

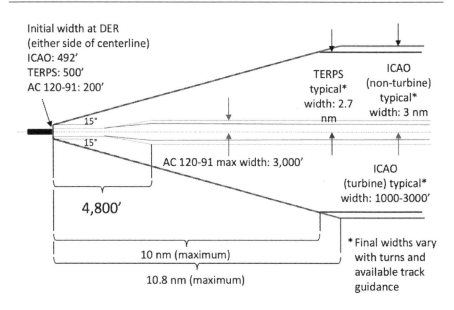

ICAO and TERPS lateral obstacle consideration area comparison

Obstacle departure procedures are designed with very wide lateral tolerances under both ICAO and TERPS. Those minimum climb gradients could be unnecessarily high because they are considering obstacles miles away from course centerline. Perhaps this was necessary back when an aircraft climbing into a cloud deck was lucky to be within a mile of course centerline. What about today? If you have an airplane with an instantaneous readout of "position uncertainty" you very seldom see your airplane more than 0.05 nautical miles off course. That's just three hundred feet! While departure procedures continue to be built off these wide lateral areas, we as pilots are allowed to narrow our gaze if we have a plan.

TERPS procedure construction can be very complicated; the lateral margins vary with distance from the departure end of the runway, relationship to the airport boundary, any turns, and available track guidance. The lateral margin starts at 200 feet either side of runway centerline and quickly expands by thousands of feet to as much as 3 miles. ICAO procedure construction mimics TERPS in many ways and becomes almost as wide. Unless the procedure says otherwise, the climb gradient on these procedures could be based on obstacles that are miles away.

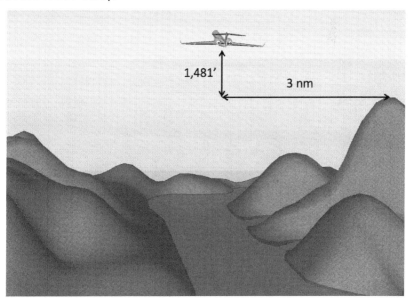

Example vertical / lateral clearances under TERPS at 10 nm

ICAO Annex 6 narrows the lateral margin that must be considered by large (more than 5,700 kg, about 12,500 lbs.) turbine aircraft. The margin can be as tight as 1,000 feet but will be no more than

3,000 feet, depending on course guidance, turns, and distance from the runway. U.S. Advisory Circular 120-91A provides a method of applying an obstacle clearance area that is narrower than the TERPS area and is almost as narrow as the tightest ICAO margin. If an aircraft can maintain course within 3,000 feet the required climb gradient can drop significantly, and that can allow much higher payloads.

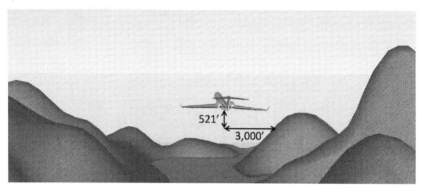

Example vertical / lateral clearances under TERPS at 10 nm

Now let's say we narrow our lateral boundaries to the maximum provided in AC 120-91A, just 3,000 feet from either wing tip. We can increase our payload since we no longer have to out-climb the more distant obstacles and will give up the TERPS 24% ROC.

That means we will cross 3,000 feet abeam another obstacle at an altitude 486 + 35 = 521 feet higher than the obstacle.

Using terrain-mapping software, such as Google-earth, we can draw the Aspen SARDD obstacle departure procedure course line from the DER all the way to the completion of the procedure. We can also diagram the borders of the obstacle clearance area and discover the most challenging obstacles are about a mile right of course.

The published climb gradient is 460 ft/nm, which comes to (460 / 6076) = 7.57 percent. The DER is 7,680 feet. We will reach 14,000 feet in (14000 - 7680) / 460 = 13.74 nm. A theoretical controlling obstacle height can be derived from the TERPS formula: CG = h / (0.76d). Solving for the height of the obstacle we see that h = (0.76)

(d) (CG) = (0.76) (13.74) (460) = 4804 feet. Our obstacle gradient appears to be (4804) / (13.74 x 6076) = 5.75 percent.

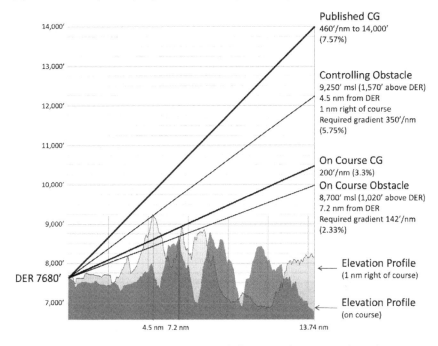

Comparing "on course" versus "1 nm right" SARDD departure obstacles, using Google-earth elevation profile feature

Looking at the chart, Google-earth allows us to trace the departure procedure and produce a terrain elevation profile for an on course departure and for one that deviates to the right inside the TERPS obstacle clearance area until it is 1 nm to the right. Right of course we see an obstacle at 9,250' MSL, 4.5 nm from the DER. This obstacle will be 9250 - 7680 = 1,570 feet above the DER. We can compute its gradient: (1570) / (4.5 x 6076) = 5.74 percent, pretty close to our theoretical gradient.

We can repeat this process for what appears to be the most challenging obstacle if the airplane were to remain precisely on course, a peak of 8,700 feet found 7.2 nm from DER. The peak is 8700 - 7680 = 1,020 feet above DER. The gradient of this obstacle is: (1020) / (7.2 x 6076) = 2.33 percent. This is less than the TERPS 152

43

ft/nm OCS, since (0.0233)(6076) = 142 ft/nm. If you could remain on course you would only need the minimum 200 ft/nm climb gradient.

Of course this kind of analysis is impractical without the benefit of extensive terrain databases and sophisticated software. Many major airlines have been using these systems for years. One such system is available from APG (Aircraft Performance Group, www.flyapg.com), available with a subscription and in many commercial flight-planning services.

```
-- ASE -KASE --            TAKEOFF PERFORMANCE              -- ASE -KASE --
                             GULFSTREAM G-450                    ASPEN, CO
   ELEVATION 7838         RR TAY MK611-8C  ENG        ASPEN-PITKIN CO/SARDY
                             AFM REVISION 40


                        TAKEOFF FLAPS 20.0 DEGREES

   ** RWY33DP    REQUIRES USE OF ATTACHED SPECIAL DEPARTURE PROCEDURE **
   ** RWY33DP1   REQUIRES USE OF ATTACHED SPECIAL DEPARTURE PROCEDURE **
   ** RWY33DP5   REQUIRES USE OF ATTACHED SPECIAL DEPARTURE PROCEDURE **

   RUNWAY         33DP           33DP1          33DP5          33
   TORA(FT)       8006           8006           8006           8006
   TODA(FT)       8006           8006           8006           8006      CLIMB
   ASDA(FT)       8006           8006           8006           8006
   SLOPE(%)      -1.97          -1.97          -1.97          -1.97      LIMIT
   TMP  EPR A/I
   DGC  OFF/ ON            RUNWAY/OBSTACLE LIMIT WEIGHT / V1

   12 1.73     72139/140      72139/140      67399/141      58929/132    74600.
   14 1.73     71900/140      71900/140      67373/141      58905/132    74600.
   16 1.73     70983/139      70983/139      66389/140      58106/131    74600.
   18 1.72     70052/138      70052/138      65330/139      57306/130    74600.
   20  0.71    69279/137      69279/137      64192/138      56367/129    74600.

   HW   +LBS/KT     68             65             56             63
   TW   -LBS/KT    404            405            233            219
   QNH  +LBS/.1    233            232            225            204
   QNH  -LBS/.1    381            381            340            378
   CWL AI ON-LBS   490            340            510            450          0
   WNG+CWL AI-LBS  730            580            930            780          0
   SPLRS INP-LBS/V1 710/ 3       710/ 3         50/ 1         0/ 0
   ASKD INOP-LBS/V1  NA/**        NA/**          NA/**         NA/**
   ACCEL ALT(MSL)  10400          10400          10350         11340

              *** OBSERVE STRUCTURAL LIMITS ***              30Jan16
```

Extract of Aircraft Performance Group example output, G450, Aspen

Plugging our Aspen example into the software yields a significant increase in gross weight, nearly an extra 20,000 lbs which would be enough to make the east coast. The program has the added benefit of factoring in low, close-in obstacles. But this software must also be used with care.

The software sometimes uses unpublished procedures that require additional steps in the event of an engine failure. You would have to file one procedure with the intent of using it under normal conditions. In the event of an engine failure, you may have to reprogram flight management systems or other avionics while letting ATC know you are deviating from the filed procedure. This is certainly possible, but not something you should burden yourself while dealing with an engine failure in mountainous terrain.

The example "33DP" procedure, however, precisely mimics the SARDD THREE procedure. In fact, it is more precise, offering bank angles, a turn based on position and not altitude, and a specific time to begin flap retraction and acceleration. We can, as a result, have confidence that we can load our G450 to 69,279 lbs and: (1) be able to stay clear of all obstacles in the event of an engine failure if we stay within 3,000 feet of our filed and planned course, (2) not have to worry about changing departure procedures in the event of an engine failure, (3) have enough fuel to make it to our destination on the east coast, and (4) avoid all low, close-in obstacles.

There still remains one loose end that the regulations do not address and that most proponents of increasing departure weights fail to recognize. If you limit your weight to the point where OEI performance will meet the AEO climb gradient you know you are okay if you lose an engine because you have (a) insured you clear all obstacles by required vertical and lateral margins, and (b) you do not have to meet the departure procedure climb gradient because you have a failed engine. But what if you don't lose the engine? If your AFM does not have AEO takeoff climb path data, how can you be sure you will meet or exceed the procedure's minimum climb gradient? The FAA is silent on this subject other than to say it is something you need to consider.

An Unspoken Loose End: Meeting All Engines Operating Climb Gradients at Higher Weights

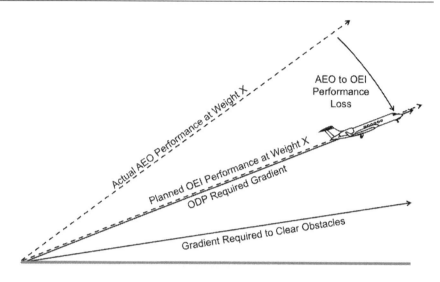

Meeting Obstacle Departure Procedure Gradients with One Engine Inoperative

Let's say, as with the Aspen example, you have an ODP climb gradient of 7.6 percent and elect to reduce that by the TERPS 24 percent ROC, lowering your OEI climb gradient to (1 - 0.24) (7.6) = 5.8 percent. You know you will clear the obstacles because the climb gradient minus the ROC is based on that. Now if you don't lose an engine can you still meet the AEO climb gradient? What follows is my personal theory.

If you are flying a two-engine aircraft you are getting half your climb gradient from each engine. If you lose an engine, your climb gradient decreases by at least 50 percent because you will also have the parasite drag from the wind-milling or seized engine.

It follows, then, that your all-engine climb gradient will be at least double your one-engine climb gradient. Since you've reduced your target climb gradient by a maximum of 24 percent and will have double the climb gradient available, you should be okay.

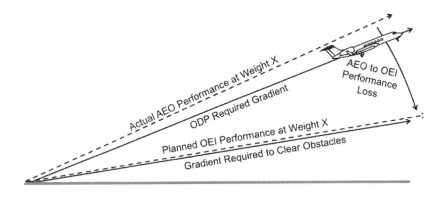

Meeting Obstacle Departure Procedure Gradients with All Engines Operating, Higher Gross weights

Since the loss of an engine in a three-engine aircraft results in 33 percent thrust loss and in a four-engine aircraft results in a 25 percent thrust loss, each aircraft should be okay since the maximum gradient reduction is 24 percent. In the case of our Gulfstream with a 5.8 percent OEI climb gradient, we can guess our AEO climb gradient will be at least 11.6 percent, much higher than the 7.6 obstacle departure procedure requirement.

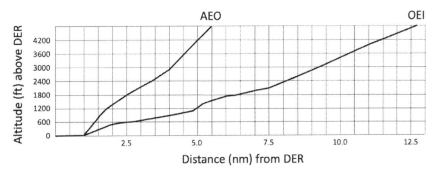

G450, KASE SARDD THREE Departure, 25°C, 63000 lbs
AEO Gradient to 4,200' Above DER: 17.3%
OEI Gradient to 4,200' Above DER: 6.6%

G450 Simulator AEO vs OEI Takeoff Climb Test

I've tested this theory in a few aircraft simulators and it appears to be valid. In the case of a G450 loaded to near APG weights, the AEO takeoff climb performance was 2.5 times greater than with OEI. Armed with this data, I believe my aircraft will meet the required climb gradient with all engines operating, even after I've increased the gross weight to underperform the climb gradient with an engine failed by the TERPS ROC margin. You can test your aircraft by having the simulator operator freeze the gross weight and run an altitude-versus-distance track on two tries, one flying AEO and another with an engine failed at V_1.

Rationalizing Your Margin of Safety

Picking a departure obstacle avoidance strategy is not as straightforward as one might think. Simply choosing to load the aircraft up so the AEO climb gradients are met with OEI does assure distant obstacle clearance and departure procedure compliance, but it does not assure all low, close-in obstacles are avoided. Electing to increase takeoff gross weight erodes the aircraft's vertical margin of safety, but in many cases the combined margins are unnecessarily wide. Using departure obstacle analysis software provides pilots with the ability to narrow the lateral margins so as to discount obstacles that are miles off course with the additional assurance that low, close-in obstacles will be avoided too.

But in every case where the vertical margin is decreased, pilots must understand how much of a margin is left over before they can decide if they are safe "enough." Let's return to our Aspen example to bring theory into practice.

Strategy one

Our G450 was grounded in Aspen with a maximum takeoff weight of 47,000 lbs. We could have flown for an hour and expected to top every obstacle within a few miles by a vertical margin that included the 24% ROC in TERPS as well as the 0.8% net takeoff path. This strategy fails to address low, close-in obstacles.

Strategy two

We could have increased our takeoff weight to 55,720 lbs by removing the TERPS 24% ROC. We still have the 0.8% net takeoff path vertical margin, but this isn't much when looking down on those jagged cliffs north of Aspen. If we found ourselves just 1 nm right of course, we would pass the mountain at 4.5 nm by just 218 feet. This strategy also fails to consider low, close-in obstacles.

Strategy three

Using computerized terrain and obstacle analysis software, we can increase our takeoff weight to over 69,000 lbs, enough to fly to the east coast. We are assured of clearing all low, close-in obstacles, as well as those that are more distant. We must fly much tighter lateral tolerances and will end up with the same reduced vertical margins as found with the second strategy.

Modern aircraft have a way to address the tighter lateral tolerances. Navigating to within 3,000' of course line is pretty easy if you ensure your GPS is operating with a good Receiver Autonomous Integrity Monitoring (RAIM) check and you are able to set your course deviation indicator to give you ample warning of a deviation. All of this electronic wizardry will be for naught, however, if you fail to "step on the good engine" and eliminate all adverse yaw with rudder.

The vertical performance is more problematic. In our Aspen example we are cutting our vertical margin over the most demanding obstacle from 500 to only 218 feet. How much of that margin will remain if you encounter a 10-knot tailwind a few hundred feet in the air? What about a temperature inversion? Finally, if the rudder isn't perfect, any adverse yaw will erode that vertical margin further. Even in ideal conditions, crossing that shear mountaintop with only 218 feet is sure to set off the Enhanced Ground Proximity Warning System.

Picking a Strategy

We are constantly required to weigh "the safest way" with "safe enough." In our Aspen example, there is a tradeoff between how much fuel and how many passengers you can carry versus the vertical clearance you can hope for in the event of an engine failure. I can't pick a strategy for you since you may not be flying the same type of aircraft and your risk tolerances are surely different than mine. But I can offer my strategy as a possible template.

Whenever I go to an unfamiliar airport I run an airport obstacle analysis using APG software. If the charts say I can load up to maximum weight on published procedures, I know I can rely on my airplane's built in performance computer and know I will beat all obstacles while meeting AEO climb gradients. Of course I need to do this for every departure because obstacles (manmade and natural) are constantly changing.

If the software says I am obstacle limited, I will consider the gross weight specified for published procedures only, and even then only as an absolute maximum. The winds and temperature at altitude have to cooperate for this plan to work.

I then brief the crew that we are about to takeoff with reduced vertical and lateral clearances and we will need to do a GPS RAIM check. Then I'll brief the other pilot on what I expect from each of us in the event of an engine failure.

I have been using airport obstacle analysis software for ten years now and I could further say I have been doing so without incident. But I haven't lost an engine in all that time. I do practice in the simulator a lot and my favorite place to practice is Aspen when loaded to APG weights. You need to see that cliff at 4.5 nm getting closer with the EGPWS going crazy to really understand how narrow that 0.8 net takeoff path percent margin really is. My aircraft has synthetic vision and a flight path vector that assures me through it all that I am not going to hit that mountain. It is still unnerving, nonetheless.

Back to Aspen. Five years after our original scenario I was back in Aspen with a new airplane and a new company. Our dispatchers were as despondent as the rest of the crews in the FBO. I loaded up our Gulfstream GV to the weight we needed to make the east coast, which split the difference between the strategy one weight and the maximum strategy three weight found in the APG software application. We departed on time and I am sure there were a few crews stuck on the ground wondering, "are those guys operating recklessly or are we missing something important?"

References

14 CFR 135, Title 14: Aeronautics and Space, Operating Requirements: Commuter and On Demand Operations and Rules Governing Persons on Board Such Aircraft, Federal Aviation Administration, Department of Transportation

Advisory Circular 120-91A, Airport Obstacle Analysis, 1/13/20, U.S. Department of Transportation

Aeronautical Information Manual

ICAO Annex 6 - Operation of Aircraft - Part 1 Commercial Aircraft, International Standards and Recommended Practices, Annex 6 to the Convention on International Civil Aviation, Part I, July 2018

ICAO Annex 8 - Airworthiness of Aircraft, International Standards and Recommended Practices, Annex 8 to the Convention on International Civil Aviation, July 2018

ICAO Doc 8168 - Aircraft Operations - Vol II - Construction of Visual and Instrument Flight Procedures, Procedures for Air Navigation Services, International Civil Aviation Organization, 2006

United States Standard for Terminal Instrument Procedures (TERPS), Federal Aviation Administration 8260.3G, 07/01/2024

Direction

While "direction" seems to be the most basic fundamental of getting from Point A to Point B, there are quite a few pitfalls in terminology. It is quite easy to get by for years and not really understand why some directions are true and others aren't. Well let's put an end to that right now.

The Numerical System for Determining Direction

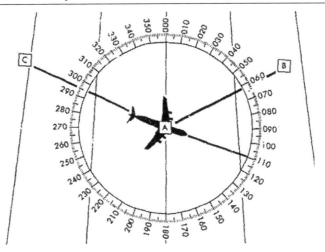

Numerical direction system, (AFM 51-40, figure 2-8)

The numerical system, [shown in the figure], divides the horizon into 360 degrees starting with north at 000 degrees, south 180 degrees, west 270 degrees, and back to north.

The circle, called a compass rose, represents the horizon divided into 360 degrees. The nearly vertical lines in the illustration are meridians of position A passing through 000 degrees and 180 degrees of the compass rose. Position B lies at a true direction of 062 degrees from A, and position C is at a true direction of 295 degrees from A.

Source: AFM 51-40, pages 2-5 to 2-6

True Course

> Course is the intended horizontal direction of travel.
>
> Heading is the horizontal direction in which an aircraft is pointed. Heading is the actual orientation of the longitudinal axis of the aircraft at any instant, while course is the direction intended to be made good.
>
> Track is the actual horizontal direction made by the aircraft over the earth.
>
> Bearing is the horizontal direction of one terrestrial point from another.
>
> Source: AFM 51-40, pages 2-5 to 2-6

A "True Course" is the relative bearing between your course and true north. It is usually found by placing a plotter over a chart and reading the angular difference to any meridian.

Variation

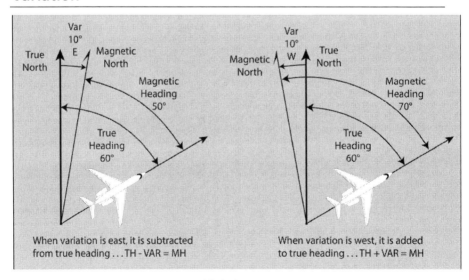

Variation

> The magnetic compass points to magnetic north. The angular difference between true and magnetic north is known as

variation and it changes for different locations on the earth. Variation must be considered when converting true course, true headings, or true winds to magnetic direction.

Source: AFM 51-37, page 1-12

This can be considered an academic exercise in understanding the difference between TRUE and MAGNETIC, except for anyone who flies at high latitudes where magnetic navigation is unreliable, or anyone who flies in Class II or oceanic airspace where plotting procedures are required. If you ever need to plot a position, variation is critical.

Variation is measured in degrees and direction either east or west. Westerly variation is positive, easterly is negative.

Note: Variation is caused by the earth's shifting magnetic field and can be further influenced by geological features like mountains or local mineral deposits. Not only can the listed variation on charts and aircraft databases be wrong, those used to calibrate VOR and other navigation aids can be in error. It is not uncommon to find a 6° error from the date a VOR was calibrated and the current known variation.

Deviation

TO FLY	STEER	TO FLY	STEER
N	001	180	179
15	016	195	194
30	031	210	209
45	046	225	224
60	062	240	238
75	077	255	253
90	092	270	268
105	107	285	283
120	122	300	298
135	135	315	314
150	149	330	330
165	164	345	346

B-16 COMPASS SWUNG 12 APR 76 BY MJR

Compass correction card, (AFM 51-37, figure 1-15)

Deviation [is] an error in compass indications caused by magnetic disturbances originating within the aircraft. The magnitude of deviation varies with operation of different electrical equipment. Periodically, the compass is checked and compensations are made to reduce the amount of deviation. Deviation errors remaining after the compass has been checked are recorded on a compass correction card in the cockpit. The STEER column on the compass correction card is the compass heading you should indicate to maintain the TO FLY magnetic heading.

Source: AFM 51-37, page 1-12

At Air Force Instrument Instructor's school we were taught to fly IFR off nothing more than an attitude indicator and a magnetic compass. These days the chances of needing to fly off one of these cards are remote, but you should know how.

Deviation is given as degrees to steer to accomplish a desired heading, but can be thought of as positive and negative numbers to apply a magnetic heading.

True / Magnetic / Course

An old sailor's mnemonic is often cited for understanding the relations between true and magnetic courses and headings: "True virgins make dull company" to which others tack on "Add Whiskey." Crude or not, the idea was to remember the order in which things are added to a true course to end up with what the sailor (and pilot) wanted, which was a course to sail (and fly):

- Start with a TRUE course using your handy plotter, to that you add
- magnetic VARIATION (explained above) to get a
- MAGNETIC course; to that add
- DEVIATION (explained: above) to get a
- COMPASS heading to steer.

The "Add Whiskey" part was to help us remember we add west variation and deviation while subtracting east variation and deviation. Another technique is to remember "East is least, west is best."

References

Air Force Manual (AFM) 51-37, Instrument Flying, 1 December 1976

Air Force Manual (AFM) 51-40, Air Navigation, Flying Training, 1 July 1973

Drift Down Techniques

As usually taught in most international procedures courses, the procedures to deal with the loss of an engine when flying an oceanic track is to add thrust to the operating engine(s), descend at "drift down" speed and end up at "drift down" altitude. It has nothing to do with navigation. That's the theory. In the real world, drift down is also a navigation problem.

The Real World

In most parts of the world, an oceanic track is designed to keep you separated from aircraft on adjacent tracks. You cannot turn off the track without considering the possibility of a midair collision first. With or without adjacent tracks, no matter where in the world you are, you need to have an idea where the nearest suitable alternate is at all times.

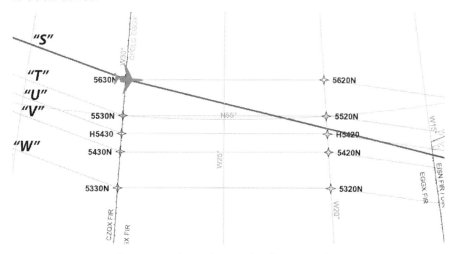

A random route above the North Atlantic Track System

Example: Let's say you are flying to Europe either on or above the northernmost North Atlantic Track when an engine quits just as you pass 56°North 030° West. You need to descend and your best option is to head to Shannon, Ireland (EINN).

Aircraft Theory

The aircraft manufacturer should have evaluated your aircraft's performance and figured out the best way to squeeze the most distance for the least amount of gas in the event of an engine failure. They will have made similar computations for a depressurization scenario and for a simple diversion while remaining at altitude.

At the very least you should have made computations to figure at what point along your route of flight you can make the decision to continue or return to a set of alternate airports in front or behind you. This point is the Equal Time Point (ETP) and is a staple of international operations. Your flight planning service very likely makes these computations for you. But what are the assumptions behind the numbers?

AFM Drift Down Procedure

Your ETP is probably designed for you to do the following:

- Set your operating engine(s) to a maximum thrust setting, while turning directly to your alternate.
- Allow your speed to decay to drift down speed while maintaining altitude (this may happen almost immediately or in a minute or so for most two-engine aircraft).
- As drift down speed is reached, descend at that speed until at drift down altitude.

This gets you to your ETP alternate at the predicted fuel level, provided the winds, temperature, and other considerations cooperate. In other words, it is a best case scenario. But what is the route of flight for this diversion?

Routing

$$\frac{Total\ Distance}{GS_r + GS_c} = \frac{ETP\ (in\ miles\ from\ departure)}{GS_r}$$

Many pilots assume that when they approach an Equal Time Point (ETP), they will have smooth sailing getting to either ETP airport. It is a safety factor, after all. But they may be surprised to hear that most ETP calculations assume a straight-line route of flight and do not provide for any additional fuel needed for the approach or APU. For more about ETP calculations, see the chapter: Equal Time Points.

Example

The ETP is based on a straight line. In a G450 at common weights, for example, the cruise speed of 0.80 Mach is identical to your drift down speed, it will take you 38 minutes and 254 nautical miles to descend to your drift down altitude of 29,000 feet. Unfortunately, this means crossing two tracks to your south.

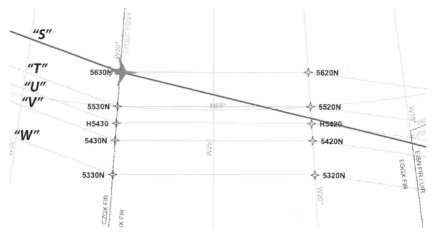

Turning direct to the alternate, descending through an adjacent track,

In our example, that would mean a twin-engine turned single-engine Gulfstream would turn right off Track "S" and would end up crossing Track "T" about 100 nm west of 020° west. The descent is begun immediately, possibly encroaching on lower traffic on Track "S" and probably also those on Track "T" using the expected descent rate. Because the center tracks are now spaced at half a degree latitude, our descent may actually cross a third track before reach an altitude below the tracks. The crew can expect to make it to

Shannon with the amount of fuel promised by their ETP calculations, provided they avoid hitting anyone.

```
ETP1 - EQUAL TIME POINT DATA FOR DEPRESS
        SAN FRANCISCO INTL (KSFO) / KAHULUI                (PHOG)
        FLIGHT LEVEL 100
ETP WAYPOINT AT N28 31.4 W139 54.8     W/C    DIST   TIME TO
ORIGIN APT TO ETP WAYPOINT                    1221    03.06
ETP WAYPOINT TO KSFO                   PO6    1034    03.51
ETP WAYPOINT TO PHOG                   M02    1008    03.51
TAS AT FLIGHT LEVEL 100           264
TEMP AT FLIGHT LEVEL 100       ISA P15
FUEL BURN TO   ETP WAYPOINT       7460
FUEL OVERHEAD ETP WAYPOINT     008690
FUEL BURN FROM ETP TO ALTN     007775
FUEL REMAINING AT ETP ALTN     000915
TOTAL ETP FUEL REQUIRED        015235
```

Fuel remaining in a CL601 flying from California to Hawaii

You may argue that it just doesn't matter, since you normally carry enough gas for every situation. That is true for some situations but not all. In the example above, a Challenger 601 can make Santa Ana, California to Kona, Hawaii without too much trouble. But if they were to lose cabin pressurization at their KSFO - PHOG Equal Time Point, they could find themselves on final with just enough gas for one approach.

What about an "ultra long range" aircraft like a GV? I once flew a GV from Wilmington, Delaware to Kona, Hawaii and landed with enough gas to make California without refueling. But a GV from Paris to Los Angeles can find itself with similarly paltry amounts of fuel flying over desolate regions of Canada. The critical lesson here is that you cannot assume you are going to be okay at an ETP alternate just because you will have lots of gas when you land at your planned destination.

Regulatory Theory

The old "Quad Four" – so called because it was contained in the ICAO Document 4444 – maneuver to turn 45° away from track, offset 15 NM, pick an altitude, etc. is gone. With the exception of lost communications timing in the Pacific, almost all of the world is on a single oceanic contingency procedure. Now you diverge from the route by at least 30°, offset by 5 NM, and then descend below FL 290 or climb above FL 410.

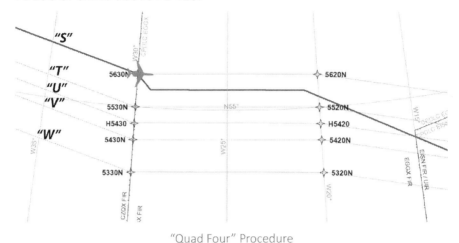

"Quad Four" Procedure

Of course, there may be regional differences that supersede these procedures and you should use your judgment to ensure safety. If you can communicate with ATC via voice or CPDLC, your options might expand.

Reality

It would seem to be a conundrum:

- a straight line to your alternate while minimizing altitude loss (as aircraft theory would demand) gets you to your alternate airport with the predicted fuel but risks a midair collision, but
- flying ICAO descents, altitudes, and routes (as regulatory theory would have you do) avoids the midair but risks a water landing.

What's a pilot to do? Every situation is different, but you need to come up with a way to minimize risk while maximizing survivability. Here is a possible solution for our example scenario. It is up to you to come up with an escape plan for each of your oceanic route segments.

Example

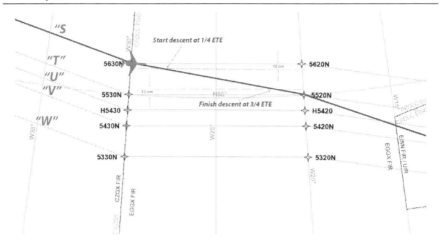

Flying the "Safe Zone" Procedure

While each situation is different, looking at the big picture you can come up with a plan to maximize the use of "safe zones" between tracks. In our example:

- We enter a direct leg to the next waypoint, one leg to the south (5520N).
- We maintain altitude (and sacrifice drift down speed) while making note of the ETE to the next waypoint.
- At one-fourth of the ETE we know we are one-fourth of the total distance between tracks (60 nm in this example) and therefore beyond 15 nm and safe to begin our descent.
- We realize that we must be below the tracks by three-quarters of our ETE so we use our FMS vertical navigation to plan a descent that has us level when 15 nm of the next track.

This method isn't as efficient as the AFM procedure but offers greater assurance of not encroaching on another aircraft's airspace. This method will, however, get us to the alternate with more gas than the purely Quad Four maneuver. Each situation is different, this should provide an example of the type of "heads up" thinking that will serve you well.

Waypoint Briefing

Depending on your aircraft, the time between an engine failure and needing to start down can be only seconds. Many twin-engine aircraft cruise right at their drift down speeds (such as a Gulfstream G450). Others give you more time (like a Challenger 605). Aircraft with three or more engines can give you 20 or 30 minutes (such as a Falcon 900). But no matter the amount of time you have, you should know what to do before it happens. A good time to think about this is at each waypoint. As your geography (distance along the route), performance (reduce weight), and endurance (reduced fuel) change, your situation changes. You need to brief a new escape plan at every waypoint.

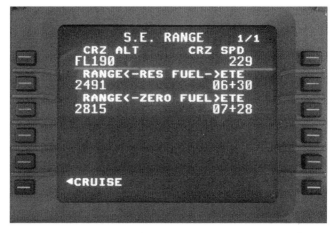

G450 Single Engine Range page

At each waypoint you should:

- Brief the aircraft's current weight.
- Look up and brief the current drift down speed and altitude.
- Update the weather at any applicable alternates.
- Brief the proximity of any organized tracks relative to the next leg.

- Brief the planned direction of turn as well as the route and altitude needed to avoid any organized tracks (your escape plan).

Improving Your Odds Before You Leave the Ground

At the very least, you can look at your ETP fuel remaining calculation and decide to takeoff with more fuel, then replan at the higher weight and possibly lower altitudes. If your flight planning service allows some customization, you might be able to dial in these extra margins automatically.

The Problem

The distance is a direct line from the ETP to the alternate airport; it doesn't make any allowance for having to circumnavigate any tracks, vectors around traffic, or to make an instrument approach.

In a depressurization scenario, you end up at 10,000 or 12,500 feet. Will the cabin be warm enough? Maybe 10,000 feet is too high? How much fuel will it take to fly lower?

In a drift down scenario, the pure math assumes you will be descending according to the manufacturer's drift down procedures. But will you be able to do that if there are any tracks between you and the alternate?

The Solution

ARINCDirect ETP presets

Your flight planning service may allow you to add factors to your ETP fuel computations. ARINCDirect, for example, adds a default 45 minutes of holding at the ETP airport at 1,500 feet AGL at AFM holding speeds. You can change many of the calculation assumptions directly on the "Create Flight Plan" page. Here are a few ideas on how to best customize this:

- 1E INOP Calculation — If your aircraft has a drift down altitude above FL 280 for most weights, lowering the value to FL 275 will add enough fuel to make sure you have enough fuel to fly below the tracks.
- Depressurized Calculation — Some aircraft have more oxygen than fuel, with others it is the opposite. No matter your situation, you should realize the passenger masks on most aircraft are only good enough to get them from altitude to unpressurized altitudes.

180 Degree Turn at Altitude

Making a 180° turn at altitude isn't as simple as one might think. At most crossing altitudes your true airspeed will be very high, 400 knots or higher. Your available bank angle will be less, say around 17° or so. If you are on track with 30 nautical mile spacing, you will be getting very close to your neighbors. With 15 nautical mile spacing? Forget about it. Within an organized track system, it may not be possible at all. It is something to consider.

A 180° turn at altitude can take 20 or more nautical miles

Computing your turn radius is simply a matter of dividing your true airspeed by the mathematical tangent of your bank angle and a magical factor:

$$r = \frac{V^2}{11.26 \tan \Theta}$$

where:

r = turn radius, ft

V = velocity, knots (TAS)

θ = bank angle, degrees

Of course, the turn diameter is double this and you also need to figure on wind effects.

In the case of a Gulfstream G450 and FL 410 doing 0.80 Mach (around 460 KTAS), limited to 17° of bank, the turn radius is just a bit over 10 nm which means the diameter is just over 20 nm. If you are on a Reduced Lateral Separation track, with only 30 nm between tracks, the distance gets eaten up quickly. If you are flying eastbound with a 2 nm Strategic Lateral Offset Procedure (SLOP) and need to turn right, you could end up 30 - 2 - 20 = 8 nm of the next track.

Polar Alternates

Imagine a scenario where you are flying above 70° North latitude and still have five hours left in the flight. One of your passengers appears to be suffering a stroke. You have an alternate right in front of you. Easy decision, right? Not so fast. See the chapter: High Latitude Operations.

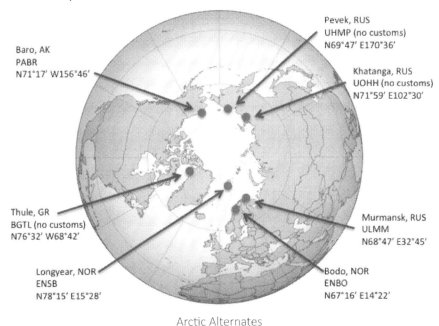

Pevek, RUS
UHMP (no customs)
N69°47′ E170°36′

Baro, AK
PABR
N71°17′ W156°46′

Khatanga, RUS
UOHH (no customs)
N71°59′ E102°30′

Thule, GR
BGTL (no customs)
N76°32′ W68°42′

Murmansk, RUS
ULMM
N68°47′ E32°45′

Longyear, NOR
ENSB
N78°15′ E15°28′

Bodo, NOR
ENBO
N67°16′ E14°22′

Arctic Alternates

The problem with some remote alternates:

- No (or very limited) medical facilities — That MedAire kit on your airplane might just be better than what you find within hours of your alternate airport. You might be better off dialing that MedAire phone number and seeing if your passenger would be better off with some of the drugs in that kit while just a few hours away from a city with a real hospital.

- No (or very limited) fuel — Sometimes you don't have an option, but you might be putting your airplane down someplace where it will have to remain for a few months.
- Very limited transportation options — If your passengers need to get out, or your mechanic needs to get in, the alternate airport may be fairly inaccessible.
- No (or very limited) lodging options — It's going to be cold and you are going to have passengers and crew that may be placed in medical jeopardy having to sleep in an unheated hangar (if they are lucky) or worse.

References

ICAO Doc 4444 - Air Traffic Management, 16th Edition, Procedures for Air Navigation Services, International Civil Aviation Organization, October 2016

Equal Time Point (ETP) Techniques

An Equal Time Point (ETP) is not a "time" at all, it is a position in space between two remote points. When you get to that point, you will have an equal time between going back or going ahead in various conditions. For example, if you lose an engine over the North Atlantic at your computed ETP, it will take you just as long to turn around and head to your alternate in Canada with the forecast headwind, as it will to continue to Ireland with the forecast tailwind. But there are other ETP situations too, such as what happens if you lose pressurization? Or what if you are able to maintain speed and altitude but have to land as soon as possible for a medical emergency? That's why we need ETPs. Your flight planning service provider can do them for you automatically, but you need to know how to compute one manually to make sure they chose the ETP airports wisely and to compute your own if they didn't.

ETPs for Navigators

From the manual Air Force navigators used back in the days the Air Force needed navigators to cross an ocean:

> The ETP is not necessarily the midpoint in time from departure to destination. Its location is somewhere near the midpoint of the route, however, and is dependent upon the wind factor.

> A wind factor is a headwind or tailwind component which is computed by comparing the average ground speed (GS) to the true airspeed (TAS). To do this, algebraically subtract the TAS from the GS. When the wind factor is a minus value (GS less than TAS), it is called a headwind factor; when it is a plus value (GS greater than TAS), it is a tailwind factor. When computing ETP, obtain a wind factor for each half of the route.

> Use the following formula to compute a ETP:

$$\frac{Total\ Distance}{GS_r + GS_c} = \frac{ETP\ (in\ miles\ from\ departure)}{GS_r}$$

Total distance is the number of nautical miles from departure to destination. Since ETP is most significant for the overwater portion of a flight, the ETP should be determined from coastal departure points and for alternate landing points. GS_r is the ground speed to return to departure from the ETP. Compute it for the first half of the route by applying the wind factor with the sign reversed to the TAS. GS_c is the GS to continue from the ETP to destination. Determine it by applying the wind factor for the second half of the route to the TAS.

Source: AFM 51-40, page 24-9

The navigator's formula is mathematically pure but hardly usable, something we can fix with a little algebra, below.

ETPs for Pilots

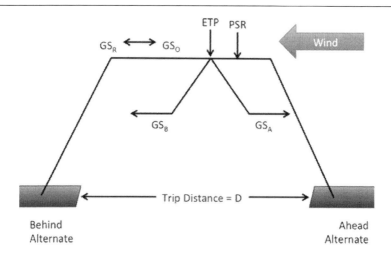

Equal Time Point and Point of Safe Return

The following formula is used to calculate the ground distance from the departure airport to ETP:

$$Ground\ Distance\ to\ ETP = \frac{(D)(GS_B)}{GS_A + GS_B}$$

Where:

D = Total Trip Distance

GS_A = Ground speed to "Ahead" airport at altitude to be flown

GS_B = Ground speed to "Behind" airport at altitude to be flown

In both the navigator and pilot versions the terms "departure" and "destination" are used when in fact they should refer to the alternate airports "ahead" and "behind." You will seldom opt return to your departure point or continue to your destination, though it could happen. Regardless, you will often see "GSR" to denote your ground speed while returning and "GSC" to denote your ground speed while continuing.

The terms GS_O and GS_R are for the Point of Safe Return (PSR), which is sometimes called the "Point of No Return" (PNR). More about that in the chapter: Point of Safe Return.

For our example, a flight from KBED to LSGG with one equal time point plotted around 37° West:

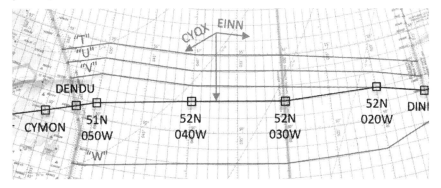

Example Plotting Chart

ETP Types

At least three types of ETPs should be considered for each location set to cover the following three contingencies:

```
1E INOP
LAT/LONG     N52 05.0/W037 17.3         CYQX                EINN
TIME TO ETP DIVRSN PT          02.51
DIST TO ETP DIVRSN PT          01510
FUEL TO ETP DIVRSN PT/RMNG   010177 /18923
FL/BURN/TIME TO ETP AP        300/05553/02.36     310/05557/02.37
TAS/ETA/DIST TO ETP AP        340/2227/000686     340/2228/001036
MAG CRS/AVG WIND COMP TO ETP AP   271/M076            105/P052
ISA TEMP DEV TO ETP AP                M000                M003
TOTAL FUEL TO ETP AP /RMNG      15730/13366         15734/13366
```

Loss of Engine ETP Example

Loss of Engine ETP

In the event of an engine loss, drift down procedures are normally used and the airplane may be required to turn to either alternate depending on its position before or after the Loss of Engine ETP.

This ETP can have other names, "1E INOP" in the example shown, but normally means you have lost an engine and must descend and slow down.

In our example this ETP occurs at N52°05.0' / W037°17.3' which is 1,510 nm along the route of flight from the takeoff point. This might seem to be a useless number when talking ETPs, but it is useful when plotting the point on a chart. For understanding the geographic position, four lines later we see the ETP is 686 nm from CYQX. In the event of an engine loss, the fuel and time are based on descending to FL 300 after reversing course to CYQX or FL 310 pressing forward to EINN. In either case, it will take around 2 hours 36 or 37 minutes at the recommended engine out speed.

```
DEPRESS - FL PROFILE: OXYGEN ALTITUDE FOR 120 MIN THEN FL150
LAT/LONG     N52 05.8/W036 28.0         CYQX                EINN
TIME TO ETP DIVRSN PT          02.55
DIST TO ETP DIVRSN PT          01541
FUEL TO ETP DIVRSN PT/RMNG   010347 /18753
FL/BURN/TIME TO ETP AP        150/11951/03.00     150/11974/02.57
TAS/ETA/DIST TO ETP AP        278/2254/000717     281/2252/001007
MAG CRS/AVG WIND COMP TO ETP AP   271/M046            105/P051
ISA TEMP DEV TO ETP AP                M016                M010
TOTAL FUEL TO ETP AP /RMNG      22298/06779         22321/06779
```

Loss of Level ETP Example

Loss of Level ETP

In the event of the loss of pressurization or other problem requiring a rapid descent without an engine loss, the airplane may be required to turn to either alternate based on its position before or after the Loss of Level ETP.

Most flight planning programs compute a rapid descent to 10,000 or 15,000 feet, depending on user preferences. A descent to 10,000 feet permits all occupants to breathe without the use of supplemental oxygen. A descent to 15,000 feet permits passengers to breathe without the use of supplemental oxygen, requires the flight crew to remain on supplemental oxygen, but provides greater endurance. This ETP can also be called "Depressurization" or some variation leading to the idea the airplane must descend.

In our example this ETP occurs just after the Engine-Out ETP, at 1,541 nm along the route of flight from our takeoff point. In the event of loss of pressurization, the aircraft would descend to 15,000' and either turn back or continue east. In either case, it will take around 3 hours at the recommended speed.

```
MEDICAL
LAT/LONG      N52 05.3/W037 00.9           CYQX                EINN
TIME TO ETP DIVRSN PT          02.52
DIST TO ETP DIVRSN PT          01521
FUEL TO ETP DIVRSN PT/RMNG  010234 /18866
FL/BURN/TIME TO ETP AP         200/11482/02.49    200/11505/02.48
TAS/ETA/DIST TO ETP AP         302/2241/000697    304/2240/001027
MAG CRS/AVG WIND COMP TO ETP AP    271/M060              105/P057
ISA TEMP DEV TO ETP AP                M012                  M010
TOTAL FUEL TO ETP AP /RMNG     21716/07361        21739/07361
```

Maintain Level ETP Example

Maintain Level ETP

In the event of a need to land as soon as possible without the need to descend, such as a medical emergency, the airplane may be required to turn to either alternate based on its position before or after the Maintain Level ETP.

This ETP can also be called "Medical" or some variation leading to the idea the airplane diverts but not need to descend or decelerate. But some vendors do select what appears to be an arbitrary descent and you may need to request a change from your vendor or compute your own.

In our example the vendor decided a medical ETP requires a descent to FL 200 to make the ETP about the same as what they call the 1E INOP (Loss of Engine) and DEPRESS (Loss of Level) ETPs. This makes flight planning and plotting easier, but it is not entirely accurate. Fortunately, with the information they've given us, we can come up with a better answer. See "Manually Computed ETPs," below.

Selecting ETP Airports

- The oceanic or remote area route of flight should be examined, and suitable diversion airports identified based on aircraft requirements, airport capability, and weather. The airport must meet the weather requirements for filing as an alternate and if operating under 14 CFR 135, the aircraft must have the performance to fly en route and hold at least 1,500 feet above all obstacles. [14 CFR 135.381]
- If using a computerized flight planning service, always look at the selected ETP airports with a eye towards judging its common sense. The flight planner may have made the airport selections prior to a significant change in winds, and it may become obvious the selected airports are no longer viable. You may also receive a routing change that negates the previously selected ETP airports.

Multiple ETP location sets may be advantageous when the route of flight is near multiple airport options.

Computer Flight Plan Computed ETPs

```
MEDICAL
LAT/LONG     N52 05.3/W037 00.9        CYQX              EINN
TIME TO ETP DIVRSN PT          02.52
DIST TO ETP DIVRSN PT          01521
FUEL TO ETP DIVRSN PT/RMNG   010234 /18866
FL/BURN/TIME TO ETP AP       200/11482/02.49    200/11505/02.48
TAS/ETA/DIST TO ETP AP       302/2241/000697    304/2240/001027
MAG CRS/AVG WIND COMP TO ETP AP    271/M060          105/P057
ISA TEMP DEV TO ETP AP                 M012              M010
TOTAL FUEL TO ETP AP /RMNG       21716/07361       21739/07361
```

Maintain Level ETP Example

Computer ETP Computations are generally superior to manually calculated ETPs because they consider a greater number of wind points and will yield more accurate ETPs. But, as we've seen with this vendor's "DIST TO ETP DIVRSN PT," you need to carefully consider what the data means before making any assumptions.

In our next example flight plan, KBED - LSGG, we elected to plot the Maintain Level ETP because it was in the middle. Our flight planning service tells us this ETP occurs 1,521 nm from our departure airport, but more importantly 697 from out "behind" airport, CYQX. The TAS going forward or back are very close but the distance covered is dramatically different because of the 62 knot wind from the west.

Manually Computed ETPs

As shown above, ETPs can be computed manually if the ground speed ahead and behind are known. To manually calculate an ETP:

$$Ground\ Distance\ to\ ETP = \frac{(D)(GS_B)}{GS_A + GS_B}$$

```
FLIGHTPLAN N7700     KBED TO LSGG  GLF4  M80 /F   IFR    29DEC13    -- AB
COMPUTED 2024Z FOR ETD 1700Z    PROGS 281200Z                  WGT IN LBS

            FUEL   TIME    DIST ARRIVE TAKEOFF   LAND    AV PLD   OPNLWT
DEST LSGG  019340 06:22    3261  2322Z  073508  054168  000500   043908
RESV       001931 00:45
ALTN       000000 00:00    0000  0000Z
HOLD       000000 00:00
REQD       029100 10:10                          ES ZFW   MX ZFW
TAXI       000400                                  44408    49000
XTRA       007829 03:03                          ES LNDG  MX LNDG
TOTL        29500 10:10                            54168   058500

KBED DCT LBSTA ENE J581 YJT CYMON DENDU 5150N 5240N 5230N 5220N
DINIM ELSOX GAPLI UL739 LIZAD UN160 PIGOP UN491 RESMI UM975 LUSAR
DCT LSGG

WIND P062    MXSH 10/LUSAR   AVG WIND 268/071
TAS 451      FL 410 YJT 390 5240N 410
```

Flight Plan Example, Top Information

All you really need is the wind factor, TAS, and distance between the behind and ahead airports. Remember that GS_B = TAS + Wind and GS_A = TAS + Wind, and the wind factor is positive if behind you and negative if in front of you.

From our plotting chart we see D = 1722

From our flight plan we see the TAS = 451 and the average wind factor is P062. This could be wildly inaccurate for the pertinent portion of the flight so it pays to scan the oceanic portion to make sure.

CPT FREQ LAT	FLT TRO	T TDV	WIND COMP	S	TAS GRS	AWY	MH MCRS	DST DSTR	ETE ATE	ETR ATR	FU AFU	FR AFR	FF/E
DENDU	390	-52	288105	7	463	DCT	083	0123	014	0435	698	22176	1531
	36	P04	P075		538		090	2315					
N50302	W052041												
5150N	390	-50	288090	4	465	DCT	095	0084	009	0426	485	21690	1531
	36	P06	P067		531		097	2231					
N51000	W050000												
5240N	390	-50	276063	2	466	DCT	106	0379	043	0343	2204	19487	1516
	52	P07	P060		527		104	1851					
N52000	W040000												
5230N	410	-51	252054	1	465	DCT	103	0371	043	0300	2076	17411	1445
	52	P06	P051		516		100	1481					
N52000	W030000												
5220N	410	-53	241060		464	DCT	124	0371	043	0217	2026	15385	1407
	31	P05	P051		515		117	1110					
N52000	W020000												
DINIM	410	-55	236069	1	462	DCT	102	0197	024	0153	1081	14305	1377
	36	P03	P040		502		097	0913					
N51000	W015000												

Flight Plan Example, Oceanic Legs

The oceanic legs reveal wind factors of P075, P067, P060, P051, P051, and P040. Rather than use a wind factor of 62 throughout, as the flight plan would suggest, we'll use P067 for our return scenario and P051 for the continue option:

GS_B = TAS + WF = 451 + (-67) = 384

GS_A = TAS + WF = 451 + (+51) = 502

Therefore:

Ground Distance to ETP = (1722)(384) / (502+384) = 746 nm

Our manually computed ETP is 50 nm further east than the computerized version because the vendor selected a descent to lower the TAS in an attempt to make the three provided ETPs about the same. If your decision is based on really staying at flight level, the actual ETP is the one we computed, 50 nm further east.

Circular Slide Rule

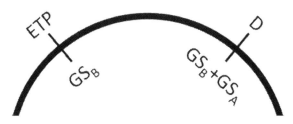

ETP With a Circular Slide Rule

With a circular slide rule, place the Total Distance (D) on the outer scale opposite the added ground speeds ($GS_B + GS_A$), and place the sliding index over the return ground speed (GSB) on the inner scale. The ETP will appear on the outer scale under the sliding index:

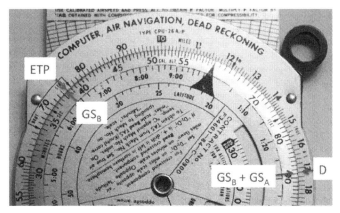

ETP With a Circular Slide Rule Example

The technique works but it introduces an opportunity for error and has been relegated to the "You can, but why would you?" category.

Three Airport Example

There are times when a third airport may become advantageous. (This occurs frequently in the North Atlantic when the route of flight is near Iceland.) For this example, we will compute only the Maintain Level ETP between CYQX-BIKF and BIKF-EINN to illustrate the positioning of the ETP on the route of flight. (The process of checking the Loss of Level and Loss of Engine ETPs is the same, using the appropriate ground speeds for those scenarios.)

- Maintain Level ETP (CYQX-BIKF). Using our FMS or by measuring the distance on the plotting chart, we see the distance between CYQX and BIKF is 1367 nm. For the example, our True Airspeed is 492 knots, but our winds will be out of the west at 10 knots.

ETP (CYQX-BIKF) = (1367 × 482) / (502 + 482) = 670 nm from CYQX

- Maintain Level ETP (BIKF-EINN). Using our FMS or by measuring the distance on the plotting chart, we see the distance between BIKF and EINN is 798 nm. Once again, our True Airspeed is 492 knots but this time our winds will be out of the west at 20 knots.

ETP (BIKF-EINN) = (798 × 472) / (512 + 472) = 383 nm from BIKF

- Each of these points are plotted on straight lines between airports. A line is then drawn from these points at a right angle towards the actual aircraft route of flight. Where the lines intersect are the appropriate equal time points:

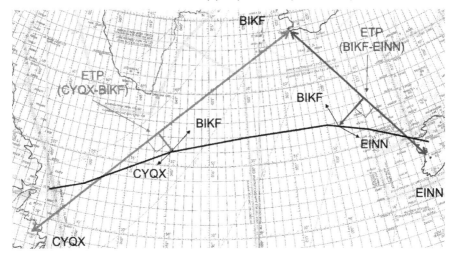

- In this example, the emergency options will be to turn back to CYQX before the first ETP, to divert north to BIKF between the first and second ETPs, and finally to press on to EINN after the second ETP.
- If the winds were especially strong up north and the route of flight was further south, we could see a case where it is never advantageous to proceed to one of the three ETP choices. In the example shown below, the flight time to either EINN or CYQX is always shorter than BIKF:

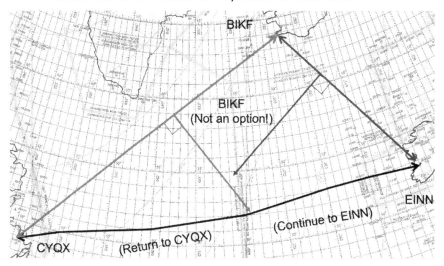

For more about how to plot ETPs, see the chapter Plotting.

References

Air Force Manual (AFM) 51-40, Air Navigation, Flying Training, 1 July 1973

Extended Diversion Time Operations (ETDO) Techniques

As turbine engines have become more and more reliable the definition of what constitutes extended operations has changed. Even the name has changed: ETOPS started out as "Extended Twin Operations" and then became "Extended Operations." ETOPS is now EDTO, "Extended Diversion Time Operations." What remains constant is confusion among many pilots as to what it means, who it impacts, and how to "comply."

ETDO is any operation that is beyond 180 minutes with one engine inoperative from a suitable airport. Who it impacts are commercial operators, 14 CFR 121 and 135. How to comply is quite complicated, involves many steps for pilots, mechanics, the airplane and the operator. This isn't an article about becoming ETOPS / EDTO eligible, it is an article on how to fly just about everywhere in the world without having to become ETOPS / EDTO certified.

Under 14 CFR 135, to fly without ETOPS / EDTO certification, you need to demonstrate that the aircraft can make it to a suitable airport in under 180 minutes, using engine-out altitudes and airspeeds of your choosing. You do not need to use Equal Time Point (ETP) altitudes and speeds. If you have the fuel and performance to do this, the rule book is satisfied. Under real engine-out situations, the actual altitudes and airspeeds are up to you, and you need not do this in under 180 minutes.

None of this make sense to you? If you fly more than 3 hours from the nearest airport under 14 CFR 135, you need to understand ETOPS / EDTO. If you fly a Challenger or Boeing it may not impact how you fly over water at all, but you need to know why. If you fly a Gulfstream or other ultra long-range aircraft, however, ETOPS / EDTO may impact your fuel loading.

Location

To find your aircraft's 180-minute range you can use the excellent website, Great Circle Mapper (http://gc.kls2.com/) and input a true airspeed to produce a chart like the one shown below. A GV's Engine-Out 180-minute footprint can be figured at 358 KTAS but the selected speed is up to the pilot. Losing an engine in the dark shaded areas means you cannot get to a suitable alternate in less than 180 minutes. To fly this under 14 CFR 135, you would need to be certified for ETOPS.

> Maximum flying time outside the United States. After August 13, 2008, no certificate holder may operate an airplane, other than an all-cargo airplane with more than two engines, on a planned route that exceeds 180 minutes flying time (at the one-engine-inoperative cruise speed under standard conditions in still air) from an Adequate Airport outside the continental United States unless the operation is approved by the FAA in accordance with Appendix G of this part, Extended Operations (ETOPS).
>
> Source: 14 CFR 135, §135.364

If you are flying under 14 CFR 135 and your planned range exceeds 14 CFR § 135.364 criteria, you and your airplane must meet 14 CFR 135 Appendix G requirements.

Aircraft not under an ETOPS / EDTO program must be able to return to an acceptable airport within 180 minutes (in still air) in the event of an engine failure.

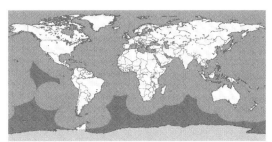

GV 180-minute, 358 KTAS ETOPS Map, from Great Circle Mapper

Obtaining ETOPS / EDTO Certification

If you want to get ETOPS / EDTO certified I recommend you contact your aircraft manufacturer and start from there. If you spend considerable time flying routes where your aircraft is impacted, it might be worth your while.

Most aircraft are grandfathered into a 180-minute engine-out capability, which means they may fly as far as 180 minutes from the nearest suitable airport engine-out, no wind, but no further.

Refer to 14 CFR 135 Appendix G to determine your 180-minute engine out qualification:

- 14 CFR 135.98, Operations in the North Polar Area
- 14 CFR 135.364, Maximum Flying Time Outside the United States
- 135.411, Maintenance Requirement Applicability
- 135 Appendix G, ETOPS

Many long-range business jets can qualify for ETOPS / EDTO, which extends that range to either 207 or 240 minutes, but the process is so time consuming and expensive, I've not heard of a single operator who has bothered. To be ETOPS / EDTO qualified, 14 CFR 135 operators must have Operations Specifications B342 and B344, as detailed under FAA 8900.1, Volume 4, Chapter 6. If you plan your 14 CFR 135 operations to be within 180 minutes, engine-out of a suitable airport, you do not need ETOPS / ETDO certification.

Example Case Study: A Gulfstream GV

The Gulfstream GV, for example, is almost never constrained in the Atlantic but cannot make many locations in the South Pacific from South America westward and remain ETOPS / EDTO compliant. Between the continental United States and Hawaii, however, the GV is capable provided crews plan fuel to allow altitudes lower than optimal and airspeeds higher than optimal in the event of an engine failure. Technique:

- If all ETPs are less than 180 minutes you are done, all requirements to fly without ETOPS / EDTO certification have been met.
- For any ETP greater than 180 minutes, examine the ETP airspeed and altitude and attempt to increase the KTAS to bring the time below 180 minutes. The GV series, for example, will have a drift down altitude and airspeed which produces the best range but a low KTAS. If the aircraft has the fuel to fly at a lower altitude and higher KTAS, you might be able to reduce the time significantly. If the time cannot be reduced below 180 minutes, the aircraft will not be allowed to fly the route under 14 CFR 135.

Note: you need only plan for the ability to fly the route from any point to a divert airport engine-out in under 180 minutes. In an actual engine-out situation, you may fly speeds and altitudes of your choosing, and you don't have to do it in under 180 minutes.

The explanation - a short story

Never since the Boeing 747 had I been so impressed with an airplane. The Gulfstream GV showed how a company can take a good idea and build on it. The Gulfstream GII was a good airplane with a lot of flaws. The Gulfstream GIII was marginally better. The Gulfstream GIV was a Gulfstream GIII with a lot of the flaws addressed. The Gulfstream GV is almost perfect. You cannot beat the wing.

While the Gulfstream GV is just about eight feet longer than a GIV, its wing has an extra sixteen feet of span. That translates into a higher ceiling, higher cruise speed, higher climb rates, and a greater payload. But what is really impressive are the things you get less of: approach speed and fuel flows. The range is incredible. We flew from Cincinnati, Ohio to Jeddah, Saudi, Arabia on one tank of gas, a trip of nearly 7,000 nautical miles. The trips from the United States to Europe were never a problem:

```
EQUAL TIME POINT DATA FOR LOSS OF ONE ENGINE
LAURENCE G HANSCOM (KBED) / LE BOURGET (LFPB)
FLIGHT LEVEL 300
ETP WAYPOINT AT N47 38.1 W034 47.6        W/C DIST TIME TO
ORIGIN APT TO ETP WAYPOINT                    1591 03.05
ETP WAYPOINT TO CYYT                      M41 0727 02.26
ETP WAYPOINT TO LPLA                      P71 1037 02.26
TAS AT FLIGHT LEVEL 300            336
TEMP AT FLIGHT LEVEL 300      ISA M02
FUEL BURN TO ETP WAYPOINT      10253
FUEL OVERHEAD ETP WAYPOINT    013341
```

Atlantic ETOPS example

The aircraft has legs, no doubt about it. That's why the flights to Hawaii surprised me. While we could fly from California to Hawaii and back without refueling, ETOPS/EDTO is an issue.

The problem was Extended Operations (ETOPS / EDTO) specified for commercial aircraft under 14 CFR 135.364: ". . . no certificate holder may operate an airplane, other than an all-cargo airplane with more than two engines, on a planned route that exceeds 180 minutes flying time (at the one engine-inoperative cruise speed under standard conditions in still air) from an Adequate Airport outside the continental United States unless the operation is approved by the FAA in accordance with Appendix G of this part, Extended Operations (ETOPS)."

Translation? If you lose an engine, you have to be within three hours of an airport. The Challenger 604— an aircraft with half the range —had no problems getting to and from Hawaii, though even with two engines that airplane was almost out of gas after the ocean hop. The Gulfstream GV? You need to understand the numbers.

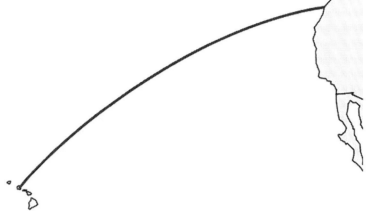

```
EQUAL TIME POINT DATA FOR LOSS OF ONE ENGINE
SAN FRANCISCO INTL(KSFO) / HONOLULU INTL (PHNL)
FLIGHT LEVEL 310
ETP WAYPOINT AT N30 42.0 W142 20.4        W/C DIST TIME TO
ORIGIN APT TO ETP WAYPOINT                    1072 03.14
ETP WAYPOINT TO KSFO                      P09 1072 03.14
ETP WAYPOINT TO PHOG                      M30 0960 03.14
TAS AT FLIGHT LEVEL 310            325
TEMP AT FLIGHT LEVEL 310      ISA P02
FUEL BURN TO ETP WAYPOINT         025197
FUEL OVERHEAD ETP WAYPOINT        015703
FUEL BURN FROM ETP TO ALTN        008356
FUEL REMAINING AT ETP ALTN        007346
```

KSFO- PHNL ETOPS example

Using standard drift down procedures — something unknown to us in the four-engine world — if you lose thrust on an engine you set the operating engine to its maximum continuous setting, allow the airplane to decelerate to an optimum speed, and then you allow the airplane to drift down to an altitude it can sustain on one engine. Most flight plan providers know this and program the equal time point calculations to do just that.

A normal airplane—one with more fuselage than wing—will have to drift down to the mid-twenties and fly a speed of around 250 or so. The Challenger 604, for example, may end up at 27,000 feet and 240 KIAS, which equates to 370 nautical miles per hour true airspeed. The airplane can make it to its divert airport in 2 hour 53 minutes, though it will be right at its minimum fuel.

The Gulfstream GV, with its massive wing, only needs to descend to 31,000 feet but can slow down to 195 KIAS. It doesn't have to, but the chart says it can. So, the flight planners use these numbers; a higher altitude translates to a lower true airspeed as does the lower indicated airspeed. The airplane, if flown at this altitude and speed, makes it to the divert airport in 3 hours and 14 minutes. An FAA examiner who doesn't understand the topic well will go ballistic and start the violation paperwork. The pilot needs to understand why the flight planning software is wrong.

In this example, the pilot need only select an altitude 4,000 feet below optimum and fly a little faster to increase to 358.2 KTAS.

Time = 1072 / 358.2 = 179 minutes.

The lower altitude will cost extra fuel, but the airplane has that to spare. So long as the pilot ensures there is fuel to do this, the aircraft doesn't need ETOPS / EDTO certification.

Of course this begs the question: can we always adjust our speed enough to keep under 180 minutes? As it turns out: no.

```
EQUAL TIME POINT DATA FOR LOSS OF ONE ENGINE
CHRISTCHURCH INTL (NZCH) / MATAVERI INTL (SCIP)
FLIGHT LEVEL 250
ETP WAYPOINT AT S51 21.2 W147 20.8          W/C DIST TIME TO
ORIGIN APT TO ETP WAYPOINT                      1744 03.20
ETP WAYPOINT TO NZCH                        M56 1672 06.12
ETP WAYPOINT TO SCIP                        P29 2241 06.12
TAS AT FLIGHT LEVEL 250           329
TEMP AT FLIGHT LEVEL 250          ISA P04
FUEL BURN TO ETP WAYPOINT         12366
FUEL OVERHEAD ETP WAYPOINT        028234
FUEL BURN FROM ETP TO ALTN        017499
FUEL REMAINING AT ETP ALTN        010597
```

NZCH- SCEL ETOPS example

While not a common flight, a trip from New Zealand to Chile is well within the range of a GV but cannot be made under 14 CFR 135 because of ETOPS-180 requirements. The total flight time is under 10 hours and not much over 5,100 nm. There is only one suitable alternate between Christchurch, New Zealand (NZCH) and Santiago, Chile (SCEL): the Isle de Pascua (SCIP).

The engine-out ETP is already calculated at an optimal altitude in terms for producing the highest available TAS, but even if the TAS is increased to the aircraft's maximum capable, the time to the ETP airport cannot be reduced to under 180 minutes. This flight cannot be accomplished in a GV under 14 CFR 135.

"Extended Range Operations"

One last note on the subject. Your Minimum Equipment List (MEL) may have restrictions for "Extended Range Operations" as "ER." Don't confuse this with any oceanic operation. The definitions section of your MEL should define it: "ER refers to extended range operations (ETOPS) of an airplane with operational approval to conduct ETOPS in accordance with applicable regulations."

References

14 CFR 135, Title 14: Aeronautics and Space, Operating Requirements: Commuter and On Demand Operations and Rules Governing Persons on Board Such Aircraft, Federal Aviation Administration, Department of Transportation

Great Circle Mapper: http://gc.kls2.com/

Fix-to-Fix Navigation Techniques

Fix-to-fix navigation was the staple of instrument pilotage in the days when avionics consisted of vacuum tubes and needles, as opposed to ones and zeroes. While at the 89th, in the 1990s, we used the method more as a manhood test than as a means of navigation. But no more; I am told the Air Force doesn't even allow the practice these days. So why should you know how to do a fix-to-fix? Because it will help you catch an error made by the box or the person programming the box. It has saved me many times, even with a Flight Management Computer.

I learned this technique in a Northrop T-38A Talon. Let's use that cockpit because it is so simple. You can use these techniques on any airplane with a bearing pointer and DME indicator.

T-38 cockpit

"Good morning studs," the instructor began day one of the T-38 instrument phase — in Air Force pilot training we were not allowed to think of ourselves as students, we were studs — "Today you learn the secret of point-to-point navigation."

The T-38 was a marvelous aircraft and had two things going for it when flying instruments that the T-37 did not: a flight director and DME, distance measuring equipment. Now by just looking at a gage, we knew our distance to a radio station. It was marvelous. What we still didn't have was an electronic method of determining our course from one point to another. It was a beautiful cockpit, but it still lacked a few creature comforts.

"You are on the 270 degree radial, 16 DME, heading north and you need to get to the 305 degree radial, 11 DME." He let his words sink in as we all soaked in the impossibility of the task. "What will you do?"

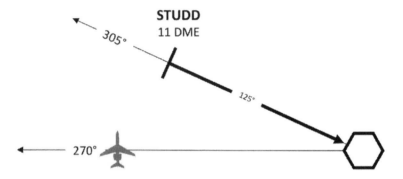

"Request vectors," said our class comic. We all laughed.

"Time to get out your crayons boys and girls," he said while turning to the chalk board.

- "You are the tail
- Target is the radial
- Higher DME is the edge of the card, lower DME is inside
- Draw a line
- Move the line
- Make the line vertical"

It didn't exactly roll of the tongue. Navigating to a named point in the sky was something all instrument pilots were expected to do and it was a skill we had to master to get our wings. Looking at your Horizontal Situation Indicator, HSI, you see:

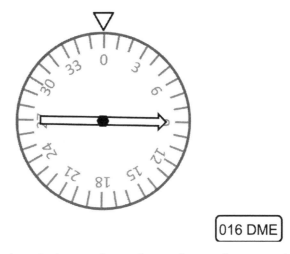

016 DME

The bearing pointer is pointing to the radio station so "you are the tail."

Your
position
line

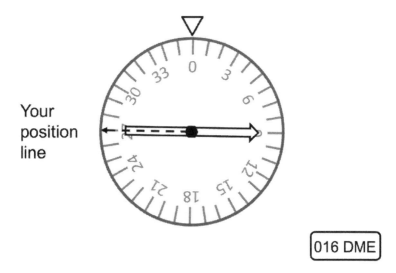

016 DME

Our desired fix is on the 305 degree radial, "target is the radial," as the rule says:

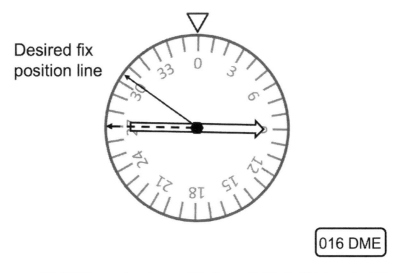

We are at 16 DME and the desired fix is at 11 DME, "higher DME is the edge of the card, lower DME is inside,"

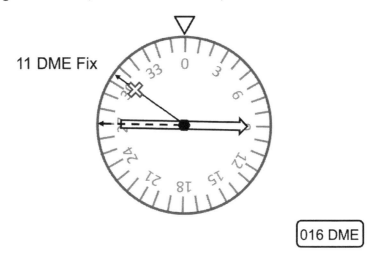

"Draw a line," the rule said:

Line from
your
position to
the fix

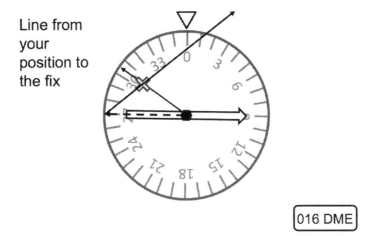

016 DME

"Make the line vertical," which meant turn the aircraft while holding
that mental image:

Make the
line vertical

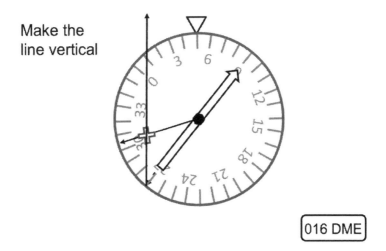

016 DME

"From here you just wait for the tail of the bearing point to . . ."

"Rise," we all said knowing our course intercept rules by now.

"Yes," he agreed, "and it really is that easy. Now: a warning." He
pulled out what looked like a popsicle stick. "I don't want to see any
of you with a popsicle stick in the cockpit. Yes, you can take one of

these and mark ratios of the compass card. Yes, you can use it to help visualize the target position. And yes, it does make fix-to-fix navigation easier. But it isn't what real pilots do. This is what they do in nav school." Being called a navigator? Unacceptable! The visualization was easy enough, but holding the visualization while turning the aircraft? Not so easy.

Soon many of our studs were hiding popsicle sticks in their flight suits. With a tandem seating of the T-38, the instructor would never know.

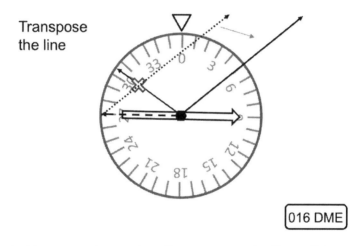

In my mind it was easier to visually transpose the line. Either way, this technique should get you within a couple of miles of the fix. Not good enough for modern day GPS standards, but good enough to QC the FMS.

Global Navigation Satellite System (GNSS)

Rules for using procedures based on the Global Navigation Satellite System (GNSS) or Global Positioning System (GPS) have changed over the years and what you can and cannot do also depends on where in the world you are. The current FAA "Instrument Procedures Handbook," FAA-H-8083-16B, continues to be an excellent resource, but deleted very good information about GPS fundamentals. I'll quote the older version, FAA-H-8083-15B, where helpful.

What about an approach that references GNSS and not GPS? Well, it depends. If your airplane lists it as a viable approach, if the country is WGS-84 compliant, and if the country's rules allow you to, then probably. See the chapter: World Geodetic System-84.

Overview

The U.S. Department of Defense (DOD) developed and deployed GPS as a space-based positioning, velocity, and time system. The DOD is responsible for the operation of the GPS satellite constellation and constantly monitors the satellites to ensure proper operation. The GPS system permits Earth-centered coordinates to be determined and provides aircraft position referenced to the DOD World Geodetic System of 1984 (WGS-84). Satellite navigation systems are unaffected by weather and provide global navigation coverage that fully meet the civil requirements for use as the primary means of navigation in oceanic airspace and certain remote areas. Properly certified GPS equipment may be used as a supplemental means of IFR navigation for domestic en route, terminal operations, and certain IAPs. Navigational values, such as distance and bearing to a waypoint and ground speed, are computed from the aircraft's current position (latitude and longitude) and the location of the next waypoint. Course guidance is provided as a linear deviation from the desired track of a great circle route between defined waypoints.

The space element [of GPS] consists of 24 Navstar satellites. This group of satellites is called a constellation. The satellites are in six orbital planes (with four in each plane) at about 11,000 miles above the Earth. At least five satellites are in view at all times. The GPS constellation broadcasts a pseudo-random code timing signal and data message that the aircraft equipment processes to obtain satellite position and status data. By knowing the precise location of each satellite and precisely matching timing with the atomic clocks on the satellites, the aircraft receiver/processor can accurately measure the time each signal takes to arrive at the receiver and, therefore, determine aircraft position.

Source: FAA-H-8083-15B (old version), p. 9-25

How GPS Works

There is much more to it than what follows, but this gives you what you need to understand how GPS works for us in aviation . . .

The Transmitted Signal

Each Navstar satellite transmits on two frequencies:

- L1: 1575.42 MHz — C/A and P codes
- L2: 1227.6 MHz — P code only

Coarse Acquisition (C/A) code is available to all users without limitations and includes

- Ephemeris (position, altitude, speed information from the satellite)

- Time (from the onboard atomic clock, including a time correction factor to make up for the clock's internal errors)

- Satellite health status

- GPS Almanac (predicted positions for entire GPS constellation, often good for months). A receiver that keeps the almanac in memory can predict from a cold start where to look for satellites, speeding acquisition times.

P-Code provides navigation/targeting data for U.S. government users with an encryption key:

• Position data

• Broadcast on both frequencies, allowing qualified receivers to compare both frequencies and correct for any ionospheric delays.

• Once decrypted P-code becomes Y-code.

Source: FAA-H-8083-15B (old version), pg. 9-25

The aircraft GPS receiver measures distance from a satellite using the travel time of a radio signal. Each satellite transmits a specific code, called a course/acquisition (CA) code, which contains information on the satellite's position, the GPS system time, and the health and accuracy of the transmitted data. Knowing the speed at which the signal traveled (approximately 186,000 miles per second) and the exact broadcast time, the distance traveled by the signal can be computed from the arrival time. The distance derived from this method of computing distance is called a pseudo-range because it is not a direct measurement of distance, but a measurement based on time. In addition to knowing the distance to a satellite, a receiver needs to know the satellite's exact position in space; this is known as its ephemeris. Each satellite transmits information about its exact orbital location. The GPS receiver uses this information to precisely establish the position of the satellite.

Source: FAA-H-8083-15 (old version), p. 7-22

Each GPS satellite transmits these two frequencies and chances are your receiver captures the L1. There are no limits to the number of receivers since there is no interaction from these receivers back to the satellites. You will need four satellites to determine your position . . .

One satellite

Each satellite sends out a signal that
includes its own position and the time. The
receiver calculates the time it took the
signal to travel and multiplies that by the
speed of light to compute the distance.
That distance ("r" in the figure) defines a

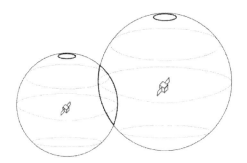

sphere. The receiver could be at any point on that sphere; more
than just the black line, it is the entire outer shell of the sphere.
This is true in theory but there is an issue with the time
synchronization when dealing with only one satellite. (The problem
goes away with more than one satellite since they can be
synchronized. But we are just illustrating a point here.)

Two satellites

With two satellites you have
an intersection of two spheres
and the receiver could be in
any position along those
intersecting spheres and any
point inside the three-
dimensional shape described
by the bolded black line.

Three satellites

With three satellites you
narrow the possible location
down to one of three points
(the three black points).

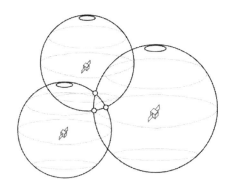

Four satellites

With one more satellite, you have narrowed the universe of possible intersections to just one point (the single black point).

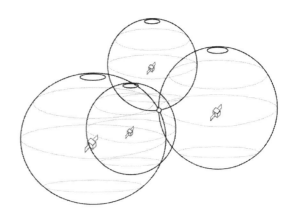

Note: There is more to it than this, but for our purposes, this is why you need four satellites.

Position Errors

Errors are possible due to:

• Minor disturbances in satellite orbits from gravitational variations from the sun and the moon or solar wind.

• Ionospheric signal delays caused by water vapor in the atmosphere; this is the biggest source of signal error.

• Slight fluctuations in the satellite atomic clocks.

• Receiver quality (faulty clocks or internal noise).

• Multi-path signal reflections off structures.

Source: AFAIS PBN Presentation

Any errors from even a single satellite can throw off the estimated distance computations and therefore your estimated position. At the speed of light, even small errors result in enormous errors. A 5 second error, for example, would throw off the position by 930,000 miles, exceeding the satellite's orbit. We must obviously be talking about very small-time errors. The performance of each satellite is measured and corrected to ensure accuracy.

GPS Ground Stations

There are 6 monitoring stations, including the master station at Colorado Springs. [These stations:]

• Collect position and timing data from satellites every 12 hours.

• Send information to master control station.

• Master control station computes corrections and uploads to satellites.

Source: AFAIS PBN Presentation

GPS ground stations, from AFAIS Presentation.

Positioning Services

Standard Positioning Service (SPS)

- Uses C/A code – for all users

- Single frequency (L1)

Precise Positioning Service (PPS)

- Uses P-code – for military

- Two frequencies (L1 and L2) – more accurate

- Requires Decryption Key do use it

Selective Availability

- Selective Availability was designed into the system to provide non-military or non-governmental users intentionally limited accuracy.

- The system was turned off in 2000 and we are told the newer satellites don't even have the capability.

Source: AFAIS PBN Presentation

As the world became more dependent on GPS they became more worried that one day the U.S. government would turn on selective availability and send airplanes into mountains. The U.S. government promises us that they've abandoned the concept entirely.

Satellite Tracks

The signal coverage is supposed to be worldwide, but the satellites do not cover the world. How can that be?

> The nominal GPS Operational Constellation consists of 24 satellites that orbit the earth in 12 hours. There are often more than 24 operational satellites as new ones are launched to replace older satellites. The satellite orbits repeat almost the same ground track (as the earth turns beneath them) once each day. The orbit altitude is such that the satellites repeat the same track and configuration over any point approximately each 24 hours (4 minutes earlier each day). There are six orbital planes (with nominally four SVs in each), equally spaced (60 degrees apart), and inclined at about fifty-five degrees with respect to the equatorial plane. This constellation provides the user with between five and eight SVs visible from any point on the earth.
>
> Source: http://www.colorado.edu/geography/gcraft /notes/gps/gps_f.html

It is true that GPS satellites never get higher than 55° but there are lots of reports of excellent GPS signals at each pole. What gives?

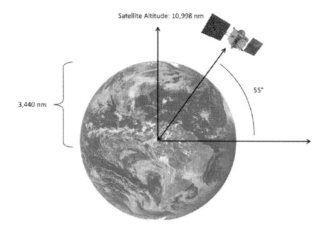

Satellite inclination

Each GPS satellite traces a track over the earth from 55° North to 55° South every twelve hours. At their maximum latitudes they are actually "looking down" on the poles:

Height Above Pole = 10998 cos(55) − 6887 = 2122

Of course, you have no guarantee you will have at least one satellite that high in its orbit. In order to have line of sight on the pole, a satellite would have to be at least 39° latitude:

Minimum Latitude to See Pole = arcsin(6887/10998) = 39

I've not found anything in writing that tells you there will always be at least four satellites above 39° North and 39° South, but it appears so. You should have a good GPS position at either pole.

GNSS versus GPS

GNSS is used internationally to indicate any satellite-based positioning system or augmentation system. The acronym 'GNSS' includes satellite constellations, such as GPS, GLONASS, Galileo, or Beidou, along with augmentation systems such as 'SBAS' and 'GBAS'; all of which provide a satellite-based positioning service.

Source: AC 20-138D, ¶1-4.e.(2)(a)

The Global Navigation Satellite System (GNSS) includes navigation satellites and ground systems that monitor satellite signals and provide corrections and integrity messages, where needed, to support specific phases of flight. Currently, there are two navigation satellite systems in orbit: the U.S. Global Positioning System (GPS) System and the Russian global navigation satellite system (GLONASS). The U.S. and Russia have offered these systems as the basis for a GNSS, free of direct user charges.

So, GPS is a subset of GNSS which means all GPS approaches are GNSS but not all GNSS approaches are GPS. If the approach is marked RNAV (GNSS) you might be okay, but you have some homework to do first: Is GNSS in your flight manual's list of allowed approaches? If you are a commercial operator, do you have the necessary OpSpec? Are there any host-nation prohibitions?

U.S. Requirements to Use GPS

General IFR requirements

(a) General Requirements. Authorization to conduct any GPS operation under IFR requires:

(1) GPS navigation equipment used for IFR operations must be approved in accordance with the requirements specified in Technical Standard Order (TSO) TSO–C129(), TSO–C196(), TSO–C145(), or TSO–C146(), and the installation must be done in accordance with Advisory Circular AC 20–138, Airworthiness Approval of Positioning and Navigation Systems. Equipment approved in accordance with TSO–C115a does not meet the requirements of TSO–C129. Visual flight rules (VFR) and hand–held GPS systems are not authorized for IFR navigation, instrument approaches, or as a principal instrument flight reference.

(2) Aircraft using un-augmented GPS (TSO-C129[] or TSO-C196[]) for navigation under IFR must be equipped with an alternate approved and operational means of navigation suitable for

navigating the proposed route of flight. (Examples of alternate navigation equipment include VOR or DME/DME/IRU capability). Active monitoring of alternative navigation equipment is not required when RAIM is available for integrity monitoring. Active monitoring of an alternate means of navigation is required when the GPS RAIM capability is lost.

(3) Procedures must be established for use in the event that the loss of RAIM capability is predicted to occur. In situations where RAIM is predicted to be unavailable, the flight must rely on other approved navigation equipment, re-route to where RAIM is available, delay departure, or cancel the flight.

(4) The GPS operation must be conducted in accordance with the FAA–approved Airplane Flight Manual (AFM) or flight manual supplement. Flight crew members must be thoroughly familiar with the particular GPS equipment installed in the aircraft, the receiver operation manual, and the AFM or flight manual supplement. Operation, receiver presentation and capabilities of GPS equipment vary. Due to these differences, operation of GPS receivers of different brands, or even models of the same brand, under IFR should not be attempted without thorough operational knowledge. Most receivers have a built–in simulator mode, which allows the pilot to become familiar with operation prior to attempting operation in the aircraft.

(5) Aircraft navigating by IFR–approved GPS are considered to be performance–based navigation (PBN) aircraft and have special equipment suffixes. File the appropriate equipment suffix in accordance with Appendix 4, TBL 4–2, on the ATC flight plan. If GPS avionics become inoperative, the pilot should advise ATC and amend the equipment suffix.

(6) Prior to any GPS IFR operation, the pilot must review appropriate NOTAMs and aeronautical information. (See GPS NOTAMs/Aeronautical Information).

Source: Aeronautical Information Manual ¶1-1-17.b.2

IFR oceanic

Conduct GPS IFR operations in oceanic areas only when approved avionics systems are installed. TSO–C196() users and TSO–C129() GPS users authorized for Class A1, A2, B1, B2, C1, or C2 operations may use GPS in place of another approved means of long–range navigation, such as dual INS. (See TBL 1–1–5 and TBL 1–1–6.) Aircraft with a single installation GPS, meeting the above specifications, are authorized to operate on short oceanic routes requiring one means of long–range navigation (reference AC 20-138, Appendix 1).

Source: Aeronautical Information Manual ¶1-1-17.b.3.(a)

Domestic en route

GPS domestic en route and terminal IFR operations can be conducted as soon as proper avionics systems are installed, provided all general requirements are met. The avionics necessary to receive all of the ground-based facilities appropriate for the route to the destination airport and any required alternate airport must be installed and operational. Ground-based facilities necessary for these routes must also be operational.

Source: Aeronautical Information Manual ¶1-1-17.b.3.(b)

ICAO Requirements to Use GPS

GPS may not be approved for IFR use in other countries. Prior to its use, pilots should ensure that GPS is authorized by the appropriate countries.

Source: FAA-H-8083-15 (old version), pg. 7-21

WGS-84

Navigation data may originate from survey observations, from equipment specifications/settings or from the airspace and procedure design process. Whatever the source, the generation and the subsequent processing of the data must take account of the following: (a) all coordinate data must be referenced to the World Geodetic System — 1984 (WGS-84).

Source: ICAO Doc 9613, Attachment 2, ¶3.4 a)

Not every country uses the same system to map coordinates. The differences can be significant on departure and approach.

Operational Approval

Aircraft equipped with basic GNSS receivers (either as stand-alone equipment or in a multi-sensor environment) that have been approved by the State of the Operator for departure and non-precision approach operations may use these systems to carry out RNAV procedures provided that before conducting any flight, the following criteria are met:

a) the GNSS equipment is serviceable;

b) the pilot has a current knowledge of how to operate the equipment so as to achieve the optimum level of navigation performance;

c) satellite availability is checked to support the intended operation;

d) an alternate airport with conventional navaids has been selected; and

e) the procedure is retrievable from an airborne navigation database.

Source: ICAO Doc 8168 Vol 1 ¶1.2.1

Navigation Database

Departure and approach waypoint information is contained in a navigation database. If the navigation database does not contain the departure or approach procedure, then the basic GNSS stand-alone receiver or FMC shall not be used for these procedures.

Source: ICAO Doc 8168 Vol 1 ¶1.2.3

Receiver Autonomous Integrity Monitoring (RAIM)

For a GPS receiver to be certified for IFR navigation, it must have RAIM or an equivalent function. RAIM is simply a computer algorithm that evaluates the integrity of the GPS signal. That means it judges whether enough satellites are in view and in a good geometry to compute a sufficiently accurate position. RAIM checked now evaluates the current satellites in view. Predictive RAIM is based solely on the Almanac. In other words, RAIM uses the Almanac data to estimate where satellites are supposed to be for the future time entered. Sometimes, the number and position of satellites may result in an accuracy good enough only for certain phases of flight, ie, en route, terminal, or approach.

Source: AFAIS PBN Presentation

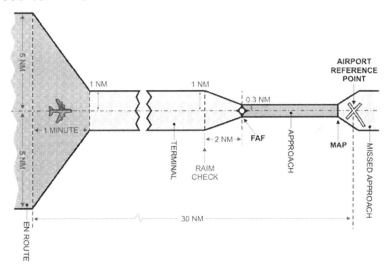

GPS CDI and RAIM Scaling, from AFAIS PBN Presentation.

Predictive RAIM

Predictive RAIM is the ability to forecast or predict when RAIM may not be available. Some systems can make the check for you while others require other measures to ensure RAIM is available when needed.

f. During the pre–flight planning phase RAIM prediction must be performed if TSO–C129() equipment is used to solely satisfy the RNAV and RNP requirement. GPS RAIM availability must be confirmed for the intended route of flight (route and time) using current GPS satellite information. In the event of a predicted, continuous loss of RAIM of more than five (5) minutes for any part of the intended flight, the flight should be delayed, canceled, or re–routed where RAIM requirements can be met. Operators may satisfy the predictive RAIM requirement through any one of the following methods:

1. Operators may monitor the status of each satellite in its plane/slot position, by accounting for the latest GPS constellation status (for example, NOTAMs or NANUs), and compute RAIM availability using model–specific RAIM prediction software;

2. Operators may use the Service Availability Prediction Tool (SAPT) on the FAA en route and terminal RAIM prediction website;

3. Operators may contact a Flight Service Station to obtain non–precision approach RAIM;

4. Operators may use a third party interface, incorporating FAA/VOLPE RAIM prediction data without altering performance values, to predict RAIM outages for the aircraft's predicted flight path and times;

5. Operators may use the receiver's installed RAIM prediction capability (for TSO–C129a/Class A1/B1/C1 equipment) to provide non–precision approach RAIM, accounting for the latest GPS constellation status (for example, NOTAMs or NANUs).

Receiver non–precision approach RAIM should be checked at airports spaced at intervals not to exceed 60 NM along the RNAV 1 procedure's flight track. "Terminal" or "Approach" RAIM must be available at the ETA over each airport checked; or,

6. Operators not using model–specific software or FAA/VOLPE RAIM data will need FAA operational approval.

Source: Source: Aeronautical Information Manual ¶5-1-16

RAIM outages

(1) RAIM outages may occur due to an insufficient number of satellites or due to unsuitable satellite geometry which causes the error in the position solution to become too large. Loss of satellite reception and RAIM warnings may occur due to aircraft dynamics (changes in pitch or bank angle). Antenna location on the aircraft, satellite position relative to the horizon, and aircraft attitude may affect reception of one or more satellites. Since the relative positions of the satellites are constantly changing, prior experience with the airport does not guarantee reception at all times, and RAIM availability should always be checked.

(2) Civilian pilots may obtain GPS RAIM availability information for nonprecision approach procedures by using a manufacturer–supplied RAIM prediction tool, or using the Service Availability Prediction Tool (SAPT) on the FAA en route and terminal RAIM prediction website. Pilots can also request GPS RAIM aeronautical information from a flight service station during preflight briefings. GPS RAIM aeronautical information can be obtained for a period of 3 hours (for example, if you are scheduled to arrive at 1215 hours, then the GPS RAIM information is available from 1100 to 1400 hours) or a 24–hour timeframe at a particular airport. FAA briefers will provide RAIM information for a period of 1 hour before to 1 hour after the ETA hour, unless a specific timeframe is requested by the pilot. If flying a published GPS departure, a RAIM prediction should also be requested for the departure airport.

(3) The military provides airfield specific GPS RAIM NOTAMs for nonprecision approach procedures at military airfields. The RAIM outages are issued as M–series NOTAMs and may be obtained for up to 24 hours from the time of request.

(4) Receiver manufacturers and/or database suppliers may supply "NOTAM" type information concerning database errors. Pilots should check these sources when available, to ensure that they have the most current information concerning their electronic database.

(5) If RAIM is not available, use another type of navigation and approach system; select another route or destination; or delay the trip until RAIM is predicted to be available on arrival. On longer flights, pilots should consider rechecking the RAIM prediction for the destination during the flight. This may provide an early indication that an unscheduled satellite outage has occurred since takeoff.

(6) If a RAIM failure/status annunciation occurs prior to the final approach waypoint (FAWP), the approach should not be completed since GPS no longer provides the required integrity. The receiver performs a RAIM prediction by 2 NM prior to the FAWP to ensure that RAIM is available as a condition for entering the approach mode. The pilot should ensure the receiver has sequenced from "Armed" to "Approach" prior to the FAWP (normally occurs 2 NM prior). Failure to sequence may be an indication of the detection of a satellite anomaly, failure to arm the receiver (if required), or other problems which preclude flying the approach.

(7) If the receiver does not sequence into the approach mode or a RAIM failure/status annunciation occurs prior to the FAWP, the pilot must not initiate the approach nor descend, but instead, proceed to the missed approach waypoint (MAWP) via the FAWP, perform a missed approach, and contact ATC as soon as practical. The GPS receiver may continue to operate after a RAIM flag/status annunciation appears, but the navigation

information should be considered advisory only. Refer to the receiver operating manual for specific indications and instructions associated with loss of RAIM prior to the FAF.

(8) If the RAIM flag/status annunciation appears after the FAWP, the pilot should initiate a climb and execute the missed approach. The GPS receiver may continue to operate after a RAIM flag/status annunciation appears, but the navigation information should be considered advisory only. Refer to the receiver operating manual for operating mode information during a RAIM annunciation.

Source: Aeronautical Information Manual ¶1-1-17.b.5.(g)

Fault Detection and Exclusion (FDE)

Definitions.

1. Primary means of navigation—Navigation equipment that provides the only required means on the aircraft of satisfying the necessary levels of accuracy, integrity, and availability for a particular area, route, procedure, or operation.

2. Class II navigation—Any en route flight operation or portion of an en route operation (irrespective of the means of navigation) which takes place outside (beyond) the designated operational service volume of ICAO standard airway navigation facilities (VOR, VOR/DME, NDB).

3. Fault detection and exclusion (FDE)—Capability of GPS to:

a. Detect a satellite failure which effects navigation; and

b. Automatically exclude that satellite from the navigation solution.

4. All operators conducting GPS primary means of Class II navigation in oceanic/remote areas under 14 CFR parts 91, 121, 125, or 135 must utilize an FAA-approved FDE prediction program for the installed GPS equipment that is capable of predicting, prior to departure, the maximum outage duration of

the loss of fault exclusion, the loss of fault detection, and the loss of navigation function for flight on a specified route. The "specified route of flight" is defined by a series of waypoints (to include the route to any required alternates) with the time specified by a velocity or series of velocities. Since specific ground speeds may not be maintained, the pre-departure prediction must be performed for the range of expected ground speeds. This FDE prediction program must use the same FDE algorithm that is employed by the installed GPS equipment and must be developed using an acceptable software development methodology (e.g., RTCA/DO-178B). The FDE prediction program must provide the capability to designate manually satellites that are scheduled to be unavailable in order to perform the prediction accurately. The FDE prediction program will be evaluated as part of the navigation system's installation approval.

5. Any predicted satellite outages that affect the capability of GPS equipment to provide the navigation function on the specified route of flight requires that the flight be canceled, delayed, or rerouted. If the fault exclusion capability outage (exclusion of a malfunctioning satellite) exceeds the acceptable duration on the specific route of flight, the flight must be canceled, delayed, or rerouted.

6. Prior to departure, the operator must use the FDE prediction program to demonstrate that there are no outages in the capability to navigate on the specified route of flight (the FDE prediction program determines whether the GPS constellation is robust enough to provide a navigation solution for the specified route of flight).

7. Once navigation function is ensured (the equipment can navigate on the specified route of flight), the operator must use the FDE prediction program to demonstrate that the maximum outage of the capability of the equipment to provide fault exclusion for the specified route of flight does not exceed the

acceptable duration (fault exclusion is the ability to exclude a failed satellite from the navigation solution). The acceptable duration (in minutes) is equal to the time it would take to exit the protected airspace (one-half the lateral separation minimum) assuming a 35-nautical mile (nm) per hour cross-track navigation system error growth rate when starting from the center of the route. For example, a 60-nm lateral separation minimum yields 51 minutes acceptable duration (30 nm divided by 35 nm per hour). If the fault exclusion outage exceeds the acceptable duration, the flight must be canceled, delayed, or rerouted.

Source: FAA Order 8900.1, Vol. 4, Ch. 1, §4, ¶4-78.C.

This can be confusing so let's break it into a few pieces:

• Class II navigation in oceanic/remote areas means anytime you are outside the service volume of authorized navigation aids.

• "GPS primary means of Class II navigation" means that the only way you have of long-range navigation is GPS. If you have an IRS, you have another means.

• If your aircraft relies on GPS, and GPS only, for Class II navigation, your manufacturer should either provide or point you to a qualified FDE program you can load on a computer device to satisfy this requirement.

Availability / NOTAMs

The status of GPS satellites is broadcast as part of the data message transmitted by the GPS satellites. GPS status information is also available by means of the U.S. Coast Guard navigation information service: (703) 313–5907, Internet: http://www.navcen.uscg.gov/?Do=constellationStatus. Additionally, satellite status is available through the Notice to Airmen (NOTAM) system.

Source: Aeronautical Information Manual, §1-1-17, ¶a.2.(a)

NOTAMs are available here: https://pilotweb.nas.faa.gov/PilotWeb/.

Satellite-Based Augmentation System (SBAS)

The acronyms 'SBAS' and 'GBAS' are the respective international designations for satellite-based and ground-based augmentation systems complying with the International Civil Aviation Organization (ICAO) standards and recommended practices (SARPs). Several countries have implemented their own versions of 'SBAS' and 'GBAS' that have specific names and acronyms. For example, WAAS is the U.S. implementation of an 'SBAS' while EGNOS is the European implementation.

Source: AC 20-138D, ¶1-4.e.(2)(b)

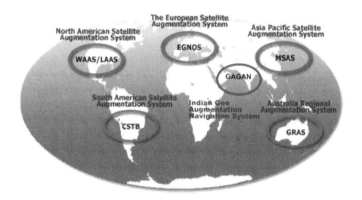

SBAS, from AFAIS PBN Presentation

An SBAS augments core satellite constellations by providing ranging, integrity and correction information via geostationary satellites. The system comprises a network of ground reference stations that observe satellite signals, and master stations that process observed data and generate SBAS messages for uplink to the geostationary satellites, which broadcast the SBAS message to the users.

By providing extra ranging signals via geostationary satellites and enhanced integrity information for each navigation satellite,

SBAS delivers a higher availability of service than the core satellite constellations.

Source: ICAO Doc 8168 - Aircraft Operations - Vol I, chapter 2, ¶2.1

These geostationary satellites are above and beyond the GPS constellation. Their positions are constantly updated by reference to the ground stations and provide a high degree of accuracy.

Accuracy

a. Lateral Accuracy - better than GPS — More like Localizer

b. Vertical Accuracy – much better than GPS — Good enough for Vertical Guidance (glideslope)

c. LPV minima — "Localizer Performance with Vertical Guidance" (GPS 95% Standard / GPS Actual Performance), (Horizontal 36m / 2.74m), (Vertical 77m / 3.89m)

Source: AFAIS PBN Presentation

	WAAS 95% Standard	WAAS Actual Performance
Horizontal	16 m	1.08 m
Vertical	4 m	1.26 m

WAAS

The U.S. implementation of SBAS is WAAS. The U.S. system is compatible with the European (EGNOS) and Asia Pacific (MSAS) systems.

WAAS improves the accuracy, integrity, availability and continuity of GPS signals. Additionally, the WAAS geostationary satellites provide ranging sources to supplement the GPS signals. If there are no airworthiness limitations on other installed navigation equipment, WAAS avionics enable aircraft navigation during all phases of flight from takeoff through vertically guided approaches and guided missed approaches. WAAS avionics with an appropriate airworthiness approval can enable aircraft to fly to the LPV, LP, LNAV/VNAV and LNAV lines of minima on RNAV (GPS) approaches. One of the major improvements WAAS provides is the ability to generate glide path guidance independent of ground equipment. Temperature and pressure extremes do not affect WAAS vertical guidance unlike when baro-VNAV is used to fly to LNAV/VNAV line of minima. However, like most other navigation services, the WAAS network has service volume limits, and some airports on the fringe of WAAS coverage may experience reduced availability of WAAS vertical guidance. When a pilot selects an approach procedure, WAAS avionics display the best level of service supported by the combination of the WAAS signal-in-space, the aircraft avionics, and the selected RNAV (GPS) instrument approach.

Source: AC 90-107 ¶6.b.

WAAS Channel Number/Approach ID

The WAAS Channel Number is an optional equipment capability that allows the use of a 5–digit number to select a specific final approach segment without using the menu method. The Approach ID is an airport unique 4–character combination for verifying the selection and extraction of the correct final approach segment information from the aircraft database. It is similar to the ILS ident, but displayed visually rather than aurally. The Approach ID consists of the letter W for WAAS, the runway number, and a letter other than L, C or R, which could be confused with Left, Center and Right, e.g., W35A. Approach IDs are assigned in the order that WAAS approaches are built to that runway number at that airport. The WAAS Channel Number and Approach ID are displayed in the upper left corner of the approach procedure pilot briefing. Depending on your avionics suite, approach verification may depend on the WAAS Channel Number, the Approach ID, or both. You will need to select the approach from a database and simply verify the necessary item for approach verification is present.

Source: AIM 5-4-5.m.7.(g)

RAIM and FDE under WAAS

e. Barometric Aiding (Baro-Aiding). A method of augmenting the GPS integrity solution in receiver autonomous integrity monitoring (RAIM) by using a barometric altitude input source. Baro-aiding requires four satellites and a barometric altimeter to detect an integrity anomaly (the current altimeter setting may need to be entered into the receiver as described in the operating manual). Baro-aiding satisfies the RAIM requirement in lieu of a fifth satellite.

h. Fault Detection and Exclusion (FDE). A receiver autonomous integrity monitoring (RAIM) algorithm that can automatically detect and exclude a faulty satellite from the position solution when measurements from six or more satellites are available. WAAS equipment uses FDE for integrity whenever a WAAS signal is not available to permit continued operation from en route through approach operations.

Source: AC 90-107 ¶4.

References

Advisory Circular 20-138D, Positioning and Navigation Systems, Change 2, 4/7/16, U.S. Department of Transportation

Advisory Circular 90-107, Guidance for Localizer Performance with Vertical Guidance and Localizer Performance without Vertical Guidance Approach Operations in the U.S. National Airspace System, 2/11/11, U.S. Department of Transportation

Aeronautical Information Manual, 4/20/23

FAA-H-8083-15B, Instrument Flying Handbook, U.S. Department of Transportation, Flight Standards Service, 2001

FAA-H-8083-16B, Instrument Flying Handbook, U.S. Department of Transportation, Flight Standards Service, 2017

FAA Order 8900.1

ICAO Doc 8168 - Aircraft Operations - Vol I - Flight Procedures, Appendix to Chapter 3, Procedures for Air Navigation Services, International Civil Aviation Organization, Appendix, 23/11/06

ICAO Doc 9613 - Performance Based Navigation (PBN) Manual, International Civil Aviation Organization, 2008

US Air Force Advanced Instrument School (AFAIS) Performance-Based Navigation Presentation, Oct 2009

High Latitude Operations Techniques

If you fly over the poles under 14 CFR 135, you need to understand everything written below about high latitude operations. It could very well be that you can't legally do what your airplane is physically capable of doing. Flying over the poles under 14 CFR 91? You still need to understand this stuff, but you might not be prevented from doing something stupid. Me? I would make sure we had all our ducks in line first. What follows will help you do just that.

Location

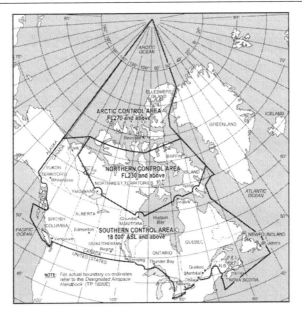

Southern, Northern, and Arctic Control Areas, (Transport Canada Aeronautical Information Manual, Figure 2.3

> The North Polar Area is defined as the entire area north of latitude 78 degrees North.
>
> The South Polar Area is defined as the entire area south of latitude 60 degrees South.
>
> Source: Advisory Circular 120-42B, ¶601

The worst magnetic compass performance is probably in the center of the Northern Control Area, home to the magnetic North Pole. This position creates a notch in the circle of magnetic unreliability, often called a "keyhole." Charts should be checked for the presence of a "T" denoting the use of True Heading instead of Magnetic. Some aircraft automatically switch to True based on airway designation or latitude. The G450, for example, automatically switches above N73° or S60° latitude.

Canadian Regulations

> Controlled airspace within the High Level Airspace is divided into three separate areas. They are the Southern Control Area (SCA), the Northern Control Area (NCA) and the Arctic Control Area (ACA).
>
> Pilots are reminded that both the NCA and the ACA are within the Northern Domestic Airspace; therefore, compass indications may be erratic, and true tracks are used in determining the flight level at which to fly. In addition, the airspace from FL 330 to FL 410 within the lateral dimensions of the NCA, the ACA and the northern part of the SCA has been designated CMNPS airspace.
>
> Source: Transport Canada Aeronautical Information Manual, ¶ 2.6

CMNPS is Canadian Minimum Navigation Performance Specifications. What we used to call "polar ops" is now "high latitude operations." The definition depends on your source of information but can be summarized as follows:

- The northern and southern poles.
- The Canadian Northern Domestic Area (NDA). The NDA includes the Northern Control Area (NCA), the Arctic Control Area (ACA) and the Area of Magnetic Unreliability (AMU). The NDA, NCA and ACA are depicted on Canadian HI en route charts and encompass the northernmost Canadian airspace.

Documentation / Certification

Operations in the North Polar Area. After February 15, 2008, no certificate holder may operate an aircraft in the region north of 78° N latitude ("North Polar Area"), other than intrastate operations wholly within the state of Alaska, unless authorized by the FAA. The certificate holder's operation specifications must include the following:

- The designation of airports that may be used for en-route diversions and the requirements the airports must meet at the time of diversion.

- Except for all-cargo operations, a recovery plan for passengers at designated diversion airports.

- A fuel-freeze strategy and procedures for monitoring fuel freezing for operations.

- A plan to ensure communication capability for operations in the North Polar Area.

- An MEL for operations in the North Polar Area.

- A training plan for operations in the North Polar Area.

- A plan for mitigating crew exposure to radiation during solar flare activity.

- A plan for providing at least two cold weather anti-exposure suits in the aircraft, to protect crewmembers during outside activity at a diversion airport with extreme climatic conditions. The FAA may relieve the certificate holder from this requirement if the season of the year makes the equipment unnecessary.

Source: 14 CFR 135, §135.98

All approvals for operations into AMUs are granted by issuing OpSpec B040, and by adding that area of en route operation to the standard OpSpec B050. A checklist for operations in AMUs is available in the guidance subsystem in association with OpSpec B040.

Source: FAA Order 8900, Volume 4, Chapter 1, §5, ¶4-103.D

Equipment

Certificate holders must have at least two cold weather anti-exposure suit(s) for the crewmembers on the airplane if outside coordination by a crewmember at a diversion airport with extreme climatic conditions is determined to be necessary. The certificate holder may be relieved of this requirement based on seasonal temperatures that would render the use of such suits unnecessary. This determination must be made with concurrence of the CHDO.

Source: Advisory Circular 135-42, Appendix 3, ¶3.f

This isn't much of a list; you would be wise to consider adding the requirements of Advisory Circular 120-42B, which do not restrict 14 CFR 135 and 91, but offer sound operating practices.

- Fuel quantity indicating system (FQIS), including the fuel tank temperature indicating system;

- APU (when the APU is necessary for an airplane to comply with ETOPS requirements), including electrical and pneumatic supply to its designed capability,

- Autothrottle system;

- Communication systems relied on by the flight crewmember to satisfy the requirement for communication capability; and

- Except for all-cargo operations, an expanded medical kit to include automated external defibrillators (AED).

Source: Advisory Circular 120-42B, ¶603.b.(5)

MEL

Before receiving approval to conduct polar operations, a certificate holder must review their MEL for such operations and should amend their MEL. The following systems and equipment should be addressed in the MEL based on specific needs applicable to this operation.

(1) Fuel Quantity Indicating System (to include a fuel tank temperature indicating system).

(2) Communication system(s) needed for effective communications by the flight crewmember while in flight.

(3) Expanded medical kit.

Source: Advisory Circular 135-42, Appendix 3, ¶3.c

Training

Before conducting polar operations, certificate holders must ensure that flight crewmembers are trained on any applicable passenger recovery plan used in this operation. Certificate holders should also ensure that flight crewmembers are trained on the following items, which should be included in a certificate holder's approved training programs:

(1) Atmospheric pressure at Field Elevation/Barometric pressure for Local Altimeter Setting and meter/feet conversion issues (flight crewmember training).

(2) Training requirements for fuel freeze (maintenance and flight crewmember training).

(3) General polar-specific training on weather patterns and aircraft system limitations (flight crewmember training).

(4) Proper use of the cold weather anti-exposure suit, if required (flight crewmember training).

(5) Radiation exposure (see AC 120-61A, In-Flight Radiation Exposure).

Source: Advisory Circular 135-42, Appendix 3, ¶3.e

Communications Issues

The FAA recognizes the limitations of satellite communications (SATCOM) in the North Polar Area above this latitude, and in such an area an alternate communication system such as HF voice or data link is to be used. The relatively short period of time that the flight is above latitude 82 degrees North in relation to the total planned flight time is a small fraction of the total flight. The ability to use SATCOM for all other portions of the flight, which for some routes could be longer than 15 hours duration, is advantageous to the flight. For flights above 82 degrees North latitude, the operator must also ensure that communications requirements can be met by the most reliable means available, taking into account the potential communication disruption due to solar flare activity. The same philosophy and commensurate requirements apply for ETOPS in the South Polar Area.

Source: AC 120-42B, ¶303.c.(7)

VHF, HF, INMARSAT, CPDLC

You can find frequencies, phone numbers, and CPDLC addresses on en route charts. I am told that VHF is sparse, HF quality is generally good, though signals may be impacted by solar activity. You may need to use either AM, USB or LSB to achieve the best clarity.

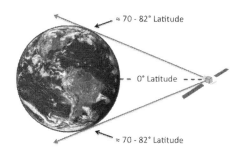

INMARSAT Line of Sight

Keep in mind that Inmarsat satellites are geostationary, generally near the equator. They may not have good line-of-sight near the poles. Geosynchronous satellites, such as Iridium, have better coverage at the poles.

Navigation Issues

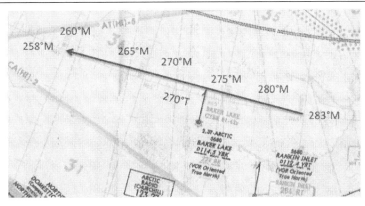

Magnetic Variation Convergence Example

Magnetic Variation and Convergence of the Meridians

The following is from an outdated navigation manual that still makes sense:

Conventional magnetic compasses sense magnetic direction by detecting the horizontal component of the earth's magnetic field. Since this horizontal component vanishes near the magnetic poles, magnetic compasses are highly unreliable and unusable in areas approximately 1,000 NM from each magnetic pole. Within these areas, air navigation is further complicated by very rapid changes in magnetic variation over small distances.

When flying "great circle" courses at latitudes greater than 67 degrees, convergence of the meridians can create rapid changes in true headings and true courses with small changes in aircraft position. As a result, relatively small errors in determining the aircraft's actual position can produce very large errors in determining the proper heading to fly and maintain the assigned flight path. When even small errors occur, very large navigation errors can develop over extremely short distances. An extreme example of this phenomenon occurs at the earth's geographic North Pole. Flight in any direction from the exact pole is initially due South (that is, the direction to Russia or the United States is South).

True Heading

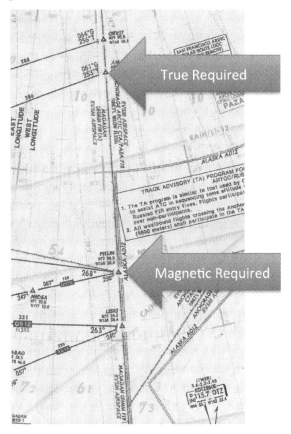

True vs. Magnetic Example, (Jeppesen Airway Manual AP(HI))

Navigating near the poles presents several issues not found anywhere else in the world. Because of these issues, the only acceptable method of navigating through the NCA and high latitude region is through the use of long-range navigation systems using inertial and GPS based FMS systems referenced to True North only. Back when I was a Strategic Air Command trained killer, our navigators would use grid navigation to head from here to there and I do believe we got lost a few times.

Other methods of navigation in the NCA are impractical or unreliable because of the inherent limitations of magnetic compasses near the magnetic and geographic North Poles, and because of the geometric problem caused by meridian convergence.

Some aircraft make the switch automatically by reference to latitude or airway, while for other the switch must be made manually. You need to dive into your aircraft manuals to find out.

Tropopause Height and ISA

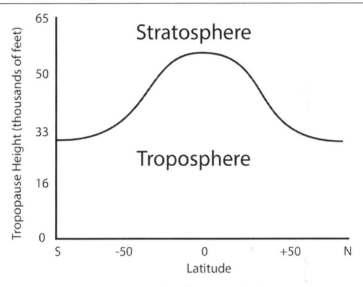

Tropopause height, generalized

The height of the tropopause depends on the location, notably the latitude, as shown in the figure (which shows annual mean conditions). It also depends on the season.

At latitudes above 60°, the tropopause is less than 9-10 km above sea level; the lowest is less than 8 km high, above Antarctica and above Siberia and northern Canada in winter. The highest average tropopause is over the oceanic warm pool of the western equatorial Pacific, about 17.5 km high, and over

Southeast Asia, during the summer monsoon, the tropopause occasionally peaks above 18 km. In other words, cold conditions lead to a lower tropopause, obviously because of less convection.

Deep convection (thunderstorms) in the Intertropical Convergence Zone, or over mid-latitude continents in summer, continuously push the tropopause upwards and as such deepen the troposphere.

On the other hand, colder regions have a lower tropopause, obviously because convective overturning is limited there, due to the negative radiation balance at the surface. In fact, convection is very rare in polar regions; most of the tropospheric mixing at middle and high latitudes is forced by frontal systems in which uplift is forced rather than spontaneous (convective). This explains the paradox that tropopause temperatures are lowest where the surface temperatures are highest.

Source: Geerts and Linacre

The tropopause at the poles is lower than at the equator; that means the altitudes where most polar-capable aircraft cruise is warmer. Knowing this, altitude selection may not be straight forward.

Surface Temperatures

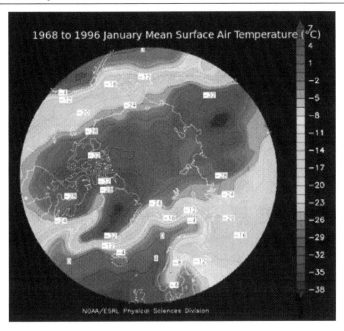

North Pole January Mean Temperatures, (Wikimedia Commons)

If a descent into lower altitudes is required, fuel freezing and other aircraft systems limitations can become issues. If an emergency landing is required, surface temperatures can be life threatening.

Fuel Freezing

Fuel Freeze Strategy and Monitoring Requirements for Polar Operations. Certificate holders must develop a fuel freeze strategy and procedures for monitoring fuel freezing for operations in the North Polar Area. A fuel freeze analysis program in lieu of using the standard minimum fuel freeze temperatures for specific types of fuel may be used. In such cases, the certificate holder's fuel freeze analysis and monitoring program for the airplane fuel load must be acceptable to the FAA Administrator. The certificate holder should have procedures for determining the fuel freeze temperature of the actual fuel load on board the airplane. These procedures relative to determining the fuel freeze temperature and monitoring the actual temperature of the fuel on board should require appropriate levels of coordination between maintenance and the flight crewmember.

Source: Advisory Circular 135-42, Appendix 3, ¶3.c

Should fuel temperatures approach the aircraft's freezing limit you should consider:

- Climbing or descending into a level of warmer air,
- Altering the route into a region of warmer air, and/or
- Increasing cruise airspeed (Fuel temperatures should increase approximately one degree for every .02 increase in Mach speed)

Your flight planning vendor should provide a temperature chart to help you plan for these contingencies. Remember, any changes in flight level, speed or route must be coordinated with ATC.

Polar Radiation Issues

Solar Flare, (Wikimedia Commons)

Less radiation will be received on a lower-latitude flight because of the greater amount of radiation shielding provided by the Earth's magnetic field. This shielding is greatest near the equator and gradually decreases to zero as one goes north or south. Galactic cosmic radiation levels over the polar regions are about twice those over the geomagnetic equator at the same altitudes. Because solar particle peak energies are much lower than galactic particle peak energies, solar cosmic radiation dose rates are negligible near the geomagnetic equator.

Source: Advisory Circular 120-61B, ¶6.a

Space radiation on the ground is very low, but increases significantly with altitude. At 30,000 to 40,000 feet, the typical altitude of a jetliner, exposure on a typical flight is still considered safe – less than a chest X-ray.

Exposure is considerably higher, however, over the Earth's poles, where the planet's magnetic field no longer provides any shielding. And with a thousand-fold rise in commercial airline flights over the North Pole in the last 10 years, exposure to radiation has become a serious concern.

A study by Mertens of polar flights during a solar storm in 2003 showed that passengers received about 12 percent of the annual radiation limit recommended by the International Committee on Radiological Protection. The exposures were greater than on typical flights at lower latitudes, and confirmed concerns about commercial flights using polar routes.

People who work on commercial airline flights are technically listed as "radiation workers" by the federal government – a classification that includes nuclear plant workers and X-ray technicians. But unlike some others in that category, flight crews do not quantify the radiation they are exposed to.

Source: NASA Study, Michael Finneran

Flights in the Polar Region at typical business jet operating altitudes are well above the tropopause where much of the atmospheric protection from solar storms is lost, increasing crew and passenger exposure to solar radiation.

For example, one New York-Tokyo flight during a solar storm could expose the passengers and crew to the normal annual exposure (1mSv) of someone who remained on the surface. If an S4 solar storm is active or predicted, polar operations are generally considered not suitable at any altitude, while operations at FL 310 or below are considered acceptable in S3 storm conditions.

Alternate Airports

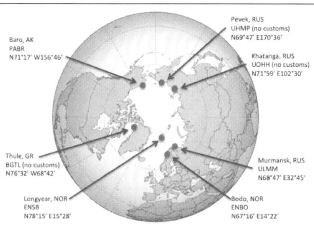

Arctic Alternates

Before each flight, certificate holders must designate alternate airports that can be used in case an en route diversion is necessary. The airplane should have a reasonable assurance that the weather during periods when the certificate holder would need the services of the airport are within the operating limits of the airplane. The airplane should be able to make a safe landing and maneuver off the runway at the diversion airport. In addition, those airports identified for use during an en route diversion should be capable of protecting the safety of all personnel by allowing:

(1) Safe offload of passengers and crewmember during possible adverse weather conditions;

(2) Providing for the physiological needs of the passengers and crewmember until a safe evacuation is completed; and

(3) Safe extraction of passengers and crewmember as soon as possible (execution and completion of the recovery should be within 12 to 48 hours following landing).

Source: Advisory Circular 135-42, Appendix 3, ¶3.a

Operators are expected to define a sufficient set of polar diversion alternate airports, such that one or more can be reasonably expected to be suitable and available in varying weather conditions (AC 120-42A, Extended Range Operation With Two-Engine Airplanes (ETOPS), provides additional guidance for two-engine airplanes).

Source: FAA Order 8900, Volume 4, Chapter 1, §5, ¶4-103.E

A recovery plan is required that will be initiated in the event of an unplanned diversion. The recovery plan should address the care and safety of passengers and flight crew at the diversion airport and include the plan of operation to extract the passengers and flight crew from that airport.

Source: FAA Order 8900, Volume 4, Chapter 1, §5, ¶4-103.G

There aren't many airports with paved runways in the Arctic, and many of those do not have regular airline service or customs. If you are flying under 14 CFR 135 your Operations Specification approval will require a list of alternates and a plan for getting passengers from the alternates within 48 hours. More on this: Advisory Circular 135-42, Appendix 3, ¶3.b.

Even if you do find a suitable alternate with a paved runway, consider what services are available. If, for example, you have a passenger suffering a stroke, will you be better off continuing six hours to your destination or landing at a remote airfield that is days away from the nearest capable healthcare facility? The same can be said for maintenance. If you have to land as soon as possible, obviously do that. But remember to consider the events following landing when weighing your decision.

References

14 CFR 135, Title 14: Aeronautics and Space, Operating Requirements: Commuter and On Demand Operations and Rules Governing Persons on Board Such Aircraft, Federal Aviation Administration, Department of Transportation

Advisory Circular 120-42B, Extended Operations (ETOPS and Polar Ops), 6/13/08, U.S. Department of Transportation

Advisory Circular 120-61B, In-flight Radiation Exposure, 11/21/14, U.S. Department of Transportation

Advisory Circular 135-42, Extended Operations (ETOPS) and Operations in the North Polar Area, 6/10/08, U.S. Department of Transportation

FAA Order 8900.1

Geerts, B. and Linacre, E, The Height of the Tropopause, University of Wyoming, Atmospheric Science 11/97

Inertial Navigation

The first description I ever read about Inertial Navigation was meant in jest, but it wasn't actually too far off: An Inertial Navigation System knows where it is because it knows where it was and where it has gone since. Before we go any further, one bit of definition is in order. An Inertial Reference System (IRS) is nothing more than something that reports your position (latitude, longitude, geometric altitude), speed, and attitude. An Inertial Navigation System (INS) adds the ability to catalog various positions as waypoints and provides a method of getting from one waypoint to another. If you have an FMS that does this for you, you don't really need an INS, so the IRS is probably what you have installed.

Evolution

As I write this, the Global Positioning System (GPS) system is the primary means of navigation for most of aviation. It may be useful to see the evolution of long-range navigation to understand how inertial navigation came to be:

- Pilotage relies on keeping an eye on landmarks and terrain to determine where you are.
- Dead reckoning uses some form of heading information and an estimate of speed to determine where you are going.
- Celestial navigation uses angles between the local horizon and known celestial objects (e.g., sun, moon, or stars), or between those celestial objects to determine position on the earth.
- Radio navigation uses frequency sources from known locations, such as VORs or NDBs.
- Inertial navigation uses a known initial position, attitude, and measured accelerations to determine velocity and the resulting position.

- GPS is a type of radio navigation that uses position and time signals from multiple satellites to determine the receiver's position.

Inertia and Newton's First Law of Motion

"A body at rest will remain at rest and a body in motion will remain in motion, unless acted upon by an unbalanced force."

Newton's First Law of Motion implies that bodies have a property called inertia. Inertia may be defined as the property of a body that results in its maintaining its velocity unchanged unless it interacts with an unbalanced force. The measure of inertia is what is technically known as mass. A few points about this first law will make all that follows easier to, well, follow:

- When there are no external forces, objects move with constant velocity.
- Inertia is resistance to changes in motion.
- The amount of inertia an object has is measured by its mass; more mass means more inertia.

So how do we measure those external forces? We first need a stable platform to measure those forces against . . .

Gyroscopes

The word gyroscope comes from the Greek gyros, which means circle. In a conventional gyroscope, the gyro is a spinning wheel mounted on two bearings inside an inner ring which itself is mounted inside another ring. When rotating, the spinning wheel maintains its position according to the conservation of angular momentum.

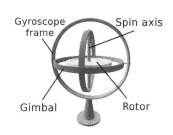

Gyroscope (Lucas Vieira)

These rings are known as gimbals. Note that the outer gimbal can be moving in various directions and the inner spinning wheel maintains its orientation in space. That becomes very useful when the outer gimbal is mounted to a moving vehicle, such as an airplane. The airplane's orientation in space can change while the inner spinning wheel's orientation remains constant.

The axle of the spinning wheel determines its axis. The ends of the axle resist any external forces exerted by the outer gimbals. They effectively "push" against the force. Measuring these forces with accelerometers provide the basis of inertial navigation.

Accelerometers

No matter how an accelerometer is constructed, we may think of it as shown in Figure 2. The accelerometer consists of a proof mass, m, suspended from a case by a pair of springs. The arrow indicates the input axis. An acceleration along this axis will cause the proof mass to be displaced from its equilibrium position. This displacement will be proportional to the acceleration. The amount of

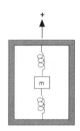

Accelerometer, Stoval, figure 2

displacement from the equilibrium position is sensed by a pick-off and scaled to provide an indication of acceleration along this axis. The equilibrium position of the proof mass is calibrated for zero acceleration. An acceleration in the plus direction will cause the proof mass to move downward with respect to the case. This downward movement indicates positive acceleration. Now imagine that the accelerometer is sitting on a bench in a gravitational field. We see that the proof mass is again displaced downward with respect to the case, which indicates positive acceleration. However, the gravitational acceleration is downward. Therefore, the output of an accelerometer due to a gravitational field is the negative of the field acceleration.

Source: Stoval, pg. 5

Accelerometers measure the deflection of the "proof mass" with something a bit more reliable than a spring. But the point is that we can measure acceleration in any axis.

Inertial Platform

An inertial platform is basically three gyroscopes placed at 90° angles with each other and three accelerometers to measure forces on the platform. If we find the forces in each direction over a specific time period, we can find the velocity in all three directions. By multiplying the velocity by time to find distance, a relative position can be determined. If the starting position was known, the relative position can be added to determine an ending position.

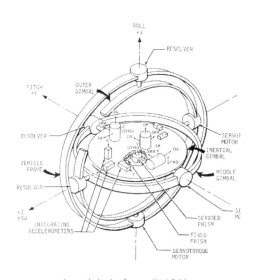

Inertial platform (NASA)

Three Dimensions – "Sort of"

With the three gyroscopes on our inertial platform, we have a way of tracking movement in three dimensions. But we, as pilots, don't actually operate in three dimensions, by the truest sense of the term. Our horizontal plane is aligned with the surface of the earth, which isn't flat.

Our inertial navigation must consider "level" to be parallel to the earth's surface or perpendicular to gravity's pull. The engineer calls this the "locally level frame" but for us pilots it is simply level flight.

There are two major problems to tackle. First, the earth is rotating. The inertial navigation system needs to compensate for that. Second, the earth isn't flat. We have to account for the fact "up" and "down" are technically different everywhere on the globe. Sounds complicated? It is . . .

We can solve many of the problems if we define our frame of reference to be Earth-Centered, Earth-Fixed, or ECEF.

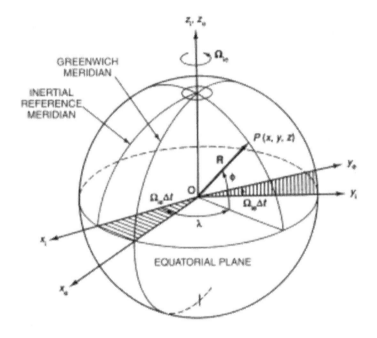

Rotating spherical earth, Stoval, figure 8

The next step in our analysis is to allow our spherical earth to rotate. We define a new coordinate frame called the inertial frame, which is fixed at the center of the earth. Ignoring the earth's orbital motion, we regard the orientation of this frame as fixed with respect to the distant stars. The inertial frame is defined to be coincident with the ECEF frame at zero time. Figure 8 shows the relationship between the inertial and ECEF frames. The ECEF frame rotates with respect to the inertial

> frame with an angular velocity (Ω) of approximately 15.04
> degrees per hour.
>
> Source: Stoval, pg. 3

As pilots we don't need to be concerned with it because the
designers have done that for us. So too with the non-flat earth.
Since we reference everything on earth to the surface of the earth,
the inertial platform must be moved to agree with the "flat earth"
concept. If we didn't do this, for example, an airplane flying from
Hawaii to Switzerland would show itself inverted at the end of the
journey.

Strapdown Systems

Gimballed inertial navigation systems are easy to understand, since
each gyroscope maintains its orientation in space no matter what
the vehicle is doing. These are called "stable platform systems"
since the platform itself is constant. The problem, however, is the
gimbal arrangement is mechanically complex and the bearing,
motors, and slip rings generate heat and friction. This makes them
somewhat expensive to maintain.

Since we are using computers to do much of the work, it isn't really
necessary to keep the platform stable, only to measure the forces
on each axis. Most inertial navigation systems today eliminate the
gimbals and simply strap the gyroscope to the system case, which is
itself strapped to the airplane. Getting rid of the gimbals certainly
reduces the number of moving parts and that increases reliability.

The problem is that the sensors used to detect forces on the gyros
now have to compensate for the movement of the vehicle itself.
But this isn't a problem with modern computers and so the
strapdown inertial is pretty much the standard solution today.

Drift Errors

With earlier inertial navigation systems, it wasn't uncommon for the
system to wander from its initial position just sitting in the chocks or

to develop an error while taxiing to the end of the runway. Friction in gyro bearings, heat in various moving parts, and even the rotation of the earth could introduce errors known as drift. Not too many years ago, a total drift of 3 to 7 miles per hour was not unusual. Replacing the mechanical gyros with light greatly reduced drift.

Ring Laser Gyros (RLGs)

In the early days of inertial navigation systems, it was thought that if we could eliminate the spinning-wheel gyros, we could greatly increase the reliability of the systems. Therein started the quest for ring laser gyros.

Ring laser gyro (Laser Sam – Wikimedia Commons)

In its most basic form, the RLG body is a solid glass block with three narrow tubes drilled to form a triangle. The tubes are filled with a helium-neon gas mixture and a mirror placed at each end. A neon lamp is used to cause the gas to generate laser light which circulates through the tubes in light particles known as photons. The light beam is split into two and the photons travel in opposite directions. Any movement of the glass block will cause the photons in one direction to arrive sooner or later than the photons going the other direction. The time difference can be used to determine the exact movement of the RLG body.

Interestingly enough, the `reliability' advantage of RLGs has turned out to be a fallacy. Good spinning-wheel gyros today have mean time between failures (MTBFs) - in an aircraft environment - of tens of thousands of hours, and virtually no life limiting wear out mechanisms. RLGs are not demonstrably better in either of these respects. In fact, it tends to be the reliability of the associated electronics that dominates an I.N. system's MTBF. A modern strapdown RLG I.N. has an MTBF of 5,000 - 10,000 hours.

Source: King

Hybrid Systems

A new feature for modern inertial navigation systems adds an embedded GPS receiver module, becoming a hybrid system. The result is a system that automatically knows where it is when first initialized, as well as a way to align itself inflight. By constantly checking with GPS, drift errors can be continuously corrected.

Flight Management Computer "Fail Down" Sensor Logic

Your FMC will navigate according to what it considers its most reliable sensor, usually GPS. Each system varies and it is important to know which sensor "comes next" in the hierarchy, when the switch is made, and when the system can restore itself to a more reliable source.

A typical system, for example, might have the following hierarchy:

- GPS
- DME/DME
- VOR/DME
- IRS

It may be as simple as saying if the GPS fails, the FMC will revert to DME/DME, if that fails then VOR/DME, and if that fails, finally to the IRS.

Some systems may place margins of accuracy to prevent nuisance switching. If the GPS, for example, is no worse than 5% than DME/DME, the GPS remains the sensor of choice.

With Hybrid Inertial Reference Systems, however, it could be that the IRS is considered more reliable, shaking up the hierarchy:

- GPS
- Hybrid IRS
- DME/DME
- VOR/DME
- IRS

It is vitally important to understand what sensors your FMC is using and how the "fail down" hierarchy works.

References

King, A. D., B.Sc, F.R.I.N., Inertial Navigation - Forty Years of Evolution, General Electric Company Review, Vol 13, No 3, 1998

Stoval, Sherryl H., Basic Inertial Navigation, Naval Air Warfare Center Weapons Division, September 1997

Initial vs. Midpoint Techniques

Your plotting chart is based on a Lambert Conformal projection, the lines of longitude converge near the poles. Except for the equator, the lines of latitude are not straight, they curve toward the equator. The measurement of your true course depends on where you place the center of your plotter and it does make a difference. In the figure shown, flying from 33°N 160°W to 33°N 150°W should, intuitively, require a 090° true course. The actual course, however, depends on what you want: the starting, mid, or ending course.

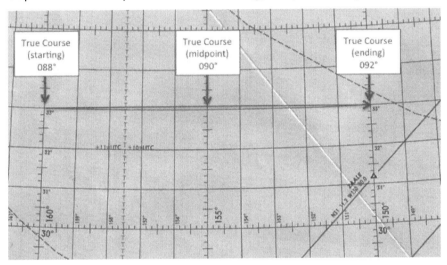

True Course initial vs. midpoint vs. ending

Most flight planning services offer either the starting or midpoint courses. Some pilots want to know what their initial course will be, others want the average course on the entire leg. It is a matter of personal preference. Using the midpoint course for plotting gives you the most line for your plotter and gives you the easiest, most accurate plot. But I think it is even more important to have a predicted magnetic heading at each waypoint to make sure the FMS is turning correctly to the next waypoint. So, life being full of compromises, we have our flight planning service use the starting course.

Example Course Line

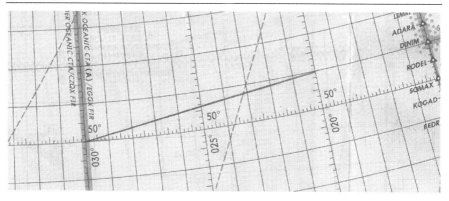

Course line in pencil

In the example we draw a line from 50°N 030°W and 51°N 020°W.

Example Initial Course

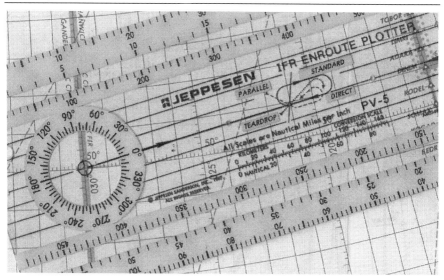

Course line with plotter on initial point

Placing the center of the plotter compass on our initial point and the course line on top of the endpoint we see our initial true course is 077°.

Example Midpoint Course

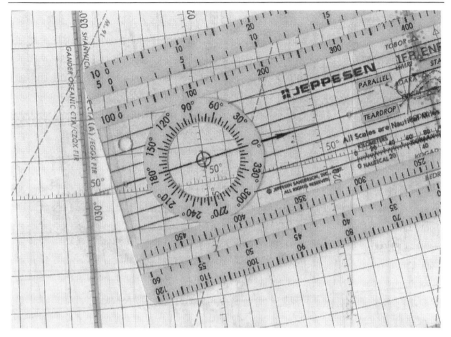

Course line with plotter on midpoint

Placing the center of the plotter compass on the midpoint, 025°W in our example, we see the true course will be 081°.

We can check this mathematically using 10 degree tables at 50°N. See the appendix: 'True Course 10 Degree Tables."

North Atlantic High Level Airspace (NAT HLA) Techniques

If you fly the North Atlantic for a living, you are in a continuing battle to keep up with the changing requirements. This page will be out of date as soon as it is written!

I think the easiest way to keep abreast of life in the North Atlantic High Level Airspace (NAT HLA) is to subscribe to OpsGroup. Nobody does a better job of keeping this complicated airspace understandable. They approach this from the standpoint of "What I've got" versus "What I don't have" and translate that to "Where can I go?" I think that works very well, so I'll copy them and add specific references.

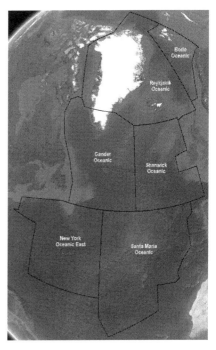

NAT HLA, NAT Doc 007, figure 1.

What I've Got: Everything

Where I can go . . .

Anywhere you like (assuming you are talking to ATC). And you have RVSM, HLA approval, CPDLC, ADS-C, more than one LRNS, a transponder, TCAS 7.1, RNP 4, HF, and PBCS.

Source: OpsGroup NAT Quick Reference Guide

Why . . .

See the "Summary of Requirements," below.

What I Don't Have: RVSM

Where I can't go . . .

> You can't cruise at levels between FL 290 - FL 410 inclusive in the NAT region.
>
> Source: OpsGroup NAT Quick Reference Guide

Where I can go . . .

> You can fly at FL 280 westbound, FL 270 eastbound, or FL 430 in either direction. If you are HLA approved: You can climb and descend through HLA RVSM airspace to reach your non-RVSM level, and ATC may approve you to fly within RVSM airspace, if you 1. Are a delivery flight, or 2. Did have RVSM approval but returning for repairs, or 3. Humanitarian. Contact the first Oceanic Centre by phone about 6 hours before you plan to enter.
>
> Source: OpsGroup NAT Quick Reference Guide

Why . . .

> To Climb/Descend Through RVSM Levels: 1.6.1 NAT HLA approved aircraft that are not approved for RVSM operation will be permitted, subject to traffic, to climb/descend through RVSM levels in order to attain cruising levels above or below RVSM airspace. Flights should climb/descend continuously through the RVSM levels without stopping at any intermediate level and should "Report leaving" current level and "Report reaching" cleared level (N.B. [Nota bene, Latin for "note well"] this provision contrasts with the regulations applicable for RVSM airspace operations in Europe, where aircraft not approved for RVSM operations are not permitted to effect such climbs or descents through RVSM levels.). Such aircraft are also permitted to flight plan and operate at FL 430 either Eastbound or Westbound above the NAT HLA.

> To Operate at RVSM Levels: 1.6.2 ATC may provide special approval for a NAT HLA approved aircraft that is not approved

for RVSM operation to fly in the NAT HLA provided that the aircraft:

a) is on a delivery flight; or

b) was RVSM approved but has suffered an equipment failure and is being returned to its base for repair and/or re-approval;

c) is on a mercy or humanitarian flight.

Source: NAT Doc 007, ¶1.6

What I Don't Have: HLA Approval

Where I can't go . . .

You can't fly in NAT HLA airspace, which is from FL 285 - FL 420.

Source: OpsGroup NAT Quick Reference Guide

Where I can go . . .

Going around HLA isn't really feasible, because it extends from about 20N to the North Pole. You can fly in the NAT region at FL 280 westbound, FL 270 eastbound, or FL 430 in either direction.

Source: OpsGroup NAT Quick Reference Guide

Why . . .

NAT HLA is that volume of airspace between flight level (FL) 285 and FL 420 within the oceanic control areas of Bodo Oceanic, Gander Oceanic, New York Oceanic East, Reykjavik, Santa Maria and Shanwick, excluding the Shannon and Brest Ocean Transition Areas.

Source: NAT Doc 007, ¶1.1.1

All flights within the NAT HLA must have the approval of either the State of Registry of the aircraft, or the State of the operator.

Source: NAT Doc 007, ¶1.2.1

What I Don't Have: CPDLC

Where I can't go . . .

> You can't operate FL 290 - FL 410 anywhere in the NAT HLA.
>
> Source: OpsGroup NAT Quick Reference Guide

Where I can go . . .

> You can cruise at FL 280 or below, or FL 410 or above anywhere in the HLA, including the tracks. There are exempted areas, where you're all good: North of 80N, Surveillance airspace (where ATC can see you on radar or ADS-B), the Tango Routes, and New York Oceanic East. If you have ADS-B and VHF, Gander will accept you on a line RATSU 61N20W 63N30W 62N40W 61N50W SAVRY or north of.
>
> Source: OpsGroup NAT Quick Reference Guide

Why . . .

> The NAT Data Link Mandate (DLM) requires aircraft to be equipped with, and operating, CPDLC and ADS-C in the NAT region. Currently, the mandate incorporates FL 290 to FL 410 inclusive.
>
> Source: NAT Doc 007, ¶1.8.1
>
> The DLM is not applicable to aircraft operating in:
>
> Airspace north of 80° North;
>
> New York Oceanic East flight information region (FIR);
>
> Airspace where an ATS surveillance service is provided by means of radar, multilateration and/or ADS-B, coupled with VHF voice communications as depicted in State Aeronautical Information Publications (AIP), provided the aircraft is suitably equipped (transponder/ADS-B extended squitter transmitter).
>
> Source: NAT Doc 007, ¶1.8.2

Certain categories of flights may be allowed to plan and operate through the mandated airspace with non-equipped aircraft. (See also NAT OPS Bulletin 2017-001.) Charts providing an indication of the likely extent of the NAT ATS Surveillance airspace are included in Attachment 8. Details will be promulgated in the future via State AIP.

Source: NAT Doc 007, ¶1.8.3

What I Don't Have: ADS-C

Where I can't go . . .

You can't operate FL 290 - FL 410 anywhere in the NAT HLA.

Source: OpsGroup NAT Quick Reference Guide

Where I can go . . .

Same as CPDLC, above.

Why . . .

The NAT Data Link Mandate (DLM) requires aircraft to be equipped with, and operating, CPDLC and ADS-C in the NAT region. Currently, the mandate incorporates FL 290 to FL 410 inclusive.

Source: NAT Doc 007, ¶1.8.1

The DLM is not applicable to aircraft operating in:

Airspace north of 80° North;

New York Oceanic East flight information region (FIR);

Airspace where an ATS surveillance service is provided by means of radar, multilateration and/or ADS-B, coupled with VHF voice communications as depicted in State Aeronautical Information Publications (AIP), provided the aircraft is suitably equipped (transponder/ADS-B extended squitter transmitter).

Source: NAT Doc 007, ¶1.8.2

Certain categories of flights may be allowed to plan and operate through the mandated airspace with non-equipped aircraft. (See also NAT OPS Bulletin 2017-001.) Charts providing an indication of the likely extent of the NAT ATS Surveillance airspace are included in Attachment 8. Details will be promulgated in the future via State AIP.

Source: NAT Doc 007, ¶1.8.3

What I Don't Have: More Than One LRNS

Where I can't go . . .

You can't fly in most of the airspace, with a few exceptions.

Source: OpsGroup NAT Quick Reference Guide

Where I can go . . .

For a full crossing, use the Blue Spruce routes. You only need a single LRNS - and HLA approval if using them between FL 285 - FL 420. You need HF for the ones that enter Shanwick OCA. You can use Tango 9 with a single LRNS, but T213, T13 and T16 need two.

Source: OpsGroup NAT Quick Reference Guide

Why . . .

Routes for Aircraft with Only One LRNS. A number of special routes have been developed for aircraft equipped with only one LRNS and carrying normal short-range navigation equipment (VOR, DME, ADF), which require to cross the North Atlantic between Europe and North America (or vice versa). It should be recognised that these routes are within the NAT HLA, and that State approval must be obtained prior to flying along them. These routes are also available for interim use by aircraft normally approved for unrestricted NAT HLA operations that have suffered a partial loss of navigation capability and have only a single remaining functional LRNS. Detailed descriptions of the special routes known as 'Blue Spruce Routes' are included in

Chapter 3 of this Document. Other routes also exist within the NAT HLA that may be flown by aircraft equipped with only a single functioning LRNS. These include routings between the Azores and the Portuguese mainland and/or the Madeira Archipelago and also routes between Northern Europe and Spain/Canaries/Lisbon FIR to the east of longitude 009° 01' W (viz.T9). Other routes available for single LRNS use are also established in the NAT HLA, including a route between Iceland and the east coast of Greenland and two routes between Kook Islands on the west coast of Greenland and Canada.

Source: NAT Doc 007, ¶1.4.1

If this single LRNS is a GPS it must be approved in accordance with FAA TSO-C129 or later standard as Class A1, A2, B1, B2, C1 or C2, or with equivalent EASA documentation ETSO- C129a. Some States may have additional requirements regarding the carriage and use of GPS (e.g. a requirement for FDE RAIM) and flight crews should check with their own State of Registry to ascertain what, if any, they are.

Source: NAT Doc 007, ¶1.4.2

What I Don't Have: Transponder

Where I can't go . . .

You cannot fly in the NAT region, at all.

Source: OpsGroup NAT Quick Reference Guide

Why . . .

All aircraft operating as IFR flights in the NAT region shall be equipped with a pressure-altitude reporting SSR transponder.

Source: NAT Doc 007, ¶10.2.1

What I Don't Have: TCAS 7.1

Where I can go . . .

> Nowhere. It's needed in the entire NAT region. And the whole world.
>
> Source: OpsGroup NAT Quick Reference Guide

Why . . .

> Turbine-engined aircraft having a maximum certificated take-off mass exceeding 5,700 kg or authorized to carry more than 19 passengers are required to carry ACAS II in the NAT region. The technical specifications for ACAS II are contained in ICAO Annex 10 Volume IV. Compliance with this requirement can be achieved through the implementation of traffic alert and collision avoidance system (TCAS) Version 7.1 as specified in RTCA/DO-185B or EUROCAE/ED-143.
>
> Source: NAT Doc 007, ¶10.4.1

What I Don't Have: ETOPS

Before we get into "Extended Twin Operations," which became "Extended Operations" (ETOPS) and are now "Extended Diversion Time Operations" (ETDO), we need to talk about applicability. ETOPS and/or ETDO only apply to commercial operators. If that's you, the following applies to you.

Where I can't go . . .

> Further than 60 minutes from adequate airports – unless you're not operating a commercial flight, or have an exemption.
>
> Source: OpsGroup NAT Quick Reference Guide

About those 60 minutes . . .

The ICAO defers to the State about how far from adequate airports you need to be. Most modern aircraft need to stay within 180 minutes without ETOPS/ETDO approval. See the chapter Extended Diversion Time Operations (ETDO) for more about this.

Where I can go . . .

> First, ATC doesn't care about your ETOPS approval status. This part is really up to you. If you're operating a noncommercial flight, or have 3+ engines, then don't worry about ETOPS. If you are required to fly ETOPS, but don't have it (recent engine change, for example) – then you'll have to pick out a route that stays within 60 minutes of adequate airports. That probably means staying within 60 mins of BIKF-BGBW-CYYR. There aren't any 60-minute options running straight across.
>
> Source: OpsGroup NAT Quick Reference Guide

Why . . .

> A large portion of NAT crossings are ETOPS operations. ETOPS rules require that one or more suitable enroute alternate airports are named prior to dispatch and then monitored while aircraft are enroute. Enroute alternate airports in the NAT region are limited to those in the Azores, Bermuda, Greenland and Iceland. In determining ETOPS alternate minima, the dispatcher must consider weather conditions, airport conditions (in addition to simple runway lengths), navigation approach aids, and the availability of ATS and ARFF facilities.
>
> Source: NAT Doc 007, ¶16.6.22

What I Don't Have: RNP 4

Where I can't go . . .

> The PBCS Tracks.
>
> Source: OpsGroup NAT Quick Reference Guide

Where I can go . . .

> Everywhere else, assuming you have RNP 10.
>
> Source: OpsGroup NAT Quick Reference Guide

Why . . .

> The navigation system accuracy requirements for NAT MNPSA/HLA operation should only be based on the PBN specifications, RNP 10 (PBN application of RNAV 10) or RNP 4.
>
> Source: NAT Doc 007, ¶1.3.4

What I Don't Have: RNP 10

Where I can't go . . .

> Then you can't enter the NAT HLA Airspace.
>
> Source: OpsGroup NAT Quick Reference Guide

Where I can go . . .

> FL 280 or below, FL 430 or above, or outside the HLA area.
>
> Source: OpsGroup NAT Quick Reference Guide

Why . . .

> The navigation system accuracy requirements for NAT MNPSA/HLA operation should only be based on the PBN specifications, RNP 10 (PBN application of RNAV 10) or RNP 4.
>
> Source: NAT Doc 007, ¶1.3.4

What I Don't Have: HF

Where I can't go . . .

> Shanwick will not welcome you. Stay out of their airspace, but the others may approve you. US operators should note: N-reg aircraft are required to have functioning HF for overwater ops.
>
> Source: OpsGroup NAT Quick Reference Guide

Where I can go . . .

> Other OCA's may approve Satcom for primary comms. If you're making a full NAT crossing, then you're basically going via Iceland. One example route is RATSU-ALDAN-KFV–EPENI–

63N30W–61N40W-OZN-58N50W-HOIST-LOACH-YYR. Canada publishes two routes that can be flown VHF only, without prior approval: below FL 195, routing Iqaluit (Frobay) – Sondre Stromfjord – Keflavík. FL 250 or above, routing Goose VOR – Prins Christian Sund (or Narsarsuaq) – Keflavik. You still need HLA approval to go above FL 285. Gander will probably approve other routes without HF, but ask ATC nicely first. In general, crossing from Greenland-Canada south of 60N, at FL 200 or above, should be fine.

Source: OpsGroup NAT Quick Reference Guide

Why . . .

Aircraft with only functioning VHF communications equipment should plan their route according to the information contained in the appropriate State AIPs and ensure that they remain within VHF coverage of appropriate ground stations throughout the flight. [. . .] Some may permit the use of SATVOICE to substitute for or supplement HF communications. However, it must also be recognised that the Safety Regulator of the operator may impose its own operational limitations on SATVOICE usage. Any operator intending to fly through the NAT HLA without fully functional HF communications or wishing to use an alternative medium should ensure that it will meet the requirements of its State of Registry and those of all the relevant ATS providers throughout the proposed route.

Source: NAT Doc 007, ¶4.2.12

What I Don't Have: SELCAL

Where I can go . . .

Fly wherever you like, but get the F/O to do radios for this leg. Listening watch required even if you have CPDLC running.

Source: OpsGroup NAT Quick Reference Guide

Why . . .

When using HF, SATVOICE, or CPDLC, flight crews should maintain a listening watch on the assigned frequency, unless SELCAL equipped, in which case they should ensure the following sequence of actions:

a) provide the SELCAL code in the flight plan; (any subsequent change of aircraft for a flight will require refiling of the flight plan or submitting a modification message (CHG) which includes the new registration and SELCAL);

b) check the operation of the SELCAL equipment, at or prior to entry into oceanic airspace, with the appropriate radio station. (This SELCAL check must be completed prior to commencing SELCAL watch); and

c) maintain thereafter a SELCAL watch.

Source: NAT Doc 007, ¶6.1.22

What I Don't Have: PBCS

Where I can't go . . .

Along the core NAT Tracks between FL 350 - 390.

Source: OpsGroup NAT Quick Reference Guide

Where I can go . . .

PBCS for the NAT means having both RCP 240 (4 minute comms loop) and RSP 180 (3 minute position reporting). If you're missing approval for either, then you can fly anywhere other than long the core NAT tracks FL 350 - 390.

Source: OpsGroup NAT Quick Reference Guide

Why . . .

Within the OTS the 42.6 km (23 NM) lateral separation minimum is implemented by applying 42.6 km (23 NM) lateral spacing through whole and half degrees of latitude between PBCS designated NAT OTS Tracks between flight levels FL 350 - 390 inclusive, except when the OTS occurs in the New York OCA East.

In the OTS this PBCS-based separation implementation supersedes and replaces the previous trials of RLatSM. In addition to requiring RNP-4 Approval, Operators must appreciate that unlike the filing criteria for the half degree spaced RLatSM Tracks, the simple equipage and operation of CPDLC and ADS-C will not be a sufficient criteria for planning and flying on the designated PBCS-based OTS Tracks. To utilize these tracks the aircraft must have formal State Authorization for filing RCP 240 and RSP 180.

Source: NAT Doc 007, ¶1.10.2

Summary of Requirements

How do you know where you can fly? It all depends on your Performance Based Communications, Navigation, Surveillance capabilities. The Navigation we know about: that's PBN, after all. The rest is now being called PBCS, at least tentatively.

If you have the following equipment:			You can fly:
Communications	Navigation	Surveillance	
VHF	VOR, DME, ADF	Mode C	Limited parts of the NAT HLA
HF (in Shanwick OCA)	1 LRNS	VHF / HF Position Reports	Limited parts of the NAT HLA

Note that we are talking about equipment for these parts of the airspace. If you want greater access, you will need communications, navigation, and surveillance capabilities and those require authorizations.

If you have the following authorizations:			You can fly:
Communications	Navigation	Surveillance	
HF	RNP 10 and 2 LRNS	HF Position Reports	NAT Tracks, NAT HLA (Except FL 350-390)
CPDLC	RNP 10 and 2 LRNS	ADS-C	NAT Tracks, NAT HLA (All Flight Levels)*
CPDLC / RCP 240	RNP 4 and 2 LRNS	ADS-C / RSP 180	NAT Tracks, NAT HLA (All Flight Levels)

* The NAT Tracks between FL 350 - 390 require RCP 240 and RSP 180.

A Summary of Authorizations

A056 — Data Link Communications (you will need this for ADS-C and CPDLC)

B036 — Required Navigation Performance Airspace (you will need this for RNP 4 or RNP 10)

B039 — North Atlantic High Level Airspace (NAT HLA), formerly North Atlantic Minimum Navigation Performance Specifications (NAT/MNPS) Airspace

B046 — Reduced Vertical Separation Minimum (RVSM) Airspace

NAT Tracks

The Organized Track System (OTS) carries with it all the restrictions of flying in the NAT HLA plus a few more. You must also be careful in that there are several layers of authorizations involved. You could be permitted the lower altitudes and standard spacing, all altitudes with the chance of decreased longitudinal spacing, and all altitudes with the chance of decreased longitudinal and lateral spacing.

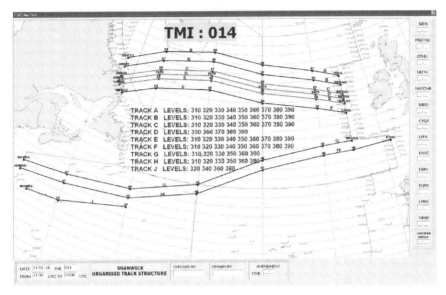

Example of Daytime Westbound NAT Organized Track System, NAT Doc 007, Fig 2

As a result of passenger demand, time zone differences and airport noise restrictions, much of the North Atlantic (NAT) air traffic contributes to two major alternating flows: a westbound flow departing Europe in the morning, and an eastbound flow departing North America in the evening. The effect of these flows is to concentrate most of the traffic uni-directionally, with peak westbound traffic crossing the 30W longitude between 1130 UTC and 1900 UTC and peak eastbound traffic crossing the 30W longitude between 0100 UTC and 0800 UTC.

The flight levels normally associated with the OTS are FL 310 to FL 400 inclusive. These flight levels, and their use have been negotiated and agreed by the NATS ATS providers and are published as the Flight Level Allocation Scheme (FLAS). The FLAS also determines flight levels available for traffic routing partly or wholly outside of the OTS as well as flights operating outside of the valid time periods of the OTS; often referred to as "transition times".

The hours of validity of the two Organised Track Systems (OTS) are as follows:

(Westbound) Day-time OTS 1130 UTC to 1900 UTC at 30°W

(Eastbound) Night-time OTS 0100 UTC to 0800 UTC at 30°W

Note: Changes to these times can be negotiated between Gander and Shanwick OACCs and the specific hours of validity for each OTS are indicated in the NAT track message. For flight planning, operators should take account of the times as specified in the relevant NAT track message(s). Tactical extensions to OTS validity times can also be agreed between OACCs when required, but these should normally be transparent to operators.

Use of the OTS tracks is not mandatory. Aircraft may flight plan on random routes which remain clear of the OTS or may fly on any route that joins, leaves, or crosses the OTS. Operators must be aware that while ATC will make every effort to clear random traffic across the OTS at requested levels, re-routes or significant changes in flight level from those planned are very likely to be necessary during most of the OTS traffic periods. A comprehensive understanding of the OTS and the FLAS may assist flight planners in determining the feasibility of flight profiles.

Source: NAT Doc 007, ¶2.1

To ensure a smooth transition from night-time to day-time OTSs and vice-versa, a period of several hours is interposed between the termination of one system and the commencement of the next. These periods are from 0801 UTC to 1129 UTC: and from 1901 UTC to 0059 UTC.

During the changeover periods some restrictions to flight planned routes and levels are imposed. Eastbound and westbound aircraft operating during these periods should file flight level requests in accordance with the Flight Level

Allocation Scheme (FLAS) as published in the UK and Canada AIPs.

It should also be recognised that during these times there is often a need for clearances to be individually co-ordinated between OACCs and cleared flight levels may not be in accordance with those flight planned. If, for any reason, a flight is expected to be level critical, operators are recommended to contact the initial OACC prior to filing of the flight plan to ascertain the likely availability of required flight levels.

Source: NAT Doc 007, ¶2.4

PBCS Tracks

Flights which are planned to follow an OTS track for its entire length (during the OTS periods) may plan any of the levels published for that track, keeping in mind PBCS and DLM requirements.

Note: PBCS tracks will be identified in Note 3 of the OTS message. Operators planning to operate in the altitude band FL 350-390 on the PBCS OTS are subject to equipage and authorization requirements as outlined in NAT OPS Bulletin, "Implementation of Performance Based Separation Minima".

Source: NAT Doc 007, ¶4.1.10

Keeping Up-to-date

In case you were thinking I was joking about this page being out of date as soon as it was written, I was not. There are so many players out there, around the world, and no central mechanism to keep everyone else current. So you can just do your best. Here are my methods.

Good sources to monitor for changes:

NAT OPS Bulletins — available at www.icao.int/EURNAT/, following "EUR & NAT Documents", then "NAT Documents", in folder "NAT OPS Bulletins".

NBAA Air Mail — https://www.nbaa.org/airmail/), several forums, including one for international operations. (Membership required.)

OpsGroup — ops.group, a platform for pilots, controllers, dispatchers, and managers to ask questions, provide answers, and to learn from peers. (Membership required.)

References

ICAO Nat Doc 007, North Atlantic Operations and Airspace Manual, v.2023-1

Ops.group

Navigation Accuracy Check Techniques

The Requirement

The requirement to do a navigation accuracy check prior to coast-out and prior to coast-in went away with the adoption of AC 91-70B in 2016, but it remains a very good idea. (AC 91-70C is now current.) We are continuing to see pilots violated for things a good navigation accuracy check would have caught. A few reasons:

- A Navigation Accuracy Check will detect when you have made a "waypoint insertion" error, one where you simply typed in the wrong waypoint, latitude, or longitude.
- A Navigation Accuracy Check will detect when the database has an error. I've seen this twice and it has happened more than a few times when half-latitude spacing was adopted a few years ago.
- Record of your Navigation Accuracy Check will impress upon an inspector that you are a careful and diligent pilot, when he or she asks for your paperwork because of a loss of separation caused by other aircraft.

The Basic Concepts

When doing a navigation accuracy check, you are basically plotting your position according to a ground station, preferably a VOR's radial and DME, and comparing that to the latitude / longitude reported by your FMS. Since the DME from the VOR is slant range – the distance from your position in the air to the ground, the DME will appear long as a result.

For basic plotting procedures, refer to the chapter: Plotting.

The How: Paper or PDF Chart

You can check your FMS's "claimed" position on a chart and compare that to your "reported" position off a VOR's radial / DME.

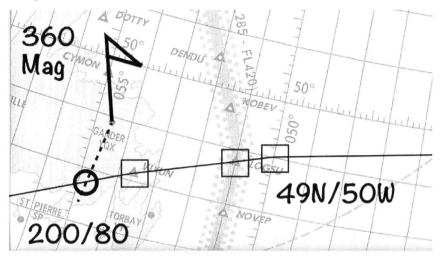

Plotting a VOR radial/DME

In the example plotting chart, a line with a flag is drawn from the Gander VOR (YQX) to magnetic north, which is 22° to the west because of the magnetic variation. We've labeled the flag "360 Mag." Our route of flight is south of Gander to VIXUN, LOGSU, 49N/50W and over the North Atlantic.

To make a navigation accuracy check, we record the VOR/DME from YQX while recording our latitude and longitude. The plotted VOR/DME position should coincide with the FMS position, differing only by the slant range of the DME.

The How: iPad Application

Many iPad navigation applications can simplify the process of a navigation accuracy check. The following screen grab was taken using ForeFlight. Using two fingers (using two hands makes this easier), simultaneously press the applicable VOR and the approximate aircraft position, fine tune the VOR position so it is exact, adjust the other until the radial and DME agree with your raw data, release both fingers. The resulting point should be right on the course line. You can take a "screen grab" on most iPads by pressing the "Home" and "Power" buttons simultaneously. The resulting photo can be saved as proof you did the navigation accuracy check.

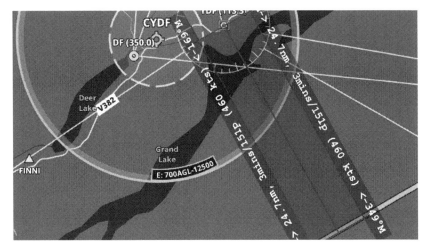

Plotting using Foreflight

The How: "Crosspoints"

Some FMS installations include a "cross points" function that computes the position of the aircraft relative to a waypoint or VOR. The applicable VOR is inputted and compared to a raw data instrument tuned to the same VOR.

Using the G450 as an example:

- Select the Nav Index by pressing the NAV key.
- Select CROSS PTS (LSK 5L).
- Select PPOS DIR (LSK 1L)
- Enter the waypoint, YQX in our example
- Tuning the YQX VOR we can see the raw data on the RMI.

In the example photo, we see that we are on the 270° radial, 113 NM from YQX.

G450 Crosspoints and EBDI

The How: Portable GPS

Using the earlier example of plotting a radial/DME using ForeFlight, we were depending on being on our cleared course to show that we were, indeed, on course. But what if we were cleared direct the next waypoint? If we have a portable GPS connected to the iPad we can compare its displayed position against a radial / DME.

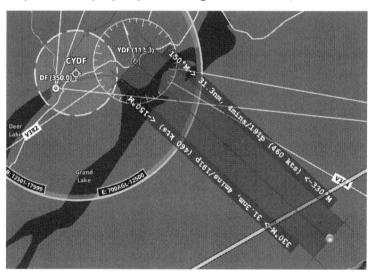

ForeFlight, nav accuracy check, with a portable GPS unit

References

Advisory Circular 91-70C, Oceanic and International Operations, 10/4/23, U.S. Department of Transportation

Performance Based Navigation (PBN)

Like the Future Air Navigation System (FANS), the Performance-Based Navigation (PBN) system is a concept of how we ensure our aircraft are where we say they are, when we say they are. The designation is mostly consistent, but not completely.

How you qualify and how you prove your qualification is pretty much up to the state (the country). But that approval isn't listed as "PBN" but as the individual levels of compliance, i.e., RNP-4.

The Concept

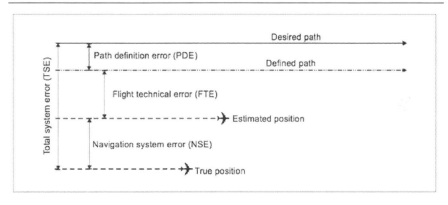

Lateral Navigation Errors, from ICAO Doc 9613, figure ii-a-2-1

The PBN concept specifies that aircraft RNAV and RNP system performance requirements be defined in terms of the accuracy, integrity, continuity and functionality, which are needed for the proposed operations in the context of a particular airspace concept. The PBN concept represents a shift from sensor-based to PBN. Performance requirements are identified in navigation specifications, which also identify the choice of navigation sensors and equipment that may be used to meet the performance requirements. These navigation specifications are defined at a sufficient level of detail to facilitate global harmonization by providing specific implementation guidance for States and operators.

> Source: ICAO Doc 9613, p. I-(iii)

This isn't to say PBN systems cannot use a particular type of sensor, only that the sensor isn't the defining characteristic of the specification. An acceptable solution could be GPS-based or even DME/DME-based. But approval for that solution for the specification depends on more than just what sensor is used.

> Under PBN, generic navigation requirements are defined based on operational requirements. Operators then evaluate options in respect of available technology and navigation services, which could allow the requirements to be met. An operator thereby has the opportunity to select a more cost-effective option, rather than a solution being imposed as part of the operational requirements. Technology can evolve over time without requiring the operation itself to be reviewed, as long as the expected performance is provided by the RNAV or RNP system.
>
> Source: ICAO Doc 9613, p. I-(iii)

The Navigation Specification

> The navigation specification is used by a State as a basis for the development of their material for airworthiness and operational approval. A navigation specification details the performance required of the RNAV system in terms of accuracy, integrity, availability and continuity; which navigation functionalities the RNAV system must have; which navigation sensors must be integrated into the RNAV system; and which requirements are placed on the flight crew.
>
> Source: ICAO Doc 9613, ¶1.2
>
> On-board performance monitoring and alerting is the main element that determines if the navigation system complies with the necessary safety level associated to an RNP application; it relates to both lateral and longitudinal navigation performance; and it allows the aircrew to detect that the navigation system is

not achieving, or cannot guarantee with 10-5 integrity, the navigation performance required for the operation.

Source: ICAO Doc 9613, ¶1.2.3.1

The 10-5 integrity is the 0.9999 probability concept. The monitoring and alerting is the key component of a PBN specification.

Both RNAV and RNP specifications include requirements for certain navigation functionalities. At the basic level, these functional requirements may include:

- continuous indication of aircraft position relative to track to be displayed to the pilot flying on a navigation display situated in his primary field of view;

- display of distance and bearing to the active (To) waypoint;

- display of ground speed or time to the active (To) waypoint;

- navigation data storage function; and

- appropriate failure indication of the RNAV system, including the sensors.

Source: ICAO Doc 9613, ¶1.2.4.1

For oceanic, remote, en-route and terminal operations, an RNP specification is designated as RNP X, e.g. RNP 4. An RNAV specification is designated as RNAV X, e.g. RNAV 1. If two navigation specifications share the same value for X, they may be distinguished by use of a prefix.

For both RNP and RNAV designations, the expression "X" (where stated) refers to the lateral navigation accuracy in nautical miles, which is expected to be achieved at least 95 per cent of the flight time by the population of aircraft operating within the airspace, route or procedure.

Approach navigation specifications cover all segments of the instrument approach. RNP specifications are designated using RNP as a prefix and an abbreviated textual suffix, e.g. RNP APCH or RNP AR APCH. There are no RNAV approach specifications.

Because functional and performance requirements are defined for each navigation specification, an aircraft approved for an RNP specification is not automatically approved for all RNAV specifications. Similarly, an aircraft approved for an RNP or RNAV specification having a stringent accuracy requirement (e.g. RNP 0.3 specification) is not automatically approved for a navigation specification having a less stringent accuracy requirement (e.g. RNP 4).

Source: ICAO Doc 9613, ¶1.2.5

This gets messy, here are two examples:

- If your airplane is approved for RNP 0.3 and RNP 10, you might think RNP 4 is automatically included. But it isn't. RNP 0.3 does not have the same communications requirements of RNP 4, specifically CPDLC and ADS-C. RNP 10 isn't a PBN specification at all. So you cannot infer you are RNP 4 qualified.
- If you have an RNP 4 qualification you are good to go for RNP 10. In fact, if you had an LOA that said RNP 10 and got approval for RNP 4, the RNP 10 disappears.

Be careful about RNP 4. Some U.S. FAA offices are granting RNP 4 LOAs based on the mistaken notion that aircraft with P-RNAV approval are more accurate than RNP 4. That might be true and it will work in the Caribbean. But it won't work in the rest of the world where RNP 4 also requires CPDLC and ADS-C.

The existing RNP 10 designation is inconsistent with PBN RNP and RNAV specifications. RNP 10 does not include requirements for on-board performance monitoring and alerting. For purposes of consistency with the PBN concept, RNP 10 is referred to as RNAV 10 in this manual. Renaming current RNP 10 routes, operational approvals, etc., to an RNAV 10 designation would be an extensive and expensive task, which is not cost-effective. Consequently, any existing or new operational approvals will continue to be designated RNP 10, and any charting annotations will be depicted as RNP 10.

In the past, the United States and member States of the European Civil Aviation Conference (ECAC) used regional RNAV specifications with different designators. The ECAC applications (P-RNAV and B-RNAV) will continue to be used only within those States. Over time, ECAC RNAV applications will migrate towards the international navigation specifications of RNAV 1 and RNAV 5. The United States migrated from the USRNAV Types A and B to the RNAV 1 specification in March 2007.

Source: ICAO Doc 9613, ¶1.2.5

Airworthiness Approval

The airworthiness approval process assures that each item of the RNAV equipment installed is of a type and design appropriate to its intended function and that the installation functions properly under foreseeable operating conditions. Additionally, the airworthiness approval process identifies any installation limitations that need to be considered for operational approval. Such limitations and other information relevant to the approval of the RNAV system installation are documented in the AFM, or AFM Supplement, as applicable. Information may also be repeated and expanded upon in other documents such as pilot operating handbooks or flight crew operating manuals. The airworthiness approval process is well established among States of the Operators and this process refers to the intended function of the navigation specification to be applied.

Approval of RNAV systems for RNAV-X operations. The RNAV system installed should be compliant with a set of basic performance requirements as described in the navigation specification, which defines accuracy, integrity and continuity criteria. It should also be compliant with a set of specific functional requirements, have a navigation database, and support each specific path terminator as required by the navigation specification.

Approval of RNP systems for RNP operations. Aircraft must be equipped with an RNP system able to support the desired navigation application, including the on-board performance monitoring and alerting function. It should also be compliant with a set of specific functional requirements, have a navigation database, and should support each specific path terminator as required by the navigation specification.

Source: ICAO Doc 9613, ¶3.4.2

You do not get approved for PBN, rather you get approved for each specification.

Reference

ICAO Doc 9613 - Performance Based Navigation (PBN) Manual, International Civil Aviation Organization, Fourth Edition, 2013

Plotting Techniques

We plot to avoid the classic one-degree error, to double-check the other pilot's FMS entries, to ensure the flight plan uplink was accurate, and to make sure the database itself is accurate. But wait, you say. The database itself has been QC'd, you've already checked the waypoints in the FMS, and your aircraft's graphical presentation makes any kind of graphical plotting completely pointless! Well, you might have a point. But Gross Navigational Errors still happen.

When is Plotting Required?

The requirement in Advisory Circular 91-70C is a bit murky. It says a plotting chart is "necessary," but doesn't require that you use it, only that you "should."

> 6.3.1 Preflight—Necessary Documents.
>
> 6.3.1.12 Plotting/orientation chart.
>
> 6.3.1.12.1 You should use an oceanic plotting/orientation chart, of appropriate scale, and with latitude and longitude depicted, to provide a visual presentation of your intended route, regardless of your type(s) of LRNS and method of cross-checking aircraft position. Plotting your route on a chart helps with situational awareness, and (together with the OFP [Operational Flight Plan]) also helps with navigation contingencies such as DR, in the event of navigation system degradation/failure.
>
> Source: AC 91-70C

If you have to do a "tabletop" with the FAA — one where they are considering giving you the authorization to fly oceanic through LOAs B036 or B039 — they will ask you to plot, so you are going to have to know how.

A Plotting Chart Should Include . . .

> Your chart should include, at a minimum:

- The route of your filed flight plan or currently effective route clearance.

- Clearly depicted waypoints using standardized symbology.

- Graphic depictions of all ETPs.

- Alternate airports.

- Proximity of other adjacent tracks.

Note: For certificated operators, if OpSpec/MSpec A061 has been issued authorizing use of an Electronic Flight Bag (EFB) and the principal inspector (PI) has authorized "interactive plotting for oceanic and remote continental navigation," the EFB application may be used in place of a paper plotting/orientation chart. The current edition of AC 120-76, Guidelines for the Certification, Airworthiness, and Operational Approval of Electronic Flight Bags, provides guidance for operators to develop associated EFB procedures. For part 91 operators, an EFB may be used, provided the criteria and considerations of the current edition of AC 91-78, Use of Class 1 or Class 2 Electronic Flight Bag (EFB), are observed.

Source: AC 91-70C, ¶6.3.1.11.2

How is a common plotting chart laid out?

Apart from saying the chart should be north up, must be based on WGS-84 and mean sea level, the chart printers are pretty much given discretion on how to print their plotting charts.

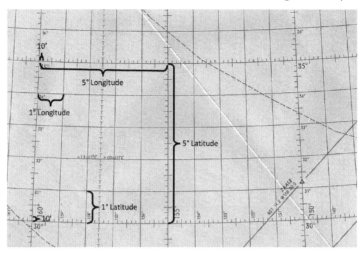

Plotting chart layout

2.1.7 Recommendation.— The charts should be True North orientated.

2.15.1 True North and magnetic variation shall be indicated. The order of resolution of magnetic variation shall be that as specified for a particular chart.

2.15.2 Recommendation.— When magnetic variation is shown on a chart, the values shown should be those for the year nearest to the date of publication that is divisible by 5, i.e. 1980, 1985, etc.

2.18.1.1 World Geodetic System — 1984 (WGS-84) shall be used as the horizontal (geodetic) reference system. Published aeronautical geographical coordinates (indicating latitude and longitude) shall be expressed in terms of the WGS-84 geodetic reference datum.

2.18.2.1 Mean sea level (MSL) datum, which gives the relationship of gravity-related height (elevation) to a surface known as the geoid, shall be used as the vertical reference system.

Source: ICAO Annex 4

There are some basic guidelines you should know for the chart you are using:

- The horizontal lines are "parallels of latitude," usually a line for every degree with a major line every five degrees.
- The vertical lines are "meridians of longitude," with a line for every degree with a major line every five degrees.
- Longitude and latitude are subdivided into 60 parts known as minutes and labeled with a single quote mark (').
- Minutes are further subdivided into 60 parts known as seconds and labeled with double quote marks (").
- Bedford (KBED) airport, for example is at 42°28'11.8" N, 71°17'20.4" W; which is pronounced "forty-two degrees, twenty-eight minutes, eleven point eight seconds north, seventy-one degrees, seventeen minutes, twenty point four seconds west.

More about this in the chapter: Coordinates.

How to Plot a Position

There are many techniques on how to do this correctly, here's mine:

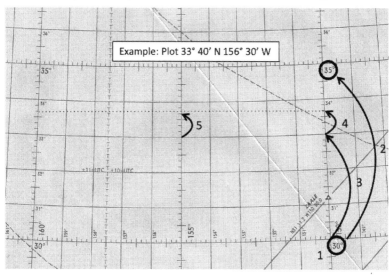

Position plotting example

- Ensure you are in the correct quadrant: In the north the latitudes increase as you go up, in the south they increase as you go down. In the west the longitudes go up as you head west, in the east the go up as you head further east. Locate the nearest five degree line in the general area of your point, in the example 30° N.
- Locate the five degree line just above your latitude, in our example 35° N.
- If your chart has one degree markings locate the nearest degree below your point, otherwise count the degree lines. In our example 33° N.
- Count the tick marks between degree lines on the chart you are using. In our example there are six so we conclude each tick mark represents 10 minutes of latitude. Counting up four tick marks we identify 30°40' N latitude.
- Notice that a line connecting 33°40' N 150° W and 33°40' N 160° W does not cross 33°40' N 155° W, it runs high. That's because the chart is a Lambert Conformal Projection which bends toward the poles. To get a more accurate position, we need to find the 33°40' point on the scale closest to our position.

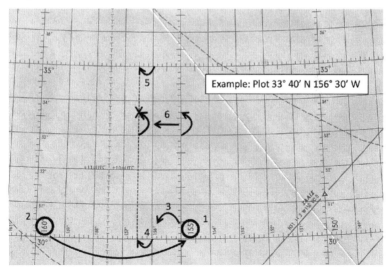

Position plotting example

- When dealing with longitude, we look for the nearest five degree line under our desired position, in our example 155° W.
- Then we look for the nearest five degree line greater than our desired position, in our example 160° W.
- We can now locate the nearest degree under our position, in our example 156° W.
- Counting the tick marks, we see there are six so 30' of longitude will be three greater.
- Unlike latitude, lines of longitude appear parallel between lines of latitude, so we can draw a line at 156°30' W between tick marks and it will remain accurate.
- We then transpose our mark identifying 33°40' N to this line of longitude and viola, we have our position.

How to Plot a Course

Part of the plotting process is to check the courses in your FMS (which are almost always in Magnetic) against those on your charts (which are in True). To convert from True to Magnetic you need Variation.

Determining a waypoint's variation

The magnetic compass points to magnetic north. The angular difference between true and magnetic north is known as variation and it changes for different locations on the earth. Variation must be considered when converting true course, true headings, or true winds to magnetic direction.

Source: AFM 51-37, page 1-12.

If you need to convert, the formula is:

True + Variation = Magnetic

Where West Variation is positive and East Variation is negative

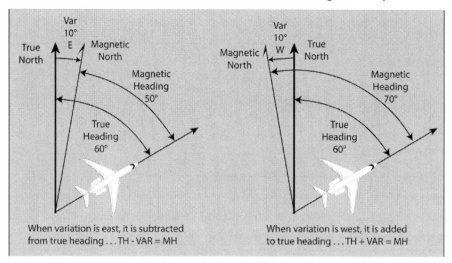

Variation, (AFM 51-37, page 1-13)

You should be able to find the variation of any waypoint by looking on the plotting chart and interpolating as needed. In the chart shown here, you would use 29° West variation for 60°N/55°W, for example.

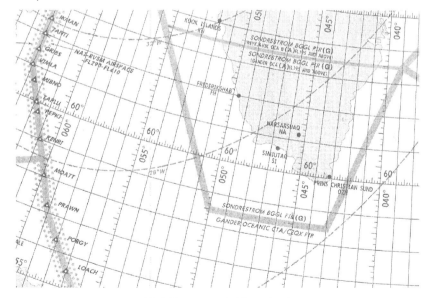

Variation on a plotting chart

Navigate – A Professional Aviator's Notebook

If you don't have a paper chart, you should be able to find the variation at each waypoint in your Flight Management System, or in an electronic tablet plotting application.

To determine the magnetic course, you will need to add or subtract the variation:

- Look for the nearest lines of magnetic variation on the chart before and after the midpoint and interpolate if necessary.
- If the variation is West, add this value to the true course to determine magnetic course. If the variation is East, subtract this value from the true course to determine magnetic course:

TC + West Variation = MC

TC - East Variation = MC

For a tutorial on magnetic variation, see the chapter: Direction.

Note: It is not uncommon to find differences of 2 or 3 degrees in the magnetic course determined from a plotting chart and that reported in a computer flight plan. The magnetic variation changes over the years and your chart may be dated.

Plotting a course

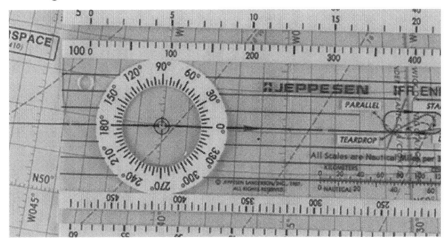

Jeppesen Plotter

A plotter is nothing more than a circular instrument designed to give angular differences between lines. A navigation plotter, such as the Jeppesen model shown, will typically have a hole in the center of a compass rose. To use:

- Decide if you want the start, mid, or ending course. Most pilots will need the start course. For more about this, see the chapter: Initial vs. Midpoint.
- Place the hole in the center of the compass rose over a line of longitude near the desired point, in our example we've used 40°W which is also the longitude of our start point.
- Align the line along the 0° mark to your desired course. You may find it helpful to insert your pencil or pen point in the hole while rotating the plotter to line up with your course.
- Read the true course along the line of selected longitude, 085° in our example.

Note: You will have two choices aligned with the line of longitude, 085° and 275° in our example. In most cases it will be the number on top, but when dealing with courses near vertical it can be confusing. Always remember to give your answer a commonsense check. In our example, we are headed to Europe and the answer should be generally easterly.

Measuring distance

One of the disadvantages of the Lambert Conformal chart is the lack of a constant scale. If the two points between which the distance is to be measured are approximately in a north-south direction and the total distance between them can be spanned, the distance can be measured on the latitude scale opposite the midpoint. However, the total distance between any two points that do not lie approximately north or south of each other should be measured as near the mid latitude as possible.

In the measurement of long distances, select a mid-latitude lying approximately half-way between the latitudes of the two points. By using dividers set to a convenient, reasonably short distance, such as 60 nautical miles picked off at the mid latitude scale, you may determine an approximate distance by marking off units along the line to be measures as shown [in the figure].

The scale at mid latitude is accurate enough if the course line does not cover more than 5 degrees of latitude (somewhat less at high latitudes). If the course line exceeds this amount or if it is crosses the equator, divide it into two or more legs and measure the length of each leg with the scale of its own mid latitude.

Source: AFM 51-40, p. 5-8

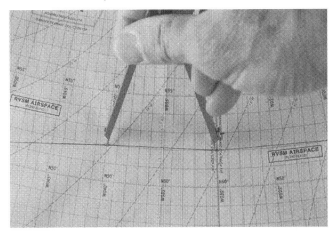

Dividers, step 1

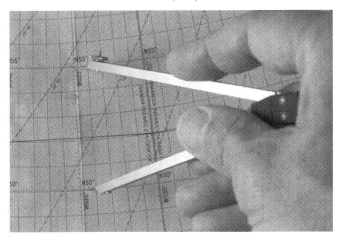

Dividers, step 2

If you have a set of dividers and a flat surface you aren't afraid to scratch, find the distance between waypoints is quite easy. First, place the points of the dividers on the start and end waypoints.

Next, find a line of longitude near the course line. It is important to use a line of longitude about the same latitude as the course, since these will change over great distances. Each degree of latitude equals 60 nautical miles.

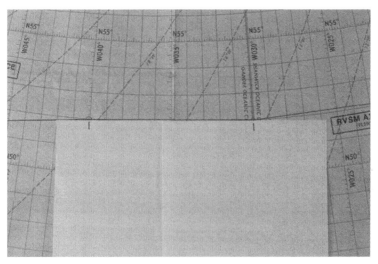

PostIt measuring tool: finding segment distance

If you don't have a set of dividers — do you really want to have such a sharp instrument in the cockpit? — you can construct your own with a PostIt note or other straight-edged paper. You will be accurate within a nautical mile if you do it this way:

- Place the straight-edged paper alongside the course. In our example, the PostIt note isn't long enough so we've used two, overlapping, notes.
- Place a tick mark at the starting and ending waypoints.

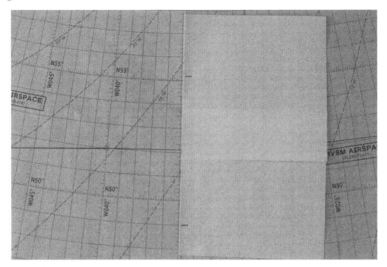

PostIt measuring tool: determining distance

- Move the straight-edged paper to the nearest line of longitude at about the same latitude. Place one tick mark over a convenient line of latitude, 49°N in our example.
- Read the distance from the ending tick mark, using 60 nautical miles per degree. In our example the distance covers at least 6° of latitude, which comes to 360 nautical miles. The mark goes further by a tenth of a degree, meaning another 10 nautical miles. We conclude the distance between waypoints is therefore 370 nautical miles.

Note: You can also determine the distance using a set of "10 Degree Tables," given in the Appendix, where we would see the exact distance is actually 369 nautical miles. (Our PostIt note was off by 1 nautical mile, or had an error rate of 0.27 percent, not bad.)

How to Determine the Position of a VOR Radial/DME

There are many ways to turn a VOR radial/DME into a latitude and longitude, the best of these may very well be inside your FMS. If you need to do this on a plotting chart, this method works well:

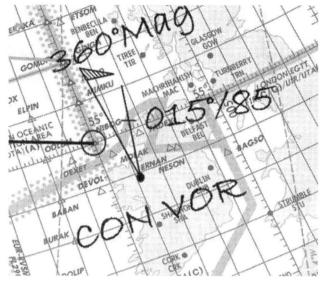

VOR/DME Plotting

- Place the plotter hole over the VOR in question and your pencil point in the hole to hold the plotter centered over the VOR. (CON in our example.)
- Find the nearest line of variation. (6° West in our example.)
- Rotate the edge of the plotter to 360° in the northern hemisphere, 180° in the southern hemisphere, and then rotate toward the magnetic pole by the amount of the variation. (Rotate 6° to the west, in our example.)
- Move your pencil from the center hole to the straight line of the plotter that describes the line to the magnetic pole, move the plotter so the straight edge connects that point to the VOR. Draw a line with a flag on it from the VOR in the direction of the pole. Label this line "360° Mag" if you like. (In our example the flag points slightly left.
- Now return the plotter center hole to the VOR and rotate it in relation to your 360° Mag line by the number of degrees in the VOR radial. Draw a line as you did earlier by placing a tick mark, moving the plotter, and drawing the line. (In our example the line is 15° clockwise from the Magnetic north line.)

- Determine the distance using the Distance Measuring techniques shown above. Place a tick mark on the VOR line. (015°/85 DME in our example.)
- The latitude and longitude can be read directly from the chart using the Plot a Position techniques shown above. (55°15'N 8°25'W in our example.)

If you are doing this to check the accuracy of your FMS, you might have easier tools at your disposal. See the chapter: Navigation Accuracy Check.

References

Advisory Circular 91-70C, Oceanic and International Operations, 10/4/23, U.S. Department of Transportation

Air Force Manual (AFM) 51-37, Instrument Flying, 1 December 1976

Air Force Manual (AFM) 51-40, Air Navigation, Flying Training, 1 July 1973

ICAO Annex 4 - Aeronautical Charts, International Standards and Recommended Practices, Annex 4 to the Convention on International Civil Aviation, July 2009

Point of Safe Return (PSR) Techniques

The Point of Safe Return (PSR) provides the pilot with the farthest point to which the aircraft can go and be able to return safely to the departure point with adequate holding, approach, landing, and alternate fuel. It is normally used when flying to remote island destinations with no diversion possibilities en route but can be useful even when alternates are available. Note: some call the last point where you can reverse course and make it back to your departure airport the "Point of No Return."

Regulatory Requirement

There is no regulatory requirement to compute a Point of No (or Safe) Return. In fact, the only regulatory mention is for 14 CFR 121 and even that is less than definitive:

(a) No certificate holder may operate an airplane outside the 48 contiguous States and the District of Columbia, when its position cannot be reliably fixed for a period of more than 1 hour, without—

- A flight crewmember who holds a current flight navigator certificate; or

- Specialized means of navigation approved in accordance with §121.355 which enables a reliable determination to be made of the position of the airplane by each pilot seated at his duty station.

(b) Notwithstanding paragraph (a) of this section, the Administrator may also require a flight navigator or special navigation equipment, or both, when specialized means of navigation are necessary for 1 hour or less. In making this determination, the Administrator considers—

- The speed of the airplane;

- Normal weather conditions en route;

- Extent of air traffic control;

- Traffic congestion;

- Area of navigational radio coverage at destination;

- Fuel requirements;

- Fuel available for return to point of departure or alternates;

- Predication of flight upon operation beyond the point of no return; and

- Any other factors he determines are relevant in the interest of safety.

(c) Operations where a flight navigator or special navigation equipment, or both, are required are specified in the operations specifications of the air carrier or commercial operator.

Source: 14 CFR 121, §121.389

The Math

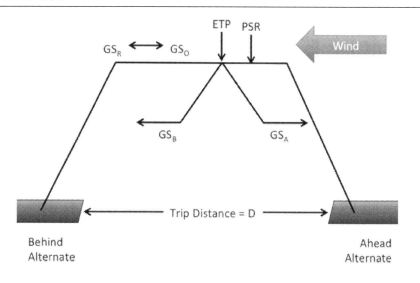

ETP / PSR Graphically

The following formula is used to calculate the ground distance from the departure airport to the Point of Safe Return:

$$Ground\ Distance\ to\ PSR = \frac{(GS_{R1})(GS_O)}{GS_O + GS_{R1}} = NM$$

Where:

Endurance = Total Fuel Quantity / Average Fuel Flow

GS_O = Normal Outbound Ground Speed at Cruise Altitude

GS_{R1} = Return Ground Speed at Normal Cruise Altitude

Notes:

- Unlike the ETP, the Point of Safe Return should be based on your original departure airport, since that is where you are likely to want to go if it becomes an issue.
- The terms GS_R, GS_C, and ETP are for the "Equal Time Point." See the chapter: Equal Time Points.

References

14 CFR 121, Operating Requirements: Domestic, Flag, and Supplemental Operations

Post Position Plot Techniques

A post-position plot is simply a check made after enough time has elapsed since crossing the waypoint to detect a navigation error, but soon enough to fix things before a loss of separation with other traffic occurs.

Requirement

D.2.9 Ten Minutes After Waypoint Passage. Cross-check navigational performance and course compliance by one of the following methods:

D.2.9.1 The "plotting" method is appropriate for all aircraft navigation configurations.

1. Verify your plotting/orientation chart reflects the currently effective route clearance.

2. Plot your present latitude/longitude and record the time on your chart.

3. You should plot your position using coordinates from the nonsteering LRNS.

4. Investigate/take corrective action if your plotted position does not agree with your currently effective route clearance.

5. Using the steering LRNS, verify the next waypoint is consistent with the currently effective route clearance.

6. Verify your autopilot steering mode is in LNAV/NAV or other appropriate mode to ensure steering to the next intended waypoint.

D.2.9.2 The "navigation display" method is appropriate for and available for use in aircraft equipped with an operable FMS.

1. Confirm the aircraft symbol is on the programmed route on the navigation display (at smallest scale).

2. Check system-generated cross-track deviation or similar indication of any deviation from the programmed route of flight.

3. Using the steering LRNS verify the "TO" waypoint is consistent with your currently effective route clearance.

4. Investigate/take correction action to address any anomalies or unexpected deviations.

5. Verify your autopilot steering mode is LNAV/NAV or other appropriate mode to ensure steering to the next intended waypoint.

D.2.9.3 You may use an alternate method with FAA acceptance.

Source: AC 91-70C, ¶D.2.9

About the "nonsteering" versus "steering"

Note: The advisory circular's use of the "nonsteering" and "steering" Long Range Navigation Systems is meant for aircraft without LRNS that self-correct and/or synchronize with each other and with GPS. The idea is that the LRNS steering the aircraft would be checked by the other.

What the post position will and will not do

The post position plot will protect you against problems between the autopilot and the FMS, but not against an improperly programmed waypoint. Let's say you entered 5230N instead of 5330N, the classic "one degree" error that will throw you 60 nm off course. Since the line drawn by the FMS on your display is looking for a latitude of 52 degrees it will draw that as a point and you will think you are on course, no matter how small the display scale is set. I recommend that if you are not going to plot, you should at the very least bring up the GPS present position display and verify you cross the correct waypoint first, and that your course to the next waypoint agrees with the master document. (Check the magnetic course, not the heading.)

Do not rely on the ARINC shorthand codes here. If you don't have a way of displaying the flight plan waypoints as latitude/longitude pairs, try bringing the waypoint into the scratch pad and then to a waypoint page to ensure your "TO" latitude and longitude points are correct.

The point is to plot the aircraft's position after about ten minutes to ensure the next waypoint wasn't entered in error. If, for example, the flight plan download (or manual entry) entered the next waypoint as 51N 040W, one degree south of the clearance, it would look perfectly normal on the cockpit displays but plotting the position would alert the crew that something is amiss.

Electronic Post Position Plots

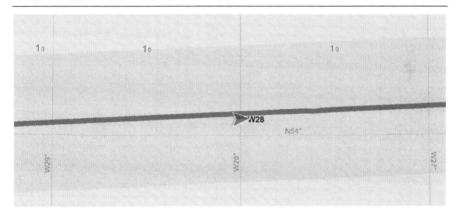

JeppFD Post Position Plot

If you are using an iPad application to track your flight progress, you can simply do a "screen grab" about ten minutes after waypoint passage to have an easy record of the post position plot. In the example photo, we took the screen grab two degrees east of 30W. (More about the two degree post position plot next.) Notice that the aircraft GPS symbol is 2 nm right of course, since we were using Strategic Lateral Offset Procedures.

A Two Degree Post Position Plot

When doing a post position plot about ten minutes after waypoint passage, you will likely have to interpolate twice. In the screen capture shown, a ten-minute check will require the pilot to estimate both the latitude and longitude, creating a chance for an error in each. When flying east-west or west-east, it may be possible to do the post position plot about ten minutes after waypoint passage by picking the nearest line of longitude. In the screen grab shown, it would be advantageous to do the post position plot when crossing 28° of longitude, eliminating the need to interpolate one part of the position.

References

Advisory Circular 91-70C, Oceanic and International Operations, 10/4/23, U.S. Department of Transportation

ICAO Nat Doc 007, North Atlantic Operations and Airspace Manual, v. 2023-1

Required Navigation Performance (RNP) and Area Navigation (RNAV)

RNAV airspace generally mandates a certain level of equipment and assumes you have a 95% chance of keeping to a stated level of navigation accuracy. RNP is a part of Performance Based Navigation (PBN) which adds to the same RNAV accuracy standards a level of system monitoring and alerting. RNAV 1 and RNP 1 both say you have a 0.95 probability of staying within 1 nm of course. RNP will let you know when the probability of you staying within 2 nm of that position goes below 0.99999.

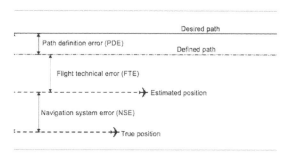

RNAV-1 versus RNP-1, from AC 20-138D, figures 1 and 2.

Under RNAV, the equipment used to achieve the navigation accuracy is specified. Under PBN, the RNP is specified, and it is up to the operator to achieve that performance.

Overview

RNAV

Area Navigation (RNAV). A method of navigation which permits aircraft operation on any desired flight path within the coverage of station-referenced navigation aids or within the limits of the capability of self-contained aids, or a combination of these. For the purposes of this AC, the specified RNAV accuracy must be met 95% of the flight time.

Source: AC 90-100A, ¶4.b

RNAV systems evolved in a manner similar to conventional ground-based routes and procedures. A specific RNAV system was identified and its performance was evaluated through a combination of analysis and flight testing. For domestic operations, the initial systems used very high frequency omnidirectional radio range (VOR) and distance measuring equipment (DME) for estimating their position; for oceanic operations, inertial navigation systems (INS) were employed. These "new" systems were developed, evaluated and certified. Airspace and obstacle clearance criteria were developed based on the performance of available equipment; and specifications for requirements were based on available capabilities. In some cases, it was necessary to identify the individual models of equipment that could be operated within the airspace concerned. Such prescriptive requirements resulted in delays to the introduction of new RNAV system capabilities and higher costs for maintaining appropriate certification.

Source: ICAO Doc 9613, pg. I-(iii)

In the old days we would navigate IFR from navaid to navaid and when we had to, we would fly fix-to-fix by mentally visualizing the airspace and estimating a course to fly. How? See the chapter: Fix-to-Fix Navigation.

Then various boxes appeared that did this better than we could and "area navigation" was born. It is simply a method of navigation that allows us to fly along any desired flight path. Inertial navigation systems allowed us to do this beyond the range of navigation aids and GNSS / GPS give us access to the best navigation aid of all just about anywhere in the world.

RNP

Performance-based navigation (PBN). The PBN concept specifies that aircraft RNAV system performance requirements be defined in terms of the accuracy, integrity, availability, continuity and functionality, which are needed for the proposed operations in the context of a particular airspace concept. The

PBN concept represents a shift from sensor-based to performance-based navigation. Performance requirements are identified in navigation specifications, which also identify the choice of navigation sensors and equipment that may be used to meet the performance requirements. These navigation specifications are defined at a sufficient level of detail to facilitate global harmonization by providing specific implementation guidance for States and operators.

Under PBN, generic navigation requirements are defined based on operational requirements. Operators then evaluate options in respect of available technology and navigation services, which could allow the requirements to be met. An operator thereby has the opportunity to select a more cost-effective option, rather than a solution being imposed as part of the operational requirements. Technology can evolve over time without requiring the operation itself to be reviewed, as long as the expected performance is provided by the RNAV system. As part of the future work of ICAO, it is anticipated that other means for meeting the requirements of the navigation specifications will be evaluated and may be included in the applicable navigation specifications, as appropriate.

Source: ICAO Doc 9613, pg. I-(iii)

Performance based navigation incorporates RNAV and adds the ability to continuously monitor the accuracy and utility of the system, alerting the pilot when the system isn't as good as it is supposed to be.

RNAV vs. RNP

The terms RNP and RNAV were once used interchangeably, but no more. The Performance Based Navigation (PBN) concept changed all that. In theory, RNP is a subset of RNAV. In actual practice, there is an exception given for RNP-10, which is another form of RNAV.

Equipment Requirements

RNAV

RNAV routes typically specify minimum equipment levels needed to satisfy navigation accuracy. For example:

U.S. RNAV operations are based upon the use of RNAV equipment that automatically determines aircraft position in the horizontal plane using inputs from the following types of positioning sensors (no specific priority).

(1) Global Navigation Satellite System (GNSS) in accordance with TSO-C145a, TSO- C146a, and TSO-C129/C129a. Positioning data from other types of navigation sensors may be integrated with the GNSS data provided it does not cause position errors exceeding the total system error requirements. As a minimum, integrity should be provided by ABAS. In addition, GPS stand-alone equipment should include the following additional functions:

- Pseudorange step detection, and

- Health word checking.

For procedures requiring GPS and/or aircraft approvals requiring GPS, if the navigation system does not automatically alert the flight crew of a loss of GPS, the operator must develop procedures to verify correct GPS operation.

(2) DME/DME RNAV equipment complying with the criteria in appendix 1. Based on current DME availability evaluations, coverage is not sufficient to support DME/DME RNAV operations without additional IRU augmentation or using GPS.

(3) DME/DME/IRU RNAV equipment complying with the criteria in appendix 2.

Source: AC 90-100A, ¶8.b

Note: ABAS is an "Aircraft-Based Augmentation System," such as Receiver Autonomous Integrity Monitoring (RAIM).

RNP

True RNP does not specify equipment but may require more than just navigation capability:

PBN offers a number of advantages over the sensor-specific method of developing airspace and obstacle clearance criteria, i.e.:

a. reduces the need to maintain sensor-specific routes and procedures, and their associated costs;

b. avoids the need for developing sensor-specific operations with each new evolution of navigation systems, which would be cost-prohibitive;

c. allows for more efficient use of airspace (route placement, fuel efficiency and noise abatement);

d. clarifies how RNAV systems are used; and

e. facilitates the operational approval process for operators by providing a limited set of navigation specifications intended for global use.

Within an airspace concept, PBN requirements will be affected by the communication, surveillance and ATM environments, the navaid infrastructure, and the functional and operational capabilities needed to meet the ATM application. PBN performance requirements also depend on what reversionary, non-RNAV means of navigation are available and what degree of redundancy is required to ensure adequate continuity of functions.

Source: ICAO Doc 9613, page I-(iii)

Monitoring ground-based NAVAIDS

The pilot is not required to monitor ground-based NAVAIDs used in position updating unless specified by the Airplane Flight Manual (AFM).

Source: AC 90-105A, ¶6.3

Total System Error (TSE)

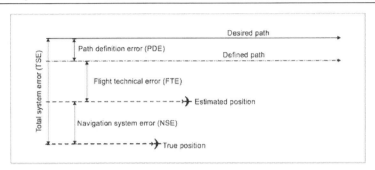

Lateral navigation errors, from ICAO Doc 9613, figure II-A-2-1.

Total System Error (TSE) is simply a measure of how far off course the airplane can be. In RNP-1 or RNAV-1 airspace, for example, the TSE = 1. Is RNP more accurate than RNAV? No.

> RNAV systems conform to the ICAO performance-based navigation specification for total system error (TSE). RNAV total system error is the 95% probability that the navigation system accuracy remains within the limits defined for the RNAV operation.

> RNP systems conform to a performance-based navigation specification based on RNAV capability that also includes requirements for on-board performance monitoring and alerting. For example, during an RNP 1.0 operation, the TSE remains within one nautical mile of the desired path 95% of the time, and on-board performance monitoring provides the pilot with an alert when the probability that TSE exceeds 2xRNP is greater than 10-5.

> RNP is an RNAV subset that also includes a requirement to provide on-board navigation system accuracy performance monitoring and alerting which means an RNP system is also an RNAV system. GNSS equipment provides accuracy performance

monitoring and alerting which, by definition, makes it both an RNAV and RNP capable system.

Source: AC 20-138D, ¶1-4.f.(2)

Both RNAV-1 and RNP-1 keep the aircraft within 1 nautical mile of centerline 95% of the flight time. The difference is that under RNP-1, the pilot is notified when the system thinks there is a greater than 0.00001 probability (.001%) that the airplane could wander outside of 2 nautical miles.

- RNAV says you should be on course,
- RNP says you should be on course, monitors system performance, and alerts you when it thinks there is a problem.

Containment

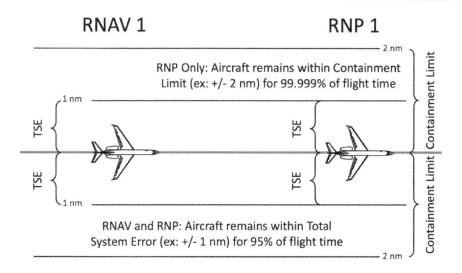

Containment Limit

So what makes RNP different than RNAV? Let's first look at what makes them the same:

- The system defines navigation accuracy as being able to stay within the total system error at least 95% of the total flight time. This applies to BOTH RNAV and RNP.
- In our example, with RNAV-1 or RNP-1, the airplane will be within 1 nautical mile 95% of the flight time.

The following applies ONLY to RNP:

- The system considers itself adequately contained as long as the probability of the airplane being inside an area twice the total system error value at least 99.999% of the time. The regulations seem to confuse the term "containment" as either the 95% navigation accuracy limit or the 99.999% alert limit.
- Regardless of the terminology, you should remember that twice the stated number is where the airplane will be 99.999% of the time before issuing an alert.
- In our example, with RNP-1, the airplane will alert the pilot if there is greater than a 0.001% chance the airplane could be more than 2 nautical miles off course.

The PBN concept uses the term on-board performance monitoring and alerting instead of the term containment. This is to avoid confusion between existing uses of containment in various documents by different areas of expertise. For example:

a. "Containment" refers to the region within which the aircraft will remain 95 per cent of the time. The associated terms have been "containment value" and "containment distance" and the related airspace protection on either side of an RNAV ATS route.

b. Within the industry standards of RTCA/DO-236 and EUROCAE/ED-75, "containment" refers to the region that the aircraft will remain when there is no alert (0.99999 probability), and defines a requirement for how often an alert occurs (0.9999). The associated terms are "containment limit", "containment integrity", "containment continuity", and "containment region".

c. Within PANS-OPS material, "containment" has referred to the region used to define the obstacle clearance, and the aircraft is expected to remain within or above that surface (regardless of alerting) with very high probability. The associated terms have been "containment area", "airspace containment", "obstacle clearance containment" and related obstacle protection areas.

Source: ICAO Doc 9613, §II-A-2-4, ¶2.3.7

The previous ICAO expressions of "containment value" and "containment distance" have been replaced by the navigation accuracy of TSE.

Source: ICAO Doc 9613, §II-A-2-4, ¶2.3.8

"On course"

All pilots are expected to maintain centerline, as depicted by onboard lateral deviation indicators and/or flight guidance during all RNP operations described in this AC unless authorized to deviate by air traffic control (ATC) or under emergency conditions. For normal operations, the cross-track (XTK) error/deviation (the difference between the RNP system computed path and the aircraft position relative to the path) should be limited to ± the RNP value. Brief deviations from this standard (e.g., overshoots or undershoots) during track changes (flyby and flyover turns), up to a maximum of one times the RNP value are allowable.

Source: AC 90-105A, ¶6.2

References

Advisory Circular 20-138D, Positioning and Navigation Systems, Change 2, 4/7/16, U.S. Department of Transportation

Advisory Circular 90-96A, Approval of U.S. Operators and Aircraft to Operate Under Instrument Flight Rules (IFR) in European Airspace Designated for Basic Area Navigation (B-RNAV) and Precision Area Navigation (P-RNAV), 1/13/05, U.S. Department of Transportation

Advisory Circular 90-100A, U.S. Terminal and En Route Area Navigation (RNAV) Operations, Change 2, 4/14/15, U.S. Department of Transportation

Advisory Circular 90-105A, Approval Guidance for RNP Operations and Barometric Vertical Navigation in the U.S. National Airspace System and in Oceanic and Remote Continental Airspace, 3/7/2016, U.S. Department of Transportation

ICAO Doc 9613 - Performance Based Navigation (PBN) Manual, International Civil Aviation Organization, Fourth Edition, 2013

Strategic Lateral Offset Procedures (SLOP) Techniques

The world has gone to SLOP. You can (and should) employ a Strategic Lateral Offset Procedures (SLOP) in almost every oceanic area. There is a debate about using SLOP over land, but the legal and official answer is you cannot with only very rare exceptions.

Most of the world only permits SLOP to the right and usually only using 1 or 2 NM distances. The ICAO has permitted "micro SLOP" in tenths since 2014, but only a few regions have adopted this. Remember that some aircraft may not SLOP: particularly those that do not have an automatic offset capability.

Why?

In the days before GPS, we would be lucky if our oceanic position was within a couple of miles of where we should have been. In the days before INS, being within 10 miles was a major accomplishment. But there were not a lot of airplanes flying oceanic and the accuracy wasn't all that important. These days, the skies are packed with airplanes but GPS allows us to navigate within a tenth or so of course centerline. It is almost all good.

It is almost all good because there is a chance a navigation or altitude error can end very badly. If someone programs the wrong course or levels off at the wrong altitude, they may be precisely on the wrong course, in position to hit someone who is properly and precisely on course. Flying a little right of course can save you when you or someone else makes a mistake.

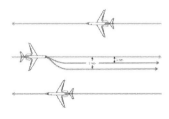

SLOP example

Regulatory

The ICAO

Strategic Lateral Offset Procedures (SLOP)

Note 1.— SLOP are approved procedures that allow aircraft to fly on a parallel track to the right of the centre line relative to the direction of flight to mitigate the lateral overlap probability due to increased navigation accuracy and wake turbulence encounters. Unless specified in the separation standard, an aircraft's use of these procedures does not affect the application of prescribed separation standards.

Note 2.— Annex 2, 3.6.2.1.1, requires authorization for the application of strategic lateral offsets from the appropriate ATS authority responsible for the airspace concerned.

16.5.1 Implementation of strategic lateral offset procedures shall be coordinated among the States involved.

Note.— Information concerning the implementation of strategic lateral offset procedures is contained in the Implementation of Strategic Lateral Offset Procedures (Circular 331).

16.5.2 Strategic lateral offsets shall be authorized only in en-route airspace as follows:

a) where the lateral separation minima or spacing between route centre lines is 42.6 km (23 NM) or more, offsets to the right of the centre line relative to the direction of flight in tenths of a nautical mile up to a maximum of 3.7 km (2 NM); and

b) where the lateral separation minima or spacing between route centre lines is 11.1 km (6 NM) or more and less than 42.6 km (23 NM), offsets to the right of the centre line relative to the direction of flight in tenths of a nautical mile up to a maximum of 0.9 km (0.5 NM).

16.5.3 The routes or airspace where application of strategic lateral offsets is authorized, and the procedures to be followed by pilots, shall be promulgated in aeronautical information publications (AIPs). In some instances, it may be necessary to impose restrictions on the use of strategic lateral offsets, e.g. where their application may be inappropriate for reasons related to obstacle clearance. Route conformance monitoring systems shall account for the application of SLOP.

16.5.4 The decision to apply a strategic lateral offset shall be the responsibility of the flight crew. The flight crew shall only apply strategic lateral offsets in airspace where such offsets have been authorized by the appropriate ATS authority and when the aircraft is equipped with automatic offset tracking capability.

Note 1.— Pilots may contact other aircraft on the inter-pilot air-to-air frequency 123.45 MHz to coordinate offsets.

Note 2.— The strategic lateral offset procedure has been designed to include offsets to mitigate the effects of wake turbulence of preceding aircraft. If wake turbulence needs to be avoided, an offset to the right and within the limits specified in 16.5.2 may be used.

Note 3.— Pilots are not required to inform ATC that a strategic lateral offset is being applied.

Source: ICAO Doc 4444, ¶16.5

The North Atlantic

Strategic Lateral Offset Procedures (SLOP)

8.4.3 This procedure provides for offsets within the following guidelines:

a) an aircraft may fly offsets right of centreline up to a maximum of 2 NM; and

b) offsets left of centreline are prohibited.

8.4.4. Distributing aircraft laterally and equally across all available positions adds an additional safety margin and reduces collision risk. SLOP is now a standard operating procedure for the entire NAT region and flight crews are required to adopt this procedure as is appropriate. In this connection, it should be noted that:

a) Aircraft without automatic offset programming capability must fly the centreline.

b) Aircraft able to perform offsets in tenths of nautical mile should do so as it contributes to risk reduction.

c) It is recommended that flight crews of aircraft capable of programming automatic offsets should randomly select flying centreline or an offset. In order to obtain lateral spacing from nearby aircraft (i.e. those immediately above and/or below), flight crews should use whatever means are available (e.g. ACAS/TCAS, communications, visual acquisition, GPWS) to determine the best flight path to fly.

d) An aircraft overtaking another aircraft should offset within the confines of this procedure, if capable, so as to minimize the amount of wake turbulence for the aircraft being overtaken.

e) For wake turbulence purposes, flight crews should fly one of the offset positions. Flight crews may contact other aircraft on the air-to-air channel, 123.450 MHz, as necessary, to co-ordinate the best wake turbulence mutual offset option. (Note. It is recognized that the flight crew will use their judgment to determine the action most appropriate to any given situation and that the pilot-in-command has the final authority and responsibility for the safe operations of the aircraft.

f) Flight crews may apply an offset outbound at the oceanic entry point and must return to centreline prior to the oceanic exit point unless otherwise authorized by the appropriate ATS authority or directed by the appropriate ATC unit.

g) There is no ATC clearance required for this procedure and it is not necessary that ATC be advised.

h) Voice Position reports should be based on the waypoints of the current ATC clearance and not the offset positions.

i) Aircraft shall not apply SLOP below F285 in the Reykjavik CTA and Bodo OCA.

j) The offset should be applied from the time the aircraft reaches its cruising level until top of descent.

Source: NAT Doc 007, ¶8.4

The US FAA

Your SOPs should include SLOP for all oceanic crossings. NOTAMs, State AIPs, and other flight planning guidance will indicate where exceptions apply and where procedures differ.

- This procedure was developed to reduce the risk associated with an altitude deviation and two highly accurate navigation systems navigating to the same point.

- SLOP also replaced the contingency procedure developed for aircraft encountering wake turbulence. Depending upon winds aloft, coordination between aircraft to avoid wake turbulence may be necessary.

- This procedure, which distributes traffic between the route centerline and up to 2 NM right of centerline, greatly reduces risk by the nature of its randomness.

Operators that have an automatic offset capability should fly up to 2 NM right of the centerline.

Aircraft that do not have an automatic offset capability (that can be programmed in the LRNS) should fly the centerline only.

Source: AC 91-70C, ¶D.2.6.5

Random SLOP

Many Gulfstream pilots feel immune to the SLOP issue, saying they always fly above the tracks and they usually fly random routing. As you can see from the drawing, there is one problem with that argument. If you are on the track, chances are you are flying the same direction as your nearest neighbor and while the sky is considerably more crowded, the chance of a collision is reduced. The guy behind you might make an altitude error but he is behind you and likely to stay behind you.

You might be on the random track because you are flying an unusual city pair or for some other reason. But what if there is somebody flying the same city pair in the opposite direction? Now what if that guy makes an altitude error? Wouldn't an extra mile of separation be nice?

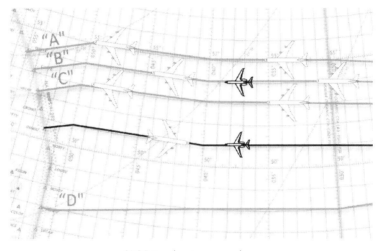

SLOP track versus random

References

Advisory Circular 91-70C, Oceanic and International Operations, 10/4/23, U.S. Department of Transportation

ICAO Doc 4444 - Air Traffic Management, 16th Edition, Procedures for Air Navigation Services, International Civil Aviation Organization, 10 November 2016

ICAO Nat Doc 007, North Atlantic Operations and Airspace Manual, v.2023-1

Weather Deviation in Oceanic Airspace Techniques

It is easy to get hung up on weather deviation procedures when in oceanic airspace. If you are in radar contact and talking to an air traffic controller, you should state your intentions and start from there. If you are not in radar contact and your only means of communication is via an ARINC radio operator or CPDLC, then things change.

General Procedures

Note.— The following procedures are intended for deviations around adverse meteorological conditions.

15.2.4.1.1 When weather deviation is required, the pilot should initiate communications with ATC via voice or CPDLC; rapid response may be obtained by either:

a) stating "WEATHER DEVIATION REQUIRED" to indicate that priority is desired on the frequency and for ATC response; or

b) requesting a weather deviation using a CPDLC lateral downlink message.

15.2.4.1.2 When necessary, the pilot should initiate the communications using the urgency call "PAN PAN" (preferably spoken three times) or by using a CPDLC urgency downlink message.

15.2.4.1.2 The pilot shall inform ATC when weather deviation is no longer required, or when a weather deviation has been completed and the aircraft has returned to its cleared route.

Source: ICAO Doc 4444 §15.2.4.1

Actions to be Taken When Controller-Pilot Communications Are Established

15.2.4.2.1 The pilot should notify ATC and request clearance to deviate from track or ATS route, advising, when possible, the extent of the deviation requested. The flight crew will use whatever means are appropriate (i.e. voice and/or CPDLC) to communicate during a weather deviation.

Note.— Pilots are advised to contact ATC as soon as possible with requests for clearance in order to provide adequate time for the request to be assessed and acted upon.

15.2.4.2.2 ATC should take one of the following actions:

a. when appropriate separation can be applied, issue clearance to deviate from track; or

b. if there is conflicting traffic and ATC is unable to establish appropriate separation, ATC shall:

- advise the pilot of inability to issue clearance for the requested deviation;

- advise the pilot of the conflicting traffic; and

- request the pilot's intentions.

15.2.4.2.3 The pilot should take the following actions:

a. comply with the ATC clearance issued; or

b. advise ATC of intentions and execute the procedures listed in 15.2.4.3.

Source: ICAO Doc 4444 §15.2.4.2

Actions to be Taken if a Revised ATC Clearance Cannot Be Obtained

Note.— The provisions of this section apply to situations where a pilot needs to exercise the authority of a pilot-in-command under the provisions of Annex 2, 2.3.1.

If the aircraft is required to deviate from track or ATS route to avoid adverse meteorological conditions and prior clearance cannot be obtained, an ATC clearance shall be obtained at the earliest possible time. Until an ATC clearance is received, the pilot shall take the following actions:

a. if possible, deviate away from an organized track or ATS route system;

b. establish communications with and alert nearby aircraft by broadcasting, at suitable intervals: aircraft identification, flight level, position (including the ATS route designator or the track code, as appropriate) and intentions, on the frequency in use and on 121.5 MHz (or, as a backup, on the inter-pilot air-to-air frequency 123.45 MHz);

c. watch for conflicting traffic both visually and by reference to ACAS (if equipped);

d. turn on all aircraft exterior lights (commensurate with appropriate operating limitations);

e. for deviations of less than 9.3 km (5 NM) from the originally cleared track or ATS route, remain at a level assigned by ATC;

f. for deviations greater than or equal to 9.3 km (5 NM) from the originally cleared track or ATS route,, when the aircraft is approximately 9.3 km (5 NM) from track, initiate a level change in accordance with Table 15-1;

g. if the pilot receives clearance to deviate from cleared track or ATS route for a specified distance and, subsequently, requests, but cannot obtain a clearance to deviate beyond that distance, the pilot should apply an altitude offset in accordance with Table 15-1 before deviating beyond the cleared distance;

h. when returning to track or ATS route, be at its assigned flight level when the aircraft is within approximately 9.3 km (5 NM) of the centre line; and

i. if contact was not established prior to deviating, continue to attempt to contact ATC to obtain a clearance. If contact was established, continue to keep ATC advised of intentions and obtain essential traffic information.

Note.— If, as a result of actions taken under the provisions of 15.2.4.3.1, the pilot determines that there is another aircraft at or near the same flight level with which a conflict may occur, then the pilot is expected to adjust the path of the aircraft, as necessary, to avoid conflict.

Source: ICAO Doc 4444 §15.2.4

Originally cleared track or ATS route centre line	Deviations ≥ 9.3 km (5.0 NM)	Level change
EAST (000° - 179° magnetic)	LEFT	DESCEND 90m (300 ft)
	RIGHT	CLIMB 90 m (300 ft)
WEST (180° - 359° magnetic)	LEFT	CLIMB 90 m (300 ft)
	RIGHT	DESCEND 90 m (300 ft)

Table 15-1

References

ICAO Doc 4444 - Air Traffic Management, 16th Edition, Procedures for Air Navigation Services, International Civil Aviation Organization, October 2016

World Geodetic System (WGS-84)

For those pilots who want to avoid all things tech, or understanding all things tech, here is what you need to know about WGS-84 in a nutshell. The United States Department of Defense first developed GPS for military uses and that eventually morphed into a worldwide civil system of navigation. Various entities around the world started cataloging the positions of things on earth as a way of finding them and, of course, avoiding them. The standard most of us use is known as the World Geodetic System of 1984, or WGS-84.

If your aircraft and its database uses WGS-84 — and most do — then it is critically important that your navigation and approach charts are based on WGS-84 too.

History

Contrary to popular folklore, it has long been obvious that the earth is a sphere of some sort, and as early as 240 BC the chief librarian at the Great Library of Alexandria, Egypt, had come up with an idea just how big the sphere is. . .

> In Egypt, a Greek scholar and philosopher, Eratosthenes, set out to make more explicit measurements. He had observed that on the day of the summer solstice, the midday sun shone to the bottom of a well in the town of Syene (Aswan). Figure 1. At the same time, he observed the sun was not directly overhead at Alexandria; instead, it cast a shadow with the vertical equal to 1/50th of a circle (7° 12'). To these observations, Eratosthenes applied certain "known" facts (1) that on the day of the summer solstice, the midday sun was directly over the line of the summer Tropic Zone (Tropic of Cancer)-Syene was therefore concluded to be on this line; (2) the linear distance between Alexandria and Syene was 500 miles; (3) Alexandria and Syene lay on a direct north south line. From these observations and "known" facts, Eratosthenes concluded that, since the angular deviation of the sun from the vertical at Alexandria was also the

angle of the subtended arc, the linear distance between Alexandria and Syene was 1/50 of the circumference of the earth or 50 x 500 = 25,000 miles. A currently accepted value for the earth's circumference at the Equator is 24,901 miles, based upon the equatorial radius of the World Geodetic System.

Source: Geodesy for the Layman, Ch. 1

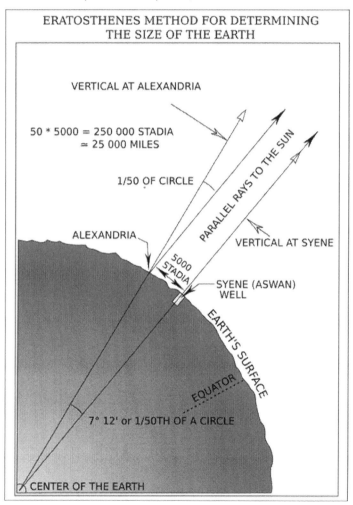

Erastothenes' Size of the Earth, from Geodesy for the Layman, Figure 1

Sphere "Flattening"

The earth isn't perfectly round, the centrifugal effects of its rotation tends to make it wider in the middle than it is tall. Technically, you would call the basic shape an oblate spheroid.

Sphere Versus Geoid

It is helpful to think of the earth's shape as a "geoid," the shape it would most closely resemble figuring the effects of gravity.

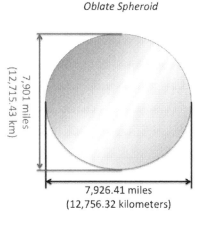

Oblate Spheroid

7,901 miles
(12,715.43 km)

7,926.41 miles
(12,756.32 kilometers)

Oblate spheroid

There have been many definitions of the "geoid" over 150 years or so. Here is the one currently adopted at NGS:

geoid: The equipotential surface of the Earth's gravity field which best fits, in a least squares sense, global mean sea level

Even though we adopt a definition, that does not mean we are perfect in the realization of that definition. For example, altimetry is often used to define "mean sea level" in the oceans, but altimetry is not global (missing the near polar regions). As such, the fit between "global" mean sea level and the geoid is not entirely confirmable.

Source: National Geodetic Survey

Notes:

- The earth doesn't conform to the geoid because the magnetic field isn't uniform and the earth's surface is filled with varying heights of land as well as a sea that does not maintain the same level throughout.

- It isn't that altimetry is "missing the near polar regions," but the shifting ice makes it unreliable at lower levels.
- The least squares method is a way of turning a curve into a mathematical formula by adding up the square of the differences between the math and the actual curve, and minimizing the result.

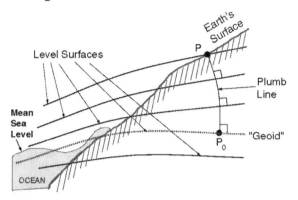

Level Surface = Equipotential Surface
H (Orthometric Height) = Distance along Plumb line (P_0 to P)

Schematic diagram, from National Geodetic Survey

Mapping the Earth

The Department of Defense, in the late 1950s began to develop the needed world system to which geodetic datums could be referred and compatibility established between the coordinates of widely separated sites of interest. Efforts of the Army, Navy and Air Force were combined leading to the DoD World Geodetic System 1960 (WGS 60).

In January 1966, a World Geodetic System Committee composed of representatives from the Army, Navy and Air Force, was charged with the responsibility of developing an improved WGS needed to satisfy mapping, charting and geodetic requirements. Additional surface gravity observations, results from the extension of triangulation and trilateration networks, and large amounts of Doppler and optical satellite data had become available since the development of WGS 60. Using the additional data and improved techniques, WGS 66 was produced which served DoD needs for about five years after its implementation in 1967.

After an extensive effort extending over a period of approximately three years, the Department of Defense World Geodetic System 1972 was completed. Selected satellite, surface gravity and astrogeodetic data available through 1972 from both DoD and non-DoD sources were used in a Unified WGS Solution (a large scale least squares adjustment).

Source: Geodesy for the Layman, Ch. 8

Adopting a Standard

The U.S. Department of Defense developed the World Geodetic System 1966 in an attempt to survey the entire earth. The survey was updated in 1984 to take advantage of GPS, and the survey name updated to WGS-84.

The ICAO adopted WGS-84 as the standard geodetic reference system for future air navigation and is used in most FMS Navigation Databases.

The Technical Stuff

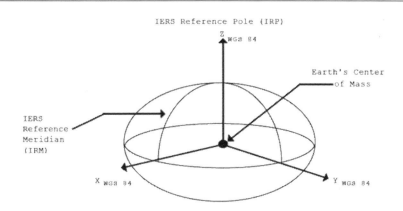

WGS84 Coordinate System Definition, from NIMA, Figure 2.1

Definition

The WGS 84 Coordinate System is a Conventional Terrestrial Reference System (CTRS). The definition of this coordinate system follows the criteria outlined in the International Earth Rotation Service (IERS) Technical Note 21 [1]. These criteria are repeated below:

- It is geocentric, the center of mass being defined for the whole Earth including oceans and atmosphere

- Its scale is that of the local Earth frame, in the meaning of a relativistic theory of gravitation

- Its orientation was initially given by the Bureau International de l'Heure (BIH) orientation of 1984.0

- Its time evolution in orientation will create no residual global rotation with regards to the crust

The WGS 84 Coordinate System is a right-handed, Earth-fixed orthogonal coordinate system and is graphically depicted in [the figure].

- Origin = Earth's center of mass

- Z-Axis = The direction of the IERS Reference Pole (IRP). This direction corresponds to the direction of the BIH Conventional Terrestrial Pole (CTP) (epoch 1984.0) with an uncertainty of 0.005

- X-Axis = Intersection of the IERS Reference Meridian (IRM) and the plane passing through the origin and normal to the Z-axis. The IRM is coincident with the BIH Zero Meridian (epoch 1984.0) with an uncertainty of 0.005

- Y-Axis = Completes a right-handed, Earth-Centered Earth-Fixed (ECEF) orthogonal coordinate system

The WGS 84 Coordinate System origin also serves as the geometric center of the WGS 84 Ellipsoid and the Z-axis serves as the rotational axis of this ellipsoid of revolution.

Source: NIMA, ¶2.1

The World Geodetic System 84 is a standard used by most of the world to define exactly where a set of coordinates are on the earth. The issues on using one standard versus another are more than just determining where something is left, right, forward, and aft. Another issue is that the world isn't a perfect sphere, or geoid, and defining where something is can also vary in height above the center of the earth.

ICAO requirement

Navigation data may originate from survey observations, from equipment specifications/settings or from the airspace and procedure design process. Whatever the source, the generation and the subsequent processing of the data must take account of the following:

a. all coordinate data must be referenced to the World Geodetic System — 1984 (WGS-84);

b. all surveys must be based upon the International Terrestrial Reference Frame;

c. all data must be traceable to their source;

d. equipment used for surveys must be adequately calibrated;

e. software tools used for surveys, procedure design or airspace design must be suitably qualified;

f. standard criteria and algorithms must be used in all designs;

g. surveyors and designers must be properly trained;

h. comprehensive verification and validation routines must be used by all data originators;

i. procedures must be subjected to ground validation and, where necessary, flight validation and flight inspection prior to publication. For guidance on the validation process see Doc 9906, Volume 5 — Validation of Instrument Flight Procedures;

j. aeronautical navigation data must be published in a standard format, with an appropriate level of detail and to the required resolution; and

k. all data originators and data processors must implement a quality management process which includes:

i) a requirement to maintain quality records;

ii) a procedure for managing feedback and error reporting from users and other processors in the data chain.

Source: ICAO Doc 9613 ¶3.4

References

Geodesy for the Layman, Defense Mapping Agency, Building 56 U.S. Naval Observatory DMA TR 80-003, Washington DC 20305, 16 March 1984

ICAO Doc 9613 - Performance Based Navigation (PBN) Manual, International Civil Aviation Organization, Fourth Edition, 2013

http://www.ngs.noaa.gov/GEOID/geoid_def.htm, National Geodetic Survey

World Geodetic System 1984, Department of Defense, National Imagery and Mapping Agency (NIMA), NSN 7643-01-402-0347, NIMA TR8350.2, Third Edition, Amendment 1, 3 January 2000

Appendix: Celestial Navigation

My first book on navigation was issued to Air Force navigators in 1972 and had this to say about celestial navigation: "When the ground is not visible and a position cannot be established with other methods, celestial observations offer the only available aid to dead reckoning." Of course, those days are long gone.

So that begs the question: why bother learning it? I offer basic celestial concepts here to show how it used to be done in hopes that it can help a modern navigator's "big picture" view of the task at hand: getting from here to there. I think having a cursory understanding – which is all I am providing here – will make you a better navigator when the GPS doesn't seem to be up to the task.

We'll cover the equipment you will need if you want to actually shoot the heavens to find where you are, some basic terminology, and then two methods to turn a view of the heavens into your latitude and longitude. The first method is easier than the second but is rarely available. Again, we aren't trying to turn you into Ferdinand Magellan. But going through the methods will make you a better navigator.

A Celestial Navigator's Toolbox

A celestial navigator needs:

- A sextant for measuring the angles between *celestial bodies* or a celestial body and the horizon.
- A watch to record the time of the observation.
- An *Air Almanac* for locating the position of the celestial body. Most Air Almanacs contain the expected positions of 57 stars, Mars, Jupiter, Saturn, Venus, the sun, and the moon for given dates and times.
- Side Reduction Tables used for computing the *Line of Position (LOP)*.

Some Terminology to Begin With

The terrestrial sphere

For the purpose of celestial navigation, the earth is considered to be a perfect sphere, called the *terrestrial sphere*, so that every point on the surface has the same distance to the center. We know that the earth rotates 360° every 24 hours, but we will normally assume the earth is not rotating for the purpose of celestial navigation.

Great circles

You can cut the sphere into slices called circles. Any slice that goes through the center of the earth is called a *great circle*. Great circles that go through the poles are called *meridians*, or lines of longitude. The *equator* and every meridian are all great circles. The meridian that goes through the Royal Observatory in Greenwich, England is called the *prime meridian*, which is 0° longitude. Lines of longitude go east and west to 180°.

Small circles

Any circle formed by a slice that doesn't go through the center is called a *small circle*. Small circles that are perpendicular to the earth's axis of the earth's rotation are called *parallels of latitude*. Latitude starts at the equator with 0° and goes north and south to the poles at 90°. The equator is often abbreviated with the letter Q.

Distances

The distance along the terrestrial sphere is known as *arc distance*. When that arc is along a line of longitude, 1° of arc equates to 60 nm, which means 1' (one minute) of arc equals 1 nm.

The celestial sphere

In celestial navigation we assume that all celestial bodies are infinitely far away on an imaginary sphere called the *celestial sphere*. This sphere (and the celestial bodies on it) rotate westward about an axis that is an extension of the earth's axis. It rotates 360° every 24 hours, 15° every hour, and 1° every 4 minutes. The axis goes through the center of the earth and the north and south poles.

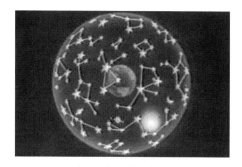

The celestial sphere

Because the celestial sphere is infinitely large, any point on earth can be considered the center of that sphere, greatly simplifying the geometry of celestial navigation. (You don't have to consider the distance from you in the air to the surface of the earth as well as from there to the center of the earth.)

Every point on earth has a corresponding point on the celestial sphere and every point on the celestial sphere has a corresponding point on earth. Accordingly, we have a celestial axis, a celestial meridian, and so forth. There are, however, a few special names.

- *Declination* is the celestial latitude.
- Parallels of declination are the celestial parallels of latitude.
- *Zenith* is your position on earth extended outward to the celestial sphere.
- *Geographic Position (GP)* is a celestial body's position drawn to the earth, also known as its subpoint on earth.

Apparent motion

We know the earth is rotating and the celestial bodies are stationary, but in celestial navigation we think of it the other way round. The celestial sphere appears to us to be moving from east to west.

Hour circle

An hour circle can be thought of as a line of longitude on the celestial sphere that contains a given celestial body. The sun, for example, has an hour circle. The star Rigel has another hour circle, and so on. Hour circles appear to us to move east to west at the standard rate of 1° every 4 minutes.

Greenwich Hour Angle (GHA)

Greenwich Hour Angle (GHA) is the angle from the Prime Celestial Meridian to the hour angle of the celestial body and is measured west of that meridian through 360°.

Prime Hour Circle and GHA-Aries

Prime Hour Circle is the hour circle of the sun when it crosses the celestial equator (the point where its declination is zero.) This is also known as the Hour Circle of Aries, or *GHA-Aries*.

This point changes the first day of every spring.

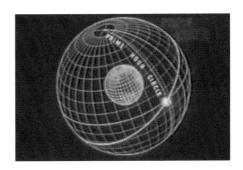

Prime Hour Circle

Local Hour Angle (LHA)

Local Hour Angle (LHA) is from the observer's celestial meridian to the hour circle of the celestial body, again measured to the west through 360°.

Sidereal Hour Angle (SHA)

Sidereal Hour Angle (SHA) is measured from GHA-Aries to the hour angle of a star (other than the sun). A star's position relative to the sun and its declination relative to the celestial equator is constant. This makes life easier since you don't need to update the GHA of the stars, only that of the sun and selected planets. If you have the GHA-Aries, adding a star's SHA will give its GHA.

Sidereal Hour Angle (SHA)

The Basic Idea

You need a rough idea of where you are through dead reckoning and a basic knowledge of which celestial bodies will be visible to you. You aim your sextant at the celestial body and measure the angle between it and the horizon. Celestial angles like this are called altitudes. Record the altitude and the time.

568   GREENWICH P. M. 1972 OCTOBER 10 (TUESDAY)

GMT	☉ SUN		ARIES	VENUS–3.7		JUPITER–1.8		SATURN 0.2		☽ MOON		Lat.	Moon-set	Diff.
	GHA	Dec.	GHA ♈	GHA	Dec.	GHA	Dec.	GHA	Dec.	GHA	Dec.			
h m	° ′	° ′	° ′	° ′	° ′	° ′	° ′	° ′	° ′	° ′	° ′	N		
12 00	3 15.6	S 6 47.2	199 11.2	41 17	N 9 50	287 23	S23 29	119 21	N21 28	330 38	S22 29	°	h m	m
10	5 45.6	47.3	201 41.6	43 47		289 53		121 52		333 03	30	72	■	*
20	8 15.7	47.5	204 12.0	46 17		292 23		124 22		335 28	32	70	■	*
30	10 45.7	· 47.6	206 42.4	48 47	·	294 54	·	126 52	·	337 53	· 33	68	■	*
40	13 15.7	47.8	209 12.9	51 17		297 24		129 23		340 19	34	66	15 17	*
50	15 45.7	48.0	211 43.3	53 47		299 54		131 53		342 44	35	64	16 03	−01
13 00	18 15.8	S 6 48.1	214 13.7	56 17	N 9 49	302 25	S23 29	134 24	N21 28	345 09	S22 36	62	16 34	+06
10	20 45.8	48.3	216 44.1	58 47		304 55		136 54		347 34	37	60	16 57	09
20	23 15.8	48.4	219 14.5	61 17		307 26		139 25		349 59	38	58	17 15	11
30	25 45.9	· 48.6	221 44.9	63 46	·	309 56	·	141 55	·	352 25	· 39	56	17 31	13
40	28 15.9	48.8	224 15.3	66 16		312 26		144 25		354 50	40	54	17 44	14
50	30 45.9	48.9	226 45.7	68 46		314 57		146 56		357 15	41	52	17 56	15

GHA examples from Air Almanac

You now need the GHA and declination of your celestial body. You can find this information for the Sun, Venus, Jupiter, Saturn, or the Moon directly in the Air Almanac on the page for your date and the row corresponding to the time of your sighting. If celestial body is outside the solar system, you will need to record the GHA-Aries.

Armed with this information, you sight the celestial body with your sextant and record its altitude. For now, let's say we sighted the Sun and have GHA-Sun and Declination-Sun.

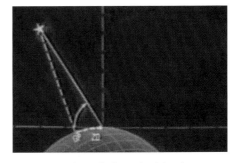

A celestial object's altitude

We have enough information to determine the location of the celestial body – the Sun in this example – and its position over the earth. That is defined as the Geographic Position (GP) of the celestial body.

The altitude of the celestial body can be seen by more than just you in your location, but also by others at other locations. Each of you sighted the same angle. The points on earth with the same angle are on what is called the *Circle of Equal Altitude*.

Circle of Equal Altitude

The entire circumference of that circle is a Line of Position (LOP). You could, theoretically, be anywhere on that LOP.

If you were to repeat the process on another celestial body and come up with a second circle of equal altitude, you will have narrowed your possible solutions to anywhere within the shared areas of those two circles.

A third circle would further reduce the uncertainty.

We've left out the math needed to pinpoint the Geographic Position (GP) of each celestial body and we've sidestepped the complexity of actually plotting these LOPs. There are two methods of note, one easier than the other. But the easier method

Two circular LOPs

requires that you are very near the GP of each celestial body. Let's look at that first. It will help understanding the harder method.

The Horizon System

When you've found a celestial body's GHA and declination, you will know its subpoint on earth, also known as its Geographic Position GP. If the celestial body was directly overhead, you would know your position. But that would be extremely rare, you are almost always a distance away from the celestial body's GP.

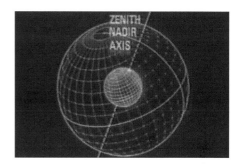

Zenith Nadir Axis

The Horizon System simplifies the process by drawing the axis of the terrestrial and celestial spheres through your position.

Zenith Nadir Axis – a line from your position to the celestial sphere

and to the center of the earth to the other side of the celestial sphere. Now draw a great circle around the earth's center perpendicular to the Zenith Nadir Axis. This is called the *celestial horizon*. The light from your celestial body comes to the earth in a narrow line. Because the

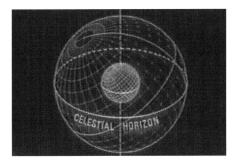

Celestial Horizon redrawn

distance between the celestial body is so great and the relative size of the earth is so small, we can assume any measurement of the angle between the celestial body and the celestial horizon will be the same.

"Tilting" the earth to put yourself on top greatly simplifies operating the sextant. You simply point the thing to your celestial object, measure the angle down to the celestial horizon, and you have a part of the puzzle solved.

Altitude (H) is the angle between celestial body and the celestial

horizon. (As opposed to declination which is measured from the celestial equator.)

Hs – Sighted Altitude

The angle you see when you sighted the celestial body is that body's Sighted Altitude (Hs). Hs cannot be more than 90° -- the celestial body

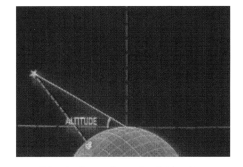

Altitude from the celestial horizon

is directly above you. Hs is normally no less than 0° -- level with you but could theoretically be at bit lower.

Ho – Corrected Altitude

The Air Almanac and other manuals have ways to correct the Sighted Altitude (Hs) for refraction and other errors. The result is Corrected Altitude Ho.

Horizon method Circle of Equal Altitude

Zenith Distance (ZD)

The distance between you and the Geographic Position of the celestial body is the Zenith Distance ZD.

Let's consider a celestial body that you've sighted, and Hs is 70°. Since the angle from you to the celestial body is 70°, you know the angle from the body straight down and to you is 20°. (The sum of the inside angles in a triangle is 180°, so 180 – 90 – 70 = 20°.) That's 20° Zenith Distance ZD over the earth, at 60 nm per degree, so the radius of that circle is 20 x 60 = 1,200 nm. That's a big circle to plot on a chart. Hence . . .

Limitations of the horizon system

Most celestial navigators think any Corrected Altitude Ho lower than 85° is too low to plot. With Ho = 85° you will have a Zenith Distance of 5° x 60 = 300 nm, which you could easily plot. Let's say your celestial object is 30° above the horizon for example. Your Zenith Distance will be 60° x 60 = 3,600 nm. Is your chart big enough to plot that? Once Ho gets lower than 85°, you will need another method . . .

The Intercept Method

As a celestial navigator, you probably have a good set of "Sight Reduction Tables" which do all the math for you. We'll cover that, but we need to go through the math first just to show what those magical tables are doing for you.

"Precomps" versus "shoot and pray"

Most competent navigators will do the computations that follow before picking up their sextants. They will usually take three shots and the time of the shots need to be very close to make the result accurate enough to use. Precomputing the shot is the way to go. If you shoot then compute, three times, the speed of the aircraft will make the first shot less relevant. We'll shoot then compute in the examples just to make it easier to explain but be aware it would be best to compute first.

Find Sighted Altitude (Hs)

As with the previous method, we begin by sighting a celestial body above the horizon with our sextant, recording the Sighted Altitude Hs and the date / time of our observation.

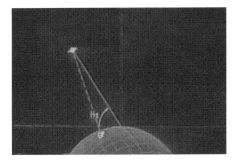

Determining Hs

Find Observed Altitude (Ho)

You then correct Hs to get Corrected Altitude Ho using correction tables in the Air Almanac:

CORRECTIONS TO BE APPLIED TO SEXTANT ALTITUDE

REFRACTION

To be subtracted from sextant altitude (referred to as observed altitude in A.P. 3270)

h	0	5	10	15	20	25	30	35	40	45	50	55	R_o	0·9 1·0 1·1 1·2
							Sextant Altitude							R
	90	90	90	90	90	90	90	90	90	90	90	90	0	0 0 0 0
	63	59	55	51	46	41	36	31	26	20	17	13	1	1 1 1 1
	33	29	26	22	19	16	14	11	9	7	6	4	2	2 2 2 2
	21	19	16	14	12	10	8	7	5	4	2 40	1 40	3	3 3 3 4
	16	14	12	10	8	7	6	5	3 10	2 20	1 30	0 40	4	4 4 4 5
	12	11	9	8	7	5	4 00	3 10	2 10	1 30	0 39	+0 05	5	5 5 5 6
	10	9	7	5 50	4 50	3 50	3 10	2 20	1 30	0 49	+0 11	−0 19	6	5 6 7 7
	8 10	6 50	5 50	4 50	4 00	3 00	2 20	1 50	1 10	0 24	−0 11	−0 38	7	6 7 8 8
	6 50	5 50	5 00	4 00	3 10	2 30	1 50	1 20	0 38	+0 04	−0 28	−0 54	8	7 8 9 10
	6 00	5 10	4 10	3 20	2 40	2 00	1 30	1 00	0 19	−0 13	−0 42	−1 08	9	8 9 10 11
	5 20	4 30	3 40	2 50	2 10	1 40	1 10	0 35	+0 03	−0 27	−0 53	−1 18	10	9 10 11 12
	4 30	3 40	2 50	2 20	1 40	1 10	0 37	+0 11	−0 16	−0 43	−1 08	−1 31	12	11 12 13 14
	3 30	2 50	2 10	1 40	1 10	0 34	+0 09	−0 14	−0 37	−1 00	−1 23	−1 44	14	13 14 15 17

$$R = R_o \times f$$

Example corrections to Hs (Air Almanac, back inside cover)

GHA and declination

Next you determine the celestial body's position using the GHA and
declination from the Air
Almanac, as before. Recall
that the Greenwich Hour
Angle GHA shows the angle
between the Prime Celestial
Meridian and the hour angle
of the celestial body,
effectively its longitude. The
declination is the celestial
body's altitude (latitude).

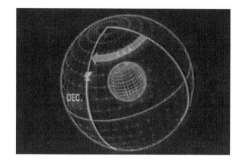

You use the GHA and declination to determine the celestial body's
Geographic Position GP on earth.

Assumed Position (AP)

Now mark your Assumed Position (AP) on a chart, based on where
your dead reckoning believes
you are. We will determine
our actual line of position
relative to our Assumed
Position AP.

To do this, we need to solve a
celestial triangle and bring
that down to earth.

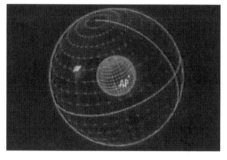

Assumed Position AP

Solving the celestial triangle

The points of the celestial triangle are the celestial body, the celestial pole (either North or South), and the Zenith of your Assumed Position AP.

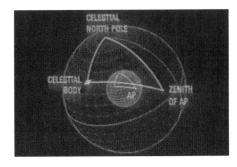

On earth, those points become the Geographic Position GP of the celestial body, the appropriate pole Pn or Ps, and your Assumed Position AP.

The points of the celestial triangle

As we know from trigonometry, if we know the length of two sides of a triangle and the included angle (the angle between those two sides), we can determine the other side and angles.

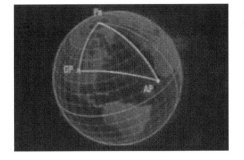

In our example, the sides of the triangle are:

The terrestrial triangle

- [Pn ↔ AP] the line between the North Pole Pn and our Assumed Position AP
- [Pn ↔ GP] is the line from the North Pole Pn to the Geographic Position GP of the celestial body.
- [GP ↔ AP] this is the line from the Geographic Position GP of the celestial body and our Assumed Position AP.

As it turns out, we already know two of those three sides and the included angle.

Co-latitude: Because we know the latitude of our Assumed Position AP, we know [Pn ↔ AP] = 90 – Lat-AP.

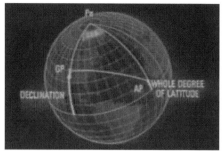

Finding two sides

Co-declination: Because we know the celestial body's declination, we know [Pn ↔ GP] = 90 - Declination.

The included angle is Local Hour Angle (LHA) from your Assumed Position (AP) to the Greenwich Hour Angle (GHA), which we looked up in the Air Almanac.

LHA = GHA – Long AP

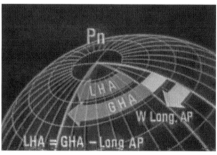

The included angle

Just remember that LHA and GHA are measured to the west, so depending on their relative locations, the math may require addition or subtraction.

Sight reduction tables

Though the math is straight forward, there is a lot of it and each computation is a chance for error. Fortunately, we have Sight Reduction Tables that do the math for us. These tables require three inputs:

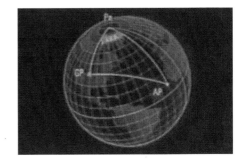

Pn, AP, GP, and LHA

- Local Hour Angle LHA of the celestial body, from the Air Almanac
- Declination of the celestial body, from the Air Almanac
- Lat-AP, the whole degree of the latitude of your Assumed Postion AP, from your dead reckoning

With these three inputs, you can turn to Sight Reduction Tables.

LAT 42°N

LHA ♈	Hc	Zn	Hc	Zn	Hc	Zn	Hc	Zn	Hc	Zn	Hc	Zn	Hc	Zn
	♦CAPELLA		ALDEBARAN		♦Diphda		FOMALHAUT		ALTAIR		♦VEGA		Kochab	
0	35 13	057	26 22	091	29 12	168	17 02	194	26 30	258	30 52	296	29 36	348
1	35 51	057	27 07	092	29 21	169	16 50	195	25 46	258	30 12	297	29 27	348
2	36 28	057	27 52	092	29 29	170	16 39	196	25 02	259	29 32	297	29 18	348
3	37 06	058	28 36	093	29 37	171	16 26	197	24 18	260	28 53	298	29 09	348
4	37 43	058	29 21	094	29 43	172	16 13	198	23 35	260	28 13	298	29 00	349
5	38 21	059	30 05	095	29 49	173	15 59	198	22 51	261	27 34	299	28 51	349
6	39 00	059	30 50	095	29 53	174	15 45	199	22 06	262	26 55	299	28 43	349
7	39 38	059	31 34	096	29 57	176	15 30	200	21 22	263	26 16	300	28 35	350
8	40 16	060	32 18	097	30 00	177	15 14	201	20 38	263	25 38	300	28 27	350
9	40 55	060	33 02	097	30 02	178	14 58	202	19 54	264	24 59	301	28 19	350
10	41 33	060	33 47	098	30 04	179	14 41	203	19 09	265	24 21	301	28 11	350
11	42 12	061	34 31	099	30 04	180	14 23	204	18 25	265	23 43	302	28 04	351
12	42 51	061	35 15	100	30 04	180	14 05	204	17 40	266	23 05	302	27 57	351
13	43 30	061	35 59	100	30 02	182	13 46	205	16 56	267	22 28	303	27 50	351
14	44 09	062	36 42	101	30 00	183	13 27	206	16 11	267	21 50	303	27 43	351

Sight Reduction Table example

To use the Site Reduction Table, select page that contains the latitude of your AP, find LHA Aries, and then move right to the celestial body you have shot. The table gives you the Computed Altitude Hc and the True Azimuth Zn, more on that in a bit.

Computed Altitude (Hc)

The Computed Altitude Hc of the celestial body is the altitude you would observe from your sextant if you were actually at your assumed position.

Once you have Hc, you can find the co-altitude, also known as the Zenith Distance, the third side to your celestial triangle.

Finding Hc with trigonometry

This gives you the linear distance from the Geographic Position GP of the celestial body and your Assumed Position AP.

Circle of Equal Altitude

The [GP ↔ AP] distance is the radius of the Circle of Equal Altitude for this sighting.

That circle includes all locations on earth that have the same angular view of the celestial body. The circle is a very large Line of Position LOP.

Circle of Equal Altitude

True Azimuth (Zn)

Sight Reduction Tables give you True Azimuth Zn. Z is the interior angle of your Assumed Position AP. True Azimuth Zn is the complement to that angle and is found in the Sight Reduction Tables.

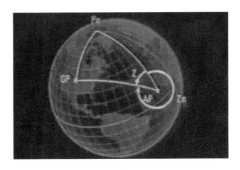

Z and Zn

If you were to plot Zn, it would be the line [AP ↔ GP]

The line along the circle of equal altitude through your Assumed Position is probably not a Line of Position, because your Assumed Position AP is probably not your actual position. The True Azimuth pointed to the Geographic Position GP of the celestial body will intercept with the actual Line of Position, either closer to or farther away than the AP. But which?

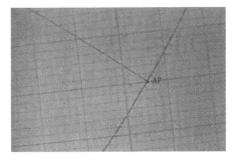

AP plotted

Comparing Corrected Altitude (Ho) and Computed Altitude (Hc)

Recall that we have two forms of altitude for our celestial body. We have the Corrected Altitude Ho derived from our sextant sighting, and we have the Computed Altitude Hc based on the very long math problem coming from the Air Almanac and the Sight Reduction Tables. Ho is tied to your Assumed Position AP. Hc is tied to your actual position.

Let's say Ho = 50°00' and Hc = 49°15', that means our actual position is (50°00' – 49°15') = 45', or 45 nm away from our Assumed Position AP. But which way, closer to or farther from the GP?

To determine if you are closer or farther, recall that the higher the altitude the closer to the celestial body you are. Since in our example our Corrected Altitude Ho is more than our Computed Altitude Hc, we are really closer to the celestial body. Celestial navigators remember "HOMOTO," if Ho is More than Hc, move the LOP toward the GP.

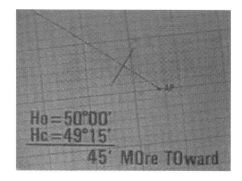

$$Ho = 50°00'$$
$$Hc = 49°15'$$
$$45' \text{ MOre TOward}$$

The Line of Position is perpendicular to the azimuth and in this example, is 45 nm toward the celestial body. We know that we are somewhere on that LOP. We now need to do two more sightings to get a more confident position:

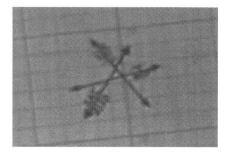

Example Problem (Intercept Method)

In my experience, most navigators prefer to do the computations first – called a precomp – and then do the observation. For sake of explanation, we'll do the observation first.

Observation

We take an observation of the sun at 1630 Z, recording that with the date. We'll say we get an Hs = 32°21'. We'll assume no corrections, so Ho = 32°21'.

Air Almanac

We will need the declination of the observed body, in this case the sun. We'll need the latitude of our assumed position, Lat-AP. And we need the LHA between the sun and our AP.

Open the Air Almanac and turn to the page for the correct date.

Look down the GMT column for the time of the observation. Read the GHA of the sun. In our example, GHA = 64°26.8' which we round to 64°27' and declination is S19°8.1'. The sun is 64°27' west of the prime celestial meridian and

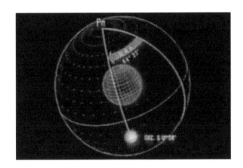

19°89' south of the celestial equator. This is one point of the celestial triangle.

Assumed Position (AP)

You then consider your DR position, in this example, N27°42' W97°12'. Since we are operating in the northern hemisphere, the north pole becomes the second point of the celestial triangle.

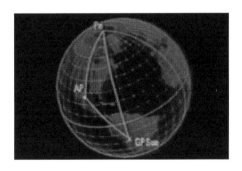

The third point is your Assumed Position AP. The Site Reduction Tables require whole degrees of latitude, so we make AP-Lat N28°. The longitude of our AP, when added or subtracted from GHA, must also result in a whole number, so we'll make it 97°27'. We are west of the sun. We've established our AP: N28° W97°27'.

We know the length of the side [Pn ↔ AP]: 90° - 28° = 62°.

The sun's declination, given in the almanac as S19°08' so we know the length of the triangle from [Pn ↔ GP] = 19°08' + 90° = 109°08'.

Local Hour Angle (LHA)

The Local Hour Angle LHA is measured west of our Assumed Position AP, so we need to add 360° to GHA-Sun before subtracting our longitude. So:

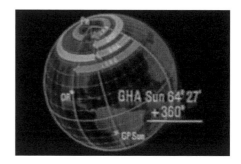

$$64°27' + 360° - 97°27' = 327° \ LHA \ Sun$$

So the inside angle at Pn = 360° - 327° = 33°. In actual practice, we don't need to do any of this math. All we need to know is:

1) The whole degree of latitude of our Assumed Position AP
2) Declination of the observed celestial body
3) The celestial body's LHA

To this we add two items from the site reduction tables:

4) Altitude Corrected Hc
5) Zn

We need to make sure we have the correct Site Reduction Tables. Volume 1 is used for selected stars while Volume 2 and 3 are for other celestial bodies, depending on latitude and declination. In this example, we need Volume 2. In Volume 2, there are two sets of latitudes, one for declinations with "same name as latitude" and another for declinations with "contrary name to latitude." Since our Assumed Position AP Latitude is 28° North and the Sun's declination is 19° South, we select the tables for 28° Latitude, declination contrary name to latitude. We read down to row LHA = 327° and over to the column declination = 19° and read Hc = 33°11', d = 49, and Z = 142°. The d = 49 is used for interpolation using a provided chart. For this example, we'll skip that chart, only to say that d = 49 corrects our Hc by -7', so that Hc = 33°4'.

DECLINATION (**15° – 19°**) <u>**CONTRARY**</u> NAME TO LATITUDE

	15°			16°			17°			18°			19°			
LHA	Hc	d	Z	Hc	d	Z	Hc	d	Z	Hc	d	Z	Hc	d	Z	LHA
	° ′	′	°	° ′	′	°	° ′	′	°	° ′	′	°	° ′	′	°	
39	32 46	−45	134	32 01	−45	134	31 16	−46	135	30 30	−46	136	29 44	−46	137	321
38	33 24	−45	135	32 39	−46	135	31 53	−47	136	31 06	−46	137	30 20	−47	138	322
37	34 02	−46	135	33 16	−47	136	32 29	−47	137	31 42	−47	138	30 55	−47	138	323
36	34 39	−47	136	33 52	−47	137	33 05	−47	138	32 18	−48	139	31 30	−47	139	324
35	35 15	−47	137	34 28	−48	138	33 40	−48	139	32 52	−48	139	32 04	−48	140	325
34	35 50	−47	138	35 03	−48	139	34 15	−48	140	33 27	−49	140	32 38	−49	141	326
33	36 25	−48	139	35 37	−48	140	34 49	−49	141	34 00	−49	141	33 11	−49	142	327

Example Site Reduction Table

Note: I've greatly truncated the chart for readability. In the resulting chart, look to the bottom row and the 19° column.

Since LHA is greater than 180°, Zn = Z. So Zn = 142°.

Recall that Ho = 32°21' and Hc = 33°4'. Since Ho is less than Hc, we are farther away from the celestial body than our Assumed Position AP. Since Hc − Ho = 33°4' − 32°21' = 43' which is 43 nm.

Plotting

We know that our actual position is 43 nm farther away from the circle of equal altitudes around the sun's GP.

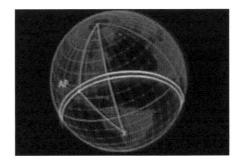

We also know that the true intercept distance is measured on a true azimuth line of 142°.

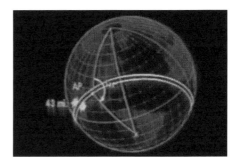

To plot, start by placing a dot at your AP.

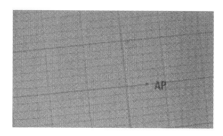

Lay your plotter over that point at an angle of 142°.

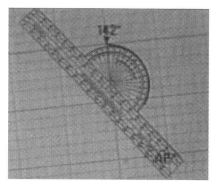

Use your dividers to find the point 43nm away from the AP.

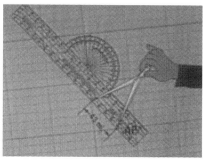

Draw a line at right angles to this line. This is your LOP.

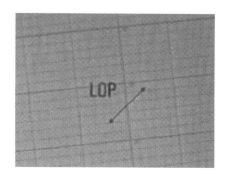

Do this two more times and you will have a triangle and can assume your position is inside the triangle. Of course, the longer it takes you to do this, as the aircraft moves, the larger that triangle will be. For this reason, it may be advantageous to precompute for three celestial objects and shoot them quickly.

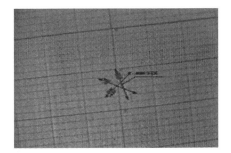

Conclusions

This only scratches the surface of celestial navigation. Let's say you are shooting in the middle of the day and the only celestial object in view is the sun. There are techniques for that! I offer this overview just to illustrate how oceanic navigation used to be and to perhaps improve your dead reckoning skills without a sextant.

References

Air Almanac: 1972, September – December, Washington, United States Naval Observatory, 1972

Celestial Navigation: Instruction Video, U.S. Army Air Force Training Film, undated

Celestial Navigation: Position Finding on the Earth, War Department Training Film 1-204, Produced by the Signal Corps in Collaboration with the Chief of Air Corps, undated

Sight Reduction Tables for Air Navigation, Pub No. 229, Vol. 1, National Geospatial-Intelligence Agency, 2010

Appendix: CR-3 / CPU-26 Techniques

Here is a primer on how to use either the military CPU-26 or the civilian Jeppesen CR-3. The procedures are similar on the front side, a bit different on the wind side.

Time / Speed / Distance

Given two of time, speed, and distance, you can find the third. If, for example, you have speed 450 knots and distance 300 nm, you can find time. (CR-3 shown, procedure on CPU-26 is identical.)

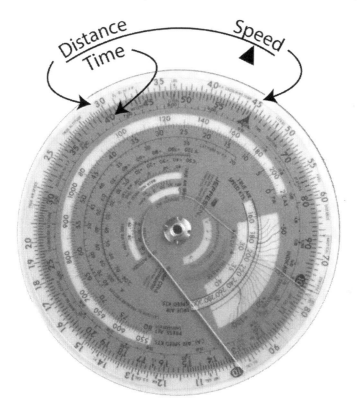

Rotate the inner dial to place the triangle (which is also the value 60) under the 45 (1/10th the speed). Look around the outer scale for the 30, which is 1/10th of 300 nm. Look to the inner scale and find the answer of 40 minutes.

Note: You may be wondering about using 1/10th for the outer scale and not the inner. This is an algebraic property where you can divide both sides of the equation by the same number and not change the answer. But you can also rationalize it in pilot terms: It takes the same time to fly 300 nm at 450 knots as it does to fly 30 nm and 45 knots.

Fuel / Time / PPH

Given two of fuel, time, and Pounds Per Hour (PPH), you can find the third. If, for example, you have 450 PPH and 30 minutes, you can find the fuel. (CPU-26 shown, procedure on CR-3 is identical.)

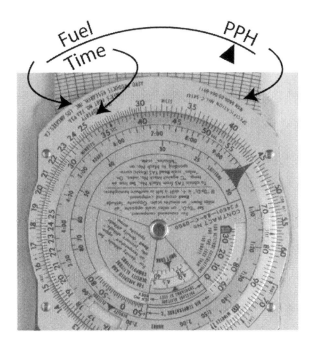

Rotate the inner dial to place the triangle (which is also the value 60) under the 45 (1/10th the PPH). Look around the inner scale for the 30 (minutes). Look opposite to the outer scale and find the answer of 22.5 which is 1/10th the fuel of 225 lbs.

Note: Once again we use 1/10th the values on the outer scale.

Conversions

One or both scales of the CR-3 and CPU-26 will have various conversions for values that are simply arithmetic formulas. You can, for example, convert nautical miles / statute miles / kilometers by locating the appropriate arrows on the outer scale, rotating the inner scale to find one value and reading the corresponding value. You will find nautical miles at 66, statute miles at 76, and kilometers at just over 12.2

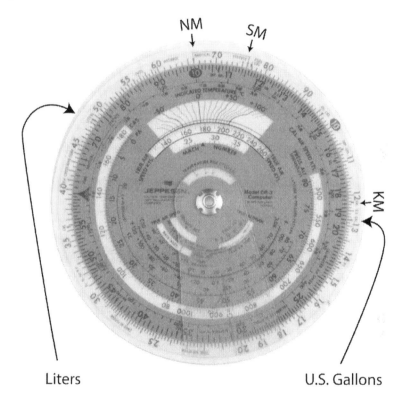

Liters   U.S. Gallons

In the photo, we see 100 nm equals 115 sm and 186 km. There are other conversions, such as liters to U.S. gallons. Some of the conversions that would appear straightforward are not. We'll cover some of those next.

Airspeed

Speed conversions require some basic definitions. To convert (I)ndicated airspeed to (T)rue airspeed, you must first find (C)alibrated airspeed and (E)quivalent airspeed. You can think of their relationship in the so-called "ICE-T" diagram.

Indicated Airspeed (IAS)

Indicated airspeed is what is reported by the pitot tube and is simply the difference in pressure from what is pointed down the tube versus the static pressure on the side, that isn't subject to the forward motion of the aircraft. On many aircraft, this is what the pilot sees on the airspeed indicator.

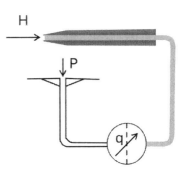

Calibrated Airspeed (CAS)

Calibrated airspeed is IAS corrected for position error (effects of the pitot tube's position on the aircraft), also known as installation error. On most aircraft, the impact is just a few knots. The correction is given in the Airplane Flight Manual. On many aircraft the correction is made by the avionics and CAS is what the pilot sees on the indicator.

Equivalent Airspeed (EAS)

Equivalent airspeed is CAS corrected for air compressibility (the air gets compacted inside the pitot tube). It can be corrected by a flight manual chart or a circular computer. The CPU-26 calls this "F-Factor."

PRESS ALT FEET	F CORRECTION FACTORS FOR TAS							
	CALIBRATED AIRSPEED KNOTS							
	200	250	300	350	400	450	500	550
10.000	1.0	1.0	.99	.99	.98	.98	.97	.97
20.000	.99	.98	.97	.97	.96	.95	.94	.93
30.000	.97	.96	.95	.94	.92	.91	.90	.89
40.000	.96	.94	.92	.90	.88	.87	.87	.86
50.000	.93	.90	.87	.86	.84	.84	.84	.84

DIRECTIONS

USE CALIBRATED AIRSPEED AND PRESS. ALT. TO OBTAIN F FACTOR. MULTIPLY F FACTOR BY TAS OBTAINED WITH COMPUTER TO OBTAIN TAS CORRECTED FOR COMPRESSIBILITY.

For example, 250 CAS at 20,000 feet yields 0.98. Place the 10 index (inner scale) opposite 250 (outer scale) and read the EAS opposite the F-Factor of 0.98 to find the answer: 245 EAS. Note the CR-3 adds this factor automatically, to be shown in a following section.

True Airspeed (TAS)

True airspeed is EAS corrected for density altitude. It can be found mathematically:

$$TAS = EAS \frac{1}{\sqrt{\sigma}}$$

The density ratio (σ) is found in a standard altitude table, extract shown below. For example, at 20,000 feet the density ratio is 0.5328 and an EAS of 245 is converted to TAS:

$$TAS = 245 \frac{1}{\sqrt{0.5328}} = 336$$

The CPU-26 converts EAS to TAS by first placing the pressure altitude opposite the air temperature.

In our example, we'll assume standard temperature which is 15° minus 2° per 1,000' altitude, so (15° - 2(20) = -25°C.

To convert 245 EAS to CAS on the CPU-26, locate the "For airspeed and density altitude computations" window and place the altitude (20) in the window opposite the

ALTITUDE FT.	DENSITY RATIO σ	$\sqrt{\sigma}$	PRESSURE RATIO δ
0	1.0000	1.0000	1.0000
1000	0.9711	0.9854	0.9644
2000	0.9428	0.9710	0.9298
3000	0.9151	0.9566	0.8962
4000	0.8881	0.9424	0.8637
5000	0.8617	0.9283	0.8320
6000	0.8359	0.9143	0.8014
7000	0.8106	0.9004	0.7716
8000	0.7860	0.8866	0.7428
9000	0.7620	0.8729	0.7148
10000	0.7385	0.8593	0.6877
15000	0.6292	0.7932	0.5643
20000	0.5328	0.7299	0.4595
25000	0.4481	0.6694	0.3711

temperature (-25) on the outer scale. Then find the EAS (245) on the inner ring of the circular computer and read the TAS on the outer ring (335).

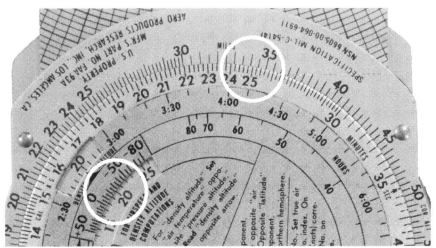

CAS to TAS and Mach Number (CR-3)

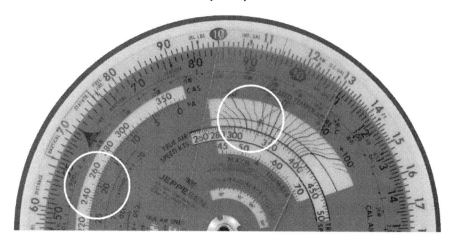

The CR-3 converts CAS to TAS without the need to consider compressibility effects.

First, place the CAS (in the CAS window) over the altitude on the scale marked "PA."

Second, look to the window with the wavy vertical lines and the inner line the spirals outward in the clockwise direction. Place the vertical line marked "C_T .8" to the outer scale showing "Indicated Temperature" at the -25° point. Follow the vertical lines downward to the spiral and place the cursor at this intersection.

Note: The C_T refers to the "temperature recovery coefficient," which for most aircraft is 1.0. The 1.0 and 0.8 lines are the same for most altitudes and we can use the 0.8 line unless the 1.0 line diverges below the spiral.

Third, read the TAS from the True Airspeed window, in this case about 330 knots. (About a 5 knot difference from the CPU-26.)

Drift, Heading, Ground speed (CPU-26)

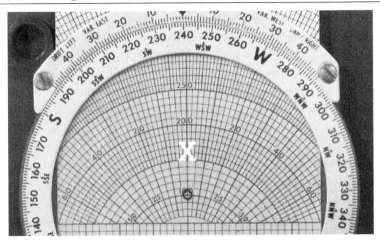

In our example, we'll use 335 TAS, 300° true course, and winds of 240° / 60 knots. Spin the wheel to place the wind direction (240°) under the True Index. Place the slide so a convenient reading is under the grommet, we've used 100 in the example. Place an "X" spaced by the winds speed (60), 160 in our example.

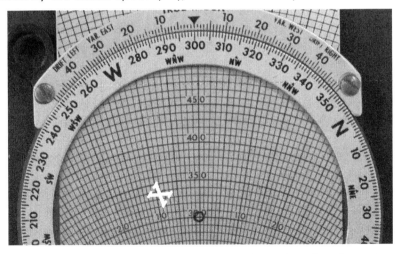

Rotate the wheel to place the true course (300°) under the index and move the slide so your TAS (335 knots) is under your drawn X. You can read the drift angle from the slide and find your ground speed under the grommet (300 knots).

Drift, Heading, Ground Speed (CR-3)

The wind side of the CR-3 easily computes drift, heading, and ground speed given aircraft course and TAS and the wind speed and direction. In our example, we'll use 335 TAS, 300° true course, and winds of 240° / 60 knots.

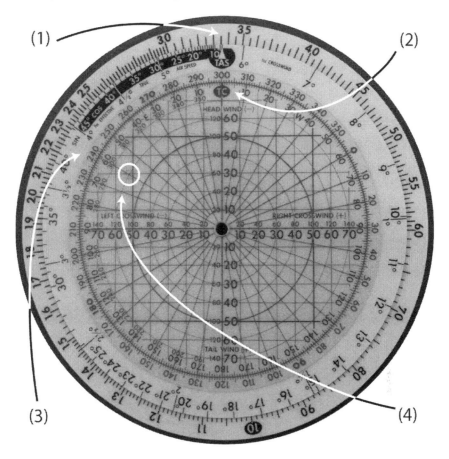

(1) Set TAS (335) above TAS index.
(2) Set True Course (300) above TC index.
(3) Find wind direction (240).
(4) Draw a circle over wind direction/speed (240/60)

(5) Draw vertical and horizontal lines from wind dot to determine headwind (30 knots) and crosswind (52 knots). Ground speed is 335 – 30 = 305 knots.

(6) Enter outer scale with crosswind (52 knots) to read the drift angle on inner scale (9°). Heading is 300 – 9 = 291°.

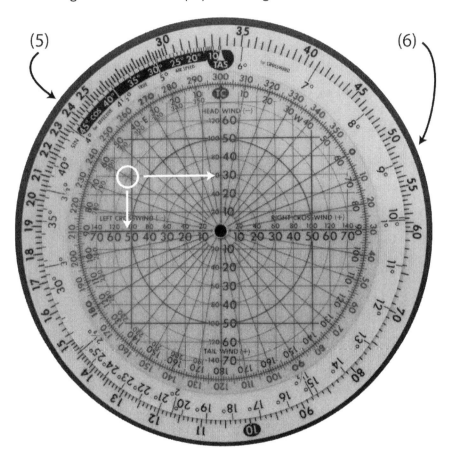

Appendix: True Course 10 Degree Tables

Back in the old days if you were presented with a reroute when oceanic, you pulled out the charts and plotter and got to work building a new flight plan. If you were good, you could churn out three thousand miles of master document in about fifteen minutes. If you were really good, you had a book of ten-degree tables and could cut that time in half.

These days I would just call in the change to my flight planning service and have them fax, e-mail, or just read them to me over the phone. What if you don't have that kind of connectivity or if you just want to be old school for a day?

Purpose

If required to fly an unplanned oceanic flight plan — you got a reroute just prior to coast out — you need to build a new master document with courses and distances between waypoints so you can still make all the necessary checks before each point and also so you can make your post position plot. The 10-degree tables below provide your true courses and distances between any two positions expressed as latitudes (to the nearest degree) and the next position expressed as a longitude 10 degrees east or west.

For example, say you are 50°N 030°W heading to Europe and your next position will be at 51°N 020°W. You could pull out a plotter and come up with a course, add the variation, and end up with the correct true course. Then you could measure the distance, compare that to the nearest line of longitude and come up with a distance. You would probably do this a few times to make sure you didn't make a mistake, either with the plotter or your ad hoc measuring device. Or you could go to the From 50° Latitude table, check the course provided on the 51° row and Northern Hemisphere / East column and see your true course will be 081° and reading across see that the distance between these two points is 386 nautical miles.

The Tables

From 0° Latitude

To Latitude	Northern Hemisphere		Southern Hemisphere		Distance (nm)
	East	West	East	West	
10°	045°	315°	135°	225°	846
09	048	312	132	228	805
08	051	309	129	231	767
07	055	305	125	235	731
06	059	301	121	239	699
05	063	297	117	243	670
04	068	292	112	248	646
03	073	287	107	253	626
02	078	282	102	258	612
01	084	276	096	264	603
00	090	270	090	270	600

From 1° Latitude

To Latitude	Northern Hemisphere		Southern Hemisphere		Distance (nm)
	East	West	East	West	
11°	044°	316°	136°	224°	846
10	048	312	132	228	805
09	051	309	129	231	766
08	055	305	125	235	731
07	059	301	121	239	698
06	063	297	117	243	670
05	068	292	112	248	645
04	073	287	107	253	626
03	079	281	101	259	611
02	084	276	096	264	603
01	090	270	090	270	600
00	096	264	084	276	603
01	101	259	079	281	612
02	106	254	074	286	626
03	112	248	068	292	646
04	117	243	063	297	670
05	121	239	059	301	699
06	125	235	055	305	732
07	129	231	051	309	767
08	132	228	048	312	806
09	135	225	045	315	847

From 2° Latitude

To Latitude	Northern Hemisphere		Southern Hemisphere		Distance (nm)
	East	West	East	West	
12°	044°	316°	136°	224°	845
11	047	313	133	227	804
10	051	309	129	231	765
09	055	305	125	235	730
08	059	301	121	239	697
07	063	297	117	243	669
06	068	292	112	248	645
05	073	287	107	253	625
04	078	282	102	258	611
03	084	276	096	264	602
02	090	270	090	270	600
01	096	264	084	276	603
00	101	259	079	281	612
01	107	253	073	287	626
02	112	248	068	292	646
03	117	243	063	297	671
04	121	239	059	301	699
05	125	235	055	305	732
06	129	231	051	309	768
07	132	228	048	312	806
08	135	225	045	315	847

From 3° Latitude

To Latitude	Northern Hemisphere		Southern Hemisphere		Distance (nm)
	East	West	East	West	
13°	044°	316°	136°	224°	844
12	047	313	133	227	803
11	051	309	129	231	764
10	054	306	126	234	729
09	058	302	122	238	697
08	063	297	117	243	668
07	068	292	112	248	644
06	073	287	107	253	625
05	078	282	102	258	610
04	084	276	096	264	602
03	090	270	090	270	599
02	096	264	084	276	602
01	101	259	079	281	611
00	107	253	073	287	626
01	112	248	068	292	646
02	117	243	063	297	671
03	121	239	059	301	699
04	125	235	055	305	732
05	129	231	051	309	768
06	132	228	048	312	807
07	135	225	045	315	848

From 4° Latitude

To Latitude	Northern Hemisphere		Southern Hemisphere		Distance (nm)
	East	West	East	West	
14°	044°	316°	136°	224°	843
13	047	313	133	227	802
12	051	309	129	231	763
11	054	306	126	234	728
10	058	302	122	238	696
09	063	297	117	243	667
08	068	292	112	248	643
07	073	287	107	253	624
06	078	282	102	258	610
05	084	276	096	264	601
04	090	270	090	270	598
03	095	265	085	275	602
02	101	259	079	281	611
01	107	253	073	287	626
00	112	248	068	292	646
01	116	244	064	296	670
02	121	239	059	301	699
03	125	235	055	305	732
04	129	231	051	309	768
05	132	228	048	312	807
06	135	225	045	315	848

From 5° Latitude

To Latitude	Northern Hemisphere		Southern Hemisphere		Distance (nm)
	East	West	East	West	
15°	044°	316°	36°	224°	841
14	047	313	133	227	801
13	050	310	130	230	762
12	054	306	126	234	727
11	058	302	122	238	694
10	063	297	117	243	666
09	068	292	112	248	642
08	073	287	107	253	623
07	078	282	102	258	609
06	084	276	096	264	600
05	090	270	090	270	598
04	095	265	085	275	601
03	101	259	079	281	610
02	106	254	074	286	625
01	112	248	068	292	645
00	116	244	064	296	670
01	121	239	059	301	699
02	125	235	055	305	732
03	129	231	051	309	768
04	132	228	048	312	807
05	135	225	045	315	848

From 6° Latitude

To Latitude	Northern Hemisphere		Southern Hemisphere		Distance (nm)
	East	West	East	West	
16°	044°	316°	136°	224°	840
15	047	313	133	227	799
14	050	310	130	230	761
13	054	306	126	234	725
12	058	302	122	238	693
11	063	297	117	243	665
10	067	293	113	247	641
09	073	287	107	253	621
08	078	282	102	258	607
07	084	276	096	264	599
06	090	270	090	270	597
05	095	265	085	275	600
04	101	259	079	281	610
03	106	254	074	286	625
02	111	249	069	291	645
01	116	244	064	296	670
00	121	239	059	301	699
01	125	235	055	305	732
02	128	232	052	308	768
03	132	228	048	312	807
04	135	225	045	315	848

From 7° Latitude

To Latitude	Northern Hemisphere		Southern Hemisphere		Distance (nm)
	East	West	East	West	
17°	043°	317°	137°	223°	839
16	047	313	133	227	797
15	050	310	130	230	759
14	054	306	126	234	724
13	058	302	122	238	692
12	062	298	118	242	663
11	067	293	113	247	639
10	072	288	108	252	620
09	078	282	102	258	606
08	084	276	096	264	598
07	090	270	090	270	595
06	095	265	085	275	599
05	101	259	079	281	609
04	106	254	074	286	624
03	111	249	069	291	644
02	116	244	064	296	669
01	121	239	059	301	698
00	125	235	055	305	731
01	128	232	052	308	767
02	132	328	048	312	806
03	135	225	045	315	848

From 8° Latitude

To Latitude	Northern Hemisphere		Southern Hemisphere		Distance (nm)
	East	West	East	West	
18	044	316	136	224	837
17	047	313	133	227	797
16	051	309	129	231	758
15	055	305	125	235	722
14	059	301	121	239	690
13	063	297	117	243	665
12	068	292	112	248	639
11	073	287	107	253	620
10	078	282	102	258	607
09	084	276	096	264	598
08	090	270	090	270	597
07	096	264	084	276	600
06	101	259	079	281	612
05	106	254	074	286	624
04	111	249	069	291	645
03	116	244	064	296	669
02	121	239	059	301	698
01	125	235	055	305	732
00	129	231	051	309	767
01	132	228	048	312	807
02	135	225	045	315	848

From 9° Latitude

To Latitude	Northern Hemisphere		Southern Hemisphere		Distance (nm)
	East	West	East	West	
19	044	316	136	224	832
18	047	313	133	227	794
17	051	309	129	231	756
16	054	306	126	234	721
15	059	301	121	239	689
14	063	297	117	243	662
13	068	292	112	248	638
12	073	287	107	253	620
11	078	282	102	258	605
10	084	276	096	264	598
09	090	270	090	270	596
08	096	264	084	276	598
07	101	259	079	281	600
06	106	254	074	286	623
05	112	248	068	292	643
04	116	244	064	296	668
03	121	239	059	301	697
02	125	235	055	305	730
01	129	231	051	309	766
00	132	228	048	312	805
01	135	225	045	315	847

From 10° Latitude

To Latitude	Northern Hemisphere		Southern Hemisphere		Distance (nm)
	East	West	East	West	
20	044	316	136	224	834
19	047	313	133	227	793
18	051	309	129	221	754
17	054	306	126	234	719
16	058	302	122	238	686
15	063	297	117	243	658
14	068	292	112	248	634
13	073	287	107	253	615
12	078	282	102	258	601
11	084	276	096	264	593
10	090	270	090	270	590
9	096	264	084	276	595
8	101	259	079	281	605
7	107	253	073	287	620
6	112	248	068	292	641
5	117	243	063	297	666
4	121	239	059	301	696
3	125	235	055	305	729
2	129	231	051	309	765
1	132	228	048	312	805
0	135	225	045	315	846

From 11° Latitude

To Latitude	Northern Hemisphere		Southern Hemisphere		Distance (nm)
	East	West	East	West	
21	044	316	136	224	832
20	047	313	133	227	791
19	050	310	130	230	752
18	054	306	126	234	716
17	058	302	122	238	684
16	063	297	117	243	656
15	068	292	112	248	632
14	073	287	107	253	613
13	078	282	102	258	599
12	084	276	096	264	591
11	090	270	090	270	589
10	096	264	084	276	593
09	101	259	079	281	603
08	107	253	073	287	619
07	112	248	068	292	639
06	117	243	063	297	665
05	121	239	059	301	695
04	125	235	055	305	728
03	129	231	051	309	765
02	132	228	048	312	804
01	135	225	045	315	846

From 12° Latitude

To Latitude	Northern Hemisphere		Southern Hemisphere		Distance (nm)
	East	West	East	West	
22	044	316	136	224	830
21	047	313	133	227	788
20	050	310	130	230	750
19	054	306	126	234	714
18	058	302	122	238	682
17	063	297	117	243	654
16	068	292	112	248	630
15	073	287	107	253	610
14	078	282	102	258	597
13	084	276	096	264	589
12	090	270	090	270	587
11	096	264	084	276	591
10	102	258	078	282	601
09	107	253	073	287	617
08	112	248	068	292	638
07	117	243	063	297	663
06	121	239	059	301	693
05	125	235	055	305	727
04	129	231	051	309	763
03	132	228	048	312	803
02	135	225	045	315	845

From 13° Latitude

To Latitude	Northern Hemisphere		Southern Hemisphere		Distance (nm)
	East	West	East	West	
23	044	316	136	224	827
22	047	313	133	227	786
21	050	310	130	230	748
20	054	306	126	234	712
19	058	302	122	238	680
18	063	297	117	243	651
17	068	292	112	248	627
16	073	287	107	253	608
15	078	282	102	258	594
14	084	276	096	264	587
13	090	270	090	270	585
12	096	264	084	276	589
11	101	259	079	281	599
10	107	253	073	287	615
09	112	248	068	292	636
08	117	243	063	297	662
07	121	239	059	301	692
06	125	235	055	305	725
05	129	231	051	309	762
04	132	228	048	312	802
03	135	225	045	315	844

From 14° Latitude

To Latitude	Northern Hemisphere		Southern Hemisphere		Distance (nm)
	East	West	East	West	
24	044	316	136	224	825
23	047	313	133	227	784
22	050	310	130	230	745
21	054	306	126	234	709
20	058	302	122	238	677
19	063	297	117	243	649
18	068	292	112	248	625
17	073	287	107	253	605
16	078	282	102	258	592
15	084	276	096	264	584
14	090	270	090	270	582
13	096	264	084	276	587
12	102	258	078	282	597
11	107	253	073	287	613
10	112	248	068	292	634
09	117	243	063	297	660
08	121	239	059	301	690
07	125	235	055	305	724
06	129	231	051	309	761
05	132	228	049	312	801
04	135	225	045	315	843

From 15° Latitude

To Latitude	Northern Hemisphere		Southern Hemisphere		Distance (nm)
	East	West	East	West	
25	043	317	137	223	823
24	046	314	134	226	781
23	050	310	130	230	743
22	054	306	126	234	707
21	058	302	122	238	674
20	062	298	118	242	646
19	067	293	113	247	622
18	073	287	107	253	603
17	078	282	102	258	589
16	084	276	096	264	581
15	090	270	090	270	580
14	096	264	084	276	584
13	102	258	078	282	594
12	107	253	073	287	610
11	112	248	068	292	632
10	117	243	063	297	658
09	121	239	059	301	688
08	125	235	055	305	722
07	129	231	051	309	759
06	132	228	048	312	799
05	135	225	045	315	842

From 16° Latitude

To Latitude	Northern Hemisphere		Southern Hemisphere		Distance (nm)
	East	West	East	West	
26	043	317	137	223	820
25	046	314	134	226	779
24	050	310	130	230	740
23	054	306	126	234	704
22	058	302	122	238	672
21	062	298	118	242	643
20	067	293	113	247	619
19	073	287	107	253	600
18	078	282	102	258	586
17	084	276	096	264	578
16	090	270	090	270	577
15	096	264	084	276	581
14	102	258	078	282	592
13	107	253	073	287	608
12	112	248	068	292	630
11	117	243	063	297	656
10	122	238	058	302	686
9	126	234	054	306	720
8	129	231	051	309	758
7	133	227	047	313	798
6	135	224	044	316	840

From 17° Latitude

To Latitude	Northern Hemisphere		Southern Hemisphere		Distance (nm)
	East	West	East	West	
27	043	317	137	223	817
26	046	314	134	226	776
25	050	310	130	230	737
24	053	307	127	233	701
23	058	302	122	238	669
22	062	298	118	242	640
21	067	293	113	247	616
20	073	287	107	253	596
19	078	282	102	258	583
18	084	276	096	264	575
17	090	270	090	270	574
16	096	264	084	276	578
15	102	258	078	282	589
14	107	253	073	287	606
13	112	248	068	292	627
12	117	243	063	297	653
11	122	238	058	302	684
10	126	234	054	306	718
09	129	231	051	309	756
08	133	227	047	313	796
07	136	224	044	316	838

From 18° Latitude

To Latitude	Northern Hemisphere		Southern Hemisphere		Distance (nm)
	East	West	East	West	
28	043	317	137	223	815
27	046	314	134	226	773
26	049	311	131	229	734
25	053	307	127	233	698
24	057	303	123	237	666
23	062	298	118	242	637
22	067	293	113	247	613
21	072	288	108	252	593
20	078	282	102	258	580
19	084	276	096	264	572
18	090	270	090	270	571
17	096	264	084	276	575
16	102	258	078	282	586
15	107	253	073	287	603
14	113	247	067	293	625
13	117	243	063	297	651
12	122	238	058	302	682
11	126	234	054	306	716
10	129	231	051	309	754
09	133	227	047	313	794
08	136	224	044	316	837

From 19° Latitude

To Latitude	Northern Hemisphere		Southern Hemisphere		Distance (nm)
	East	West	East	West	
29	043	317	137	223	812
28	046	314	134	226	770
27	049	311	131	229	731
26	053	307	127	233	695
25	057	303	123	237	662
24	062	298	118	242	633
23	067	293	113	247	609
22	072	288	108	252	590
21	078	282	102	258	576
20	084	276	096	264	569
19	090	270	090	270	567
18	096	264	084	276	572
17	102	258	078	282	583
16	107	253	073	287	600
15	113	247	067	293	622
14	118	242	002	298	649
13	122	238	058	302	680
12	126	234	054	306	714
11	130	230	050	310	752
10	133	227	047	313	793
09	136	224	044	316	835

From 20° Latitude

To Latitude	Northern Hemisphere		Southern Hemisphere		Distance (nm)
	East	West	East	West	
30	042	318	138	222	809
29	045	315	135	225	767
28	049	311	131	229	728
27	053	307	127	233	692
26	057	303	123	237	659
25	062	298	118	242	630
24	067	293	113	247	606
23	072	288	108	252	586
22	078	282	102	258	573
21	084	276	096	264	565
20	090	270	090	270	564
19	096	264	084	276	569
18	102	258	078	282	580
17	108	252	072	288	597
16	113	247	067	293	619
15	118	242	062	298	646
14	122	238	058	302	677
13	126	234	054	306	712
12	130	230	050	310	750
11	133	227	047	313	791
10	136	224	044	316	834

From 21° Latitude

To Latitude	Northern Hemisphere		Southern Hemisphere		Distance (nm)
	East	West	East	West	
31	042	318	138	222	806
30	045	315	135	225	764
29	049	311	131	229	725
28	053	307	127	233	688
27	057	303	123	237	655
26	062	298	118	242	626
25	067	293	113	247	602
24	072	288	108	252	583
23	078	282	102	258	569
22	084	276	096	264	561
21	090	270	090	270	560
20	096	264	084	276	565
19	102	258	078	282	576
18	108	252	072	288	593
17	113	247	067	293	616
16	118	242	062	298	643
15	122	238	058	302	674
14	126	234	054	306	709
13	130	230	050	310	748
12	133	227	047	313	788
11	136	224	044	316	832

From 22° Latitude

To Latitude	Northern Hemisphere		Southern Hemisphere		Distance (nm)
	East	West	East	West	
32	042	318	138	222	803
31	045	315	135	225	761
30	048	312	132	228	721
29	052	308	128	232	685
28	057	303	123	237	652
27	061	299	119	241	623
26	066	294	114	246	598
25	072	288	108	252	579
24	078	282	102	258	565
23	084	276	096	264	558
22	090	270	090	270	556
21	096	264	084	276	561
20	102	258	078	282	573
19	108	252	072	288	590
18	113	247	067	293	613
17	118	242	062	298	640
16	122	238	058	302	672
15	126	234	054	306	707
14	130	230	050	310	745
13	133	227	047	313	786
12	136	224	044	316	830

From 23° Latitude

To Latitude	Northern Hemisphere		Southern Hemisphere		Distance (nm)
	East	West	East	West	
33	042	318	138	222	800
32	045	315	135	225	757
31	048	312	132	228	718
30	052	308	128	232	681
29	056	304	124	236	648
28	061	299	119	241	619
27	066	294	114	246	594
26	072	288	108	252	575
25	078	282	102	258	561
24	084	276	096	264	553
23	090	270	090	270	552
22	096	264	084	276	558
21	102	258	078	282	569
20	108	252	072	288	586
19	113	247	067	293	609
18	118	242	062	298	637
17	123	237	057	303	669
16	127	233	053	307	704
15	130	230	050	310	743
14	133	227	047	313	784
13	136	224	044	316	827

From 24° Latitude

To Latitude	Northern Hemisphere		Southern Hemisphere		Distance (nm)
	East	West	East	West	
34	041	319	13	221	796
33	044	316	136	224	754
32	048	312	132	228	714
31	052	308	128	232	677
30	056	304	124	236	644
29	061	299	119	241	615
28	066	294	114	246	590
27	072	288	108	252	570
26	078	282	102	258	557
25	084	276	096	264	549
24	090	270	090	270	548
23	096	264	084	276	553
22	102	258	078	282	565
21	108	252	072	288	583
20	113	247	067	293	606
19	118	242	062	298	633
18	123	237	057	303	665
17	127	233	053	307	701
16	130	230	050	310	740
15	134	226	046	314	781
14	137	223	043	317	825

From 25° Latitude

To Latitude	Northern Hemisphere		Southern Hemisphere		Distance (nm)
	East	West	East	West	
35	041	319	139	221	793
34	044	316	136	224	750
33	048	312	132	228	710
32	052	308	128	232	673
31	056	304	124	236	640
30	061	299	119	241	610
29	066	294	114	246	586
28	072	288	108	252	566
27	078	282	102	258	552
26	084	276	096	264	545
25	090	270	090	270	544
24	096	264	084	276	549
23	102	258	078	282	561
22	108	252	072	288	579
21	113	247	067	293	602
20	118	242	062	298	630
19	123	237	057	303	662
18	127	233	053	307	698
17	131	229	049	311	737
16	134	226	046	314	779
15	137	223	043	317	823

From 26° Latitude

To Latitude	Northern Hemisphere		Southern Hemisphere		Distance (nm)
	East	West	East	West	
36	041	319	139	221	789
35	044	316	136	224	747
34	047	313	133	227	707
33	051	309	129	231	670
32	056	304	124	236	636
31	060	300	120	240	606
30	066	294	114	246	581
29	071	289	109	251	562
28	077	283	103	257	547
27	084	276	096	264	540
26	090	220	090	270	539
25	096	264	084	276	545
24	102	258	078	282	557
23	108	252	072	288	575
22	114	246	066	294	598
21	119	241	061	299	626
20	123	237	057	303	659
19	127	233	053	307	695
18	131	229	049	311	734
17	134	226	046	314	776
16	137	223	043	317	820

From 27° Latitude

To Latitude	Northern Hemisphere		Southern Hemisphere		Distance (nm)
	East	West	East	West	
37	040	320	140	220	786
36	044	316	136	224	743
35	047	313	133	227	703
34	051	309	129	231	665
33	055	305	125	235	632
32	060	300	120	240	602
31	066	294	114	246	577
30	071	289	109	251	557
29	077	283	103	255	543
28	084	276	096	264	535
27	090	270	090	270	534
26	096	264	084	276	540
25	102	258	078	282	552
24	108	252	072	288	571
23	114	246	066	294	594
22	119	241	063	299	623
21	123	237	057	303	655
20	127	233	053	307	692
19	131	229	049	311	731
18	134	226	046	314	773
17	137	223	043	317	817

From 28° Latitude

To Latitude	Northern Hemisphere		Southern Hemisphere		Distance (nm)
	East	West	East	West	
38	040	320	140	220	782
37	043	317	137	223	739
36	047	313	133	227	699
35	051	309	129	231	661
34	055	305	125	235	627
33	060	300	120	240	597
32	065	255	115	245	572
31	071	289	109	251	552
30	077	283	103	257	538
29	084	276	096	263	531
28	090	270	090	270	530
27	096	264	084	276	535
26	103	257	077	283	548
25	109	251	071	289	566
24	114	246	066	294	590
23	119	241	061	299	619
22	123	237	057	303	652
21	128	232	052	308	688
20	131	229	049	311	728
19	134	226	046	314	770
18	137	223	043	317	815

From 29° Latitude

To Latitude	Northern Hemisphere		Southern Hemisphere		Distance (nm)
	East	West	East	West	
39	040	320	140	210	778
38	043	317	137	223	735
37	046	314	134	226	695
36	050	310	130	230	657
35	055	305	125	233	623
34	060	300	120	240	593
33	065	295	115	245	567
32	071	289	109	251	547
31	077	283	103	257	333
30	083	274	109	263	526
29	090	270	090	270	325
28	097	263	083	277	530
27	103	257	077	283	543
26	109	251	071	289	562
25	114	246	066	294	586
24	119	241	061	299	615
23	124	236	056	304	648
22	128	232	052	308	685
21	131	229	049	311	725
20	135	225	045	315	767
19	138	222	042	318	812

From 30° Latitude

To Latitude	Northern Hemisphere		Southern Hemisphere		Distance (nm)
	East	West	East	West	
40	039	321	141	219	775
39	043	317	137	223	731
38	046	314	134	226	690
37	050	310	130	230	653
36	055	305	125	235	618
35	059	301	121	239	588
34	065	295	115	245	562
33	071	289	109	251	542
32	077	283	103	257	528
31	083	2770	097	263	520
30	090	270	090	270	519
29	096	264	084	276	525
28	103	237	077	283	538
27	109	251	071	289	55
26	114	246	066	294	581
25	119	241	061	299	611
24	124	236	056	304	644
23	128	232	052	308	681
22	132	228	048	312	721
21	135	225	045	315	764
20	138	222	042	318	809

From 31° Latitude

To Latitude	Northern Hemisphere		Southern Hemisphere		Distance (nm)
	East	West	East	West	
41	039	321	141	219	771
40	042	318	138	222	727
39	046	314	134	226	686
38	050	310	130	230	648
37	054	306	126	234	613
36	059	301	127	239	583
35	065	295	115	245	557
34	071	289	109	231	537
33	077	283	103	257	523
32	083	277	097	263	515
31	090	270	095	270	514
30	097	263	083	277	520
29	103	257	077	283	533
28	109	251	071	289	552
27	115	245	065	295	577
26	120	240	060	300	606
25	124	236	056	304	640
24	128	232	052	308	677
23	132	228	048	312	718
22	135	225	045	315	761
21	138	222	042	318	806

From 32° Latitude

To Latitude	Northern Hemisphere		Southern Hemisphere		Distance (nm)
	East	West	East	West	
42	039	321	141	219	767
41	042	318	138	222	723
40	045	315	135	225	682
39	049	311	131	229	644
38	054	306	126	234	609
37	059	301	121	239	578
36	064	296	116	244	552
35	070	290	110	250	531
34	077	283	103	257	517
33	083	277	097	263	509
32	090	270	090	270	508
31	097	263	083	277	515
30	103	257	077	283	528
29	109	251	071	289	547
28	115	245	065	295	572
27	120	240	060	300	602
26	124	236	056	304	636
25	128	232	052	308	674
24	132	228	048	312	714
23	135	225	045	315	757
22	138	222	042	318	803

From 33° Latitude

To Latitude	Northern Hemisphere		Southern Hemisphere		Distance (nm)
	East	West	East	West	
43	038	322	142	218	763
42	042	318	138	222	719
41	045	315	135	225	677
40	049	311	131	229	639
39	054	306	126	234	604
38	059	301	121	239	573
37	064	296	116	244	547
36	070	290	110	250	526
35	077	283	103	257	511
34	083	274	097	263	504
33	090	270	090	270	503
32	097	263	083	277	509
31	103	257	077	283	523
30	109	251	071	289	542
29	115	245	065	295	567
28	120	240	060	300	597
27	125	235	055	305	632
26	129	231	051	309	670
25	132	228	048	312	711
24	136	224	044	316	754
23	138	222	042	318	800

From 34° Latitude

To Latitude	Northern Hemisphere		Southern Hemisphere		Distance (nm)
	East	West	East	West	
44	038	322	142	218	759
43	041	319	139	221	715
42	045	315	135	225	673
41	049	311	131	229	634
40	053	307	127	233	599
39	058	302	122	238	568
38	064	296	116	244	541
37	070	290	110	250	520
36	076	284	104	256	506
35	083	277	097	263	498
34	090	270	090	270	497
33	097	263	083	277	504
32	103	257	077	283	517
31	110	250	071	289	537
30	115	245	065	295	562
29	120	240	060	300	593
28	125	235	055	305	627
27	129	231	051	309	665
26	133	227	047	313	707
25	136	224	044	316	750
24	139	221	041	319	796

From 35° Latitude

To Latitude	Northern Hemisphere		Southern Hemisphere		Distance (nm)
	East	West	East	West	
45	038	322	142	218	754
44	041	319	139	221	710
43	044	316	136	224	668
42	048	312	132	228	629
41	053	307	127	233	594
40	058	302	122	238	562
39	064	296	116	244	536
38	070	290	110	250	515
37	076	284	104	256	500
36	083	277	097	263	492
35	090	270	090	270	491
34	097	263	083	277	498
33	104	256	076	283	511
32	110	250	070	290	531
31	115	245	065	295	557
30	121	239	059	301	588
29	125	235	055	305	623
28	129	231	051	309	661
27	133	227	047	333	703
26	136	224	044	316	747
25	139	221	041	319	793

From 36° Latitude

To Latitude	Northern Hemisphere		Southern Hemisphere		Distance (nm)
	East	West	East	West	
46	037	323	143	217	750
45	040	320	140	220	706
44	044	316	136	224	664
43	048	312	132	228	624
42	052	308	128	232	588
41	058	302	122	238	557
40	063	297	117	243	530
39	069	291	111	249	509
38	076	284	104	256	494
37	083	277	097	263	486
36	090	270	090	270	485
35	097	263	083	277	492
34	104	256	076	284	506
33	110	250	070	293	526
32	116	244	064	296	552
31	121	239	059	301	583
30	126	234	054	306	618
29	130	230	050	310	657
28	133	227	047	313	699
27	136	224	044	316	743
26	139	221	041	319	789

From 37° Latitude

To Latitude	Northern Hemisphere		Southern Hemisphere		Distance (nm)
	East	West	East	West	
47	037	323	143	217	746
46	040	320	140	220	701
45	043	317	137	223	659
44	048	312	132	228	619
43	052	308	128	232	583
42	057	303	123	237	551
41	063	297	117	243	524
40	069	291	111	249	503
39	076	284	104	256	488
38	083	277	097	263	480
37	090	270	090	270	478
36	097	263	083	277	486
35	104	256	076	284	500
34	110	250	070	290	520
33	116	244	064	296	547
32	121	238	059	301	578
31	126	234	054	306	613
30	130	230	050	310	653
29	134	226	046	314	695
28	137	223	043	317	739
27	140	220	040	320	786

From 38° Latitude

To Latitude	Northern Hemisphere		Southern Hemisphere		Distance (nm)
	East	West	East	West	
48	036	324	144	216	742
47	039	321	141	219	697
46	043	317	137	223	654
45	047	313	133	227	614
44	052	308	128	232	579
43	057	303	123	237	545
42	063	297	117	243	518
41	069	291	111	249	496
40	076	284	104	256	481
39	083	277	097	263	473
38	090	270	090	270	472
37	097	263	083	277	479
36	104	256	076	284	494
35	110	250	070	290	515
34	116	244	064	296	541
33	122	238	058	302	573
32	126	234	054	306	609
31	130	230	050	310	648
30	134	226	046	314	690
29	137	223	043	317	735
28	140	220	040	320	782

From 39° Latitude

To Latitude	Northern Hemisphere		Southern Hemisphere		Distance (nm)
	East	West	East	West	
49	036	324	144	216	738
48	039	321	141	219	692
47	043	317	137	223	649
46	047	313	133	227	609
45	051	309	129	231	572
44	056	304	124	236	540
43	062	298	118	242	512
42	069	291	111	249	490
41	075	285	105	255	474
40	083	277	097	263	467
39	090	270	090	270	466
38	097	263	083	277	473
37	104	256	076	284	487
36	111	249	069	291	509
35	117	243	063	297	536
34	122	238	058	302	568
33	127	233	053	307	604
32	131	229	049	311	644
31	134	226	046	314	686
30	137	223	043	317	731
29	140	220	040	320	778

From 40° Latitude

To Latitude	Northern Hemisphere		Southern Hemisphere		Distance (nm)
	East	West	East	West	
50	035	325	145	215	733
49	039	321	141	219	688
48	042	318	138	222	644
47	046	314	134	226	604
46	051	309	129	231	567
45	056	304	124	236	534
44	062	298	118	242	506
43	068	292	112	248	484
42	075	285	105	255	468
41	083	277	097	263	460
40	090	270	090	270	459
39	097	263	083	277	467
38	104	256	076	284	481
37	111	249	069	291	503
36	117	243	063	297	530
35	122	238	058	302	562
34	127	233	053	301	599
33	131	229	049	311	639
32	135	225	045	315	682
31	138	222	042	318	727
30	141	219	039	321	775

From 41° Latitude

To Latitude	Northern Hemisphere		Southern Hemisphere		Distance (nm)
	East	West	East	West	
51	03	325	145	215	729
50	038	322	142	218	683
49	042	318	138	222	640
48	046	314	134	226	599
47	050	310	130	230	561
46	056	304	124	236	528
45	061	299	119	241	500
44	068	292	112	248	477
43	075	285	105	255	461
42	082	228	098	262	453
41	090	270	090	270	453
40	098	262	082	278	460
39	105	255	075	285	475
38	111	249	069	291	496
37	117	243	063	297	524
36	123	237	057	303	557
35	127	233	053	307	594
34	131	229	049	311	634
33	13	225	045	315	677
32	138	222	042	318	723
31	141	219	039	321	771

From 42° Latitude

To Latitude	Northern Hemisphere		Southern Hemisphere		Distance (nm)
	East	West	East	West	
52	034	326	146	214	725
51	038	322	142	218	679
50	041	319	139	221	635
49	045	315	135	225	593
48	050	310	130	230	556
47	055	305	125	235	522
46	061	299	119	241	493
45	068	292	112	248	471
44	075	285	105	255	455
43	082	278	098	262	446
42	090	270	090	270	446
41	098	262	082	278	453
40	105	255	075	285	468
39	112	248	068	292	490
38	118	242	062	298	518
37	123	237	057	303	551
36	128	232	052	308	588
35	132	228	048	312	629
34	135	225	045	315	673
33	139	221	041	319	719
32	141	219	039	321	767

From 43° Latitude

To Latitude	Northern Hemisphere		Southern Hemisphere		Distance (nm)
	East	West	East	West	
53	034	326	146	214	720
52	037	323	143	217	674
51	041	319	139	221	630
50	045	315	135	225	588
49	049	311	131	229	550
48	055	305	125	235	516
47	061	299	119	241	487
46	067	293	113	247	464
45	075	285	105	255	448
44	082	278	098	262	439
43	090	270	090	270	439
42	098	262	082	278	446
41	105	255	075	285	461
40	112	248	068	292	484
39	118	242	062	298	512
38	123	237	057	303	545
37	128	232	052	308	583
36	132	228	048	312	624
35	136	224	044	316	668
34	139	221	041	319	715
33	142	218	038	322	763

From 44° Latitude

To Latitude	Northern Hemisphere		Southern Hemisphere		Distance (nm)
	East	West	East	West	
54	031	327	147	213	716
53	037	323	143	217	669
52	040	320	140	220	625
51	044	316	166	224	583
50	049	311	131	229	544
49	054	306	126	234	510
48	060	300	120	240	480
47	067	293	113	247	457
46	074	286	106	254	441
45	082	278	098	262	432
44	090	270	090	270	431
43	098	262	082	278	439
42	105	255	075	285	455
41	112	248	068	292	477
40	118	242	062	298	506
39	124	236	056	304	540
38	128	232	052	308	578
37	133	227	047	313	619
36	136	224	044	316	664
35	139	221	041	319	710
34	142	218	038	322	759

From 45° Latitude

To Latitude	Northern Hemisphere		Southern Hemisphere		Distance (nm)
	East	West	East	West	
55	033	327	147	213	712
54	036	324	144	216	665
53	039	321	141	219	620
52	044	346	136	224	577
51	048	312	132	228	538
50	054	306	126	234	504
49	060	300	120	240	474
48	067	293	113	247	450
47	074	286	106	254	433
46	082	278	098	262	425
45	090	270	090	270	424
44	098	262	082	278	432
43	106	254	074	286	448
42	112	248	068	292	471
41	119	241	061	299	500
40	124	236	056	304	534
39	129	231	051	309	522
38	133	227	047	313	614
37	137	223	043	317	659
36	140	220	040	320	706
35	142	218	038	322	755

From 46° Latitude

To Latitude	Northern Hemisphere		Southern Hemisphere		Distance (nm)
	East	West	East	West	
56	032	328	148	212	707
55	035	325	145	215	660
54	039	321	141	219	615
53	043	317	137	223	572
52	048	312	132	228	533
51	053	307	127	233	497
50	059	301	121	239	467
49	066	294	114	246	443
48	074	286	106	254	426
47	082	278	098	262	417
46	090	270	090	270	417
45	098	262	082	278	425
44	106	254	074	286	441
43	113	247	067	293	464
42	119	241	061	299	493
41	125	235	055	305	528
40	129	231	051	309	567
39	133	227	047	313	609
38	137	223	043	317	654
37	140	220	040	320	701
36	143	217	037	323	750

From 47° Latitude

To Latitude	Northern Hemisphere		Southern Hemisphere		Distance (nm)
	East	West	East	West	
57	032	328	148	212	703
56	035	325	145	215	655
55	038	322	142	218	610
54	042	318	138	222	566
53	047	313	133	227	527
52	053	307	127	233	491
51	059	301	121	239	460
50	066	294	114	246	436
49	073	287	107	253	419
48	082	278	098	262	410
47	090	270	090	270	409
46	098	262	082	278	417
45	106	254	074	286	433
44	113	247	067	293	457
43	119	241	061	299	487
42	125	235	055	305	522
41	130	230	050	310	561
40	134	226	046	314	604
39	138	222	042	318	649
38	141	219	039	321	697
37	143	217	037	323	746

From 48° Latitude

To Latitude	Northern Hemisphere		Southern Hemisphere		Distance (nm)
	East	West	East	West	
58	031	329	149	211	699
57	034	326	146	214	651
56	038	322	142	218	604
55	042	318	138	222	561
54	047	313	133	227	521
53	052	308	128	232	485
52	058	302	122	238	454
51	065	295	115	245	428
50	073	287	107	253	401
49	081	279	099	261	402
48	090	270	090	270	401
47	098	262	082	278	410
46	106	254	074	286	426
45	114	246	066	294	450
44	120	240	060	300	480
43	125	235	055	305	516
42	130	230	050	310	556
41	134	226	046	314	599
40	138	222	042	318	644
39	141	219	039	321	692
38	144	216	036	324	742

From 49° Latitude

To Latitude	Northern Hemisphere		Southern Hemisphere		Distance (nm)
	East	West	East	West	
59	031	329	149	211	694
58	034	326	146	214	646
57	037	323	143	217	599
56	041	319	139	221	556
55	046	314	134	226	515
54	051	309	129	231	478
53	058	302	122	238	447
52	065	295	115	245	422
51	073	287	107	253	404
50	081	279	099	261	394
49	090	270	090	270	393
48	099	261	081	279	402
47	107	253	073	287	419
46	114	246	066	294	443
45	120	240	060	300	474
44	126	234	054	306	510
43	131	229	049	311	550
42	135	225	045	315	593
41	138	222	042	318	640
40	142	218	038	322	688
39	144	215	036	324	738

From 50° Latitude

To Latitude	Northern Hemisphere		Southern Hemisphere		Distance (nm)
	East	West	East	West	
60	030	330	150	210	690
59	033	327	147	213	641
58	036	324	144	216	594
57	040	320	140	220	550
56	045	315	135	225	509
55	051	309	129	231	472
54	057	303	123	237	440
53	064	296	116	244	414
52	072	288	108	252	396
51	081	279	099	261	386
50	090	270	090	270	385
49	099	261	081	279	394
48	107	253	073	287	411
47	114	246	066	294	436
46	121	239	059	301	467
45	126	234	054	306	504
44	131	229	049	311	544
43	135	225	045	315	588
42	139	221	041	319	635
41	142	218	038	322	683
40	145	215	035	325	733

From 51° Latitude

To Latitude	Northern Hemisphere		Southern Hemisphere		Distance (nm)
	East	West	East	West	
61	029	331	151	209	686
60	032	328	148	212	637
59	036	324	144	126	589
58	040	320	140	220	545
57	045	315	135	225	503
56	050	310	130	230	465
55	057	303	123	237	433
54	064	296	116	244	407
53	072	288	108	252	388
52	081	229	099	261	378
51	090	270	090	270	377
50	099	261	081	279	386
49	107	253	073	287	404
48	115	245	065	295	429
47	121	239	059	301	460
46	127	233	053	307	497
45	132	228	048	312	538
44	136	224	044	316	583
43	140	220	040	320	630
42	143	217	037	323	679
41	145	215	035	325	729

From 52° Latitude

To Latitude	Northern Hemisphere		Southern Hemisphere		Distance (nm)
	East	West	East	West	
62	029	331	151	209	682
61	032	328	148	212	632
60	035	325	145	215	584
59	039	321	141	219	539
58	044	316	136	224	497
57	049	311	131	229	459
56	056	304	124	236	426
55	063	297	117	243	399
54	072	288	108	252	380
53	081	279	099	261	370
52	090	270	090	270	369
51	099	261	081	279	378
50	108	252	072	288	396
49	115	245	065	295	422
48	122	238	058	302	454
47	128	232	052	308	491
46	132	228	048	312	533
45	137	223	043	317	577
44	140	220	040	320	625
43	143	217	037	323	674
42	146	214	034	326	725

From 53° Latitude

To Latitude	Northern Hemisphere		Southern Hemisphere		Distance (nm)
	East	West	East	West	
63	028	332	152	208	677
62	031	329	149	211	627
61	034	326	146	214	579
60	038	322	142	218	534
59	043	317	137	223	491
58	049	311	131	229	453
57	055	303	125	235	419
56	063	297	117	243	392
55	071	289	109	251	372
54	081	279	099	261	362
53	090	270	090	270	361
52	099	261	081	279	370
51	108	252	072	288	388
50	116	244	064	296	414
49	122	238	058	302	447
48	128	232	052	308	485
47	133	227	047	313	527
46	137	223	043	317	572
45	141	219	039	321	620
44	144	216	036	324	669
43	146	214	034	326	720

From 54° Latitude

To Latitude	Northern Hemisphere		Southern Hemisphere		Distance (nm)
	East	West	East	West	
64	027	333	153	207	673
63	030	330	150	210	623
62	034	326	146	214	574
61	038	322	142	218	528
60	042	318	138	222	485
59	048	312	132	228	446
58	055	305	125	235	412
57	062	298	118	242	384
56	071	289	109	251	364
55	080	280	100	260	353
54	090	270	090	270	352
53	100	260	080	280	362
52	108	252	072	288	380
51	116	244	064	296	407
50	123	237	057	303	440
49	129	231	051	309	478
48	134	226	046	314	521
47	138	222	042	318	566
46	141	219	039	321	615
45	144	216	036	324	665
44	147	213	033	327	716

From 55° Latitude

To Latitude	Northern Hemisphere		Southern Hemisphere		Distance (nm)
	East	West	East	West	
65	027	333	153	207	669
64	030	330	150	210	618
63	033	327	147	213	570
62	037	323	143	217	523
61	042	318	138	222	479
60	047	313	133	227	440
59	054	306	126	234	405
58	062	298	118	242	376
57	070	290	110	250	356
56	080	280	100	260	345
55	090	270	090	270	344
54	100	260	080	280	353
53	109	251	071	289	372
52	117	243	063	297	399
51	124	236	056	304	433
50	129	231	051	309	472
49	134	226	046	314	515
48	138	222	042	318	561
47	142	218	038	322	610
46	145	215	035	325	660
45	147	213	033	327	712

From 56° Latitude

To Latitude	Northern Hemisphere		Southern Hemisphere		Distance (nm)
	East	West	East	West	
66	026	334	154	206	665
65	029	331	151	209	614
64	032	328	148	212	565
63	036	324	144	216	318
62	041	319	139	221	473
61	046	314	134	226	433
60	053	307	127	233	398
59	061	299	119	241	369
58	070	290	110	250	348
57	080	280	100	260	336
56	090	270	090	270	335
55	100	260	080	280	345
54	109	251	071	289	364
53	117	243	063	297	392
52	124	236	056	304	426
51	130	230	050	310	465
50	134	226	046	314	509
49	139	221	041	319	556
48	142	218	038	322	604
47	145	215	035	325	655
46	148	212	032	328	707

From 57° Latitude

To Latitude	Northern Hemisphere		Southern Hemisphere		Distance (nm)
	East	West	East	West	
67	025	335	155	205	661
66	028	332	152	208	610
65	031	329	149	211	560
64	035	325	145	215	512
63	040	320	140	220	468
62	046	314	134	226	427
61	052	308	128	232	391
60	060	300	120	240	361
59	069	291	111	249	339
58	079	281	101	259	328
57	090	270	090	270	327
56	100	260	080	280	336
55	110	250	070	290	355
54	118	242	062	298	384
53	125	235	055	305	419
52	131	229	049	311	459
51	136	224	044	316	503
50	140	220	040	320	550
49	143	217	037	323	599
48	146	214	034	326	651
47	148	212	032	328	703

From 58° Latitude

To Latitude	Northern Hemisphere		Southern Hemisphere		Distance (nm)
	East	West	East	West	
68	025	335	155	205	657
67	027	333	153	207	605
66	031	329	149	211	555
65	034	326	146	214	507
64	039	321	141	219	462
63	045	315	135	225	420
62	051	309	129	231	384
61	060	300	120	240	353
60	069	291	111	249	331
59	079	281	101	259	319
58	090	270	090	270	318
57	101	259	079	281	328
56	110	250	070	290	348
55	119	241	061	299	376
54	126	234	054	306	412
53	131	229	049	311	453
52	136	224	044	316	497
51	140	220	040	320	545
50	144	216	036	324	594
49	146	214	034	326	646
48	149	211	031	329	699

From 59° Latitude

To Latitude	Northern Hemisphere		Southern Hemisphere		Distance (nm)
	East	West	East	West	
69	024	336	156	204	653
68	027	333	153	207	601
67	030	330	150	210	550
66	034	326	146	214	502
65	038	322	142	218	456
64	044	316	136	224	414
63	051	309	129	231	376
62	059	301	121	239	345
61	068	292	112	248	323
60	079	281	101	259	310
59	090	270	090	270	309
58	101	259	079	281	319
57	111	249	069	291	339
56	119	241	061	299	369
55	126	234	054	306	405
54	132	228	048	312	446
53	137	223	043	317	491
52	141	219	039	321	539
51	144	216	036	324	589
50	147	213	033	327	641
49	150	210	030	330	694

From 60° Latitude

To Latitude	Northern Hemisphere		Southern Hemisphere		Distance (nm)
	East	West	East	West	
70	023	337	157	203	649
69	026	334	154	206	597
68	029	331	151	209	546
67	033	327	147	213	497
66	037	323	143	217	450
65	043	317	137	223	408
64	050	310	130	230	369
63	058	302	122	238	338
62	068	292	112	248	314
61	079	281	101	259	301
60	090	270	090	270	300
59	101	259	079	281	310
58	111	249	069	291	331
57	120	240	060	300	361
56	127	233	053	307	398
55	133	227	047	313	440
54	138	222	042	318	485
53	142	218	038	322	534
52	145	215	035	325	584
51	148	212	032	328	637
50	150	210	030	330	690

From 61° Latitude

To Latitude	Northern Hemisphere		Southern Hemisphere		Distance (nm)
	East	West	East	West	
71	022	338	158	202	646
70	025	335	155	205	593
69	028	332	152	208	541
68	032	328	148	212	492
67	036	324	144	216	445
66	042	318	138	222	401
65	049	311	131	229	362
64	057	303	123	237	330
63	067	293	113	247	306
62	078	282	102	258	292
61	090	270	090	270	291
60	102	258	078	282	301
59	112	248	068	292	323
58	121	239	059	301	353
57	128	232	052	308	391
56	134	226	046	314	433
55	139	221	041	319	479
54	142	218	038	322	528
53	146	214	034	326	579
52	148	212	032	328	632
51	151	209	029	331	686

From 62° Latitude

To Latitude	Northern Hemisphere		Southern Hemisphere		Distance (nm)
	East	West	East	West	
72	021	339	159	201	642
71	024	336	156	204	589
70	027	333	153	207	537
69	031	329	149	211	487
68	035	325	145	215	439
67	041	319	139	221	395
66	048	312	132	228	355
65	056	304	124	236	322
64	066	294	114	246	297
63	078	282	102	258	283
62	090	270	090	270	281
61	102	258	078	282	292
60	112	248	068	292	314
59	121	239	059	301	345
58	129	231	051	309	384
57	135	225	045	315	427
56	139	221	041	319	473
55	143	217	037	323	523
54	146	216	034	326	574
53	149	211	031	329	627
52	151	209	029	331	682

From 63° Latitude

To Latitude	Northern Hemisphere		Southern Hemisphere		Distance (nm)
	East	West	East	West	
73	021	339	159	201	639
72	023	337	157	203	585
71	026	334	154	206	533
70	030	330	150	210	482
69	034	326	146	214	434
68	040	320	140	220	389
67	047	313	133	227	348
66	055	305	125	235	314
65	066	294	114	246	289
64	077	283	103	257	274
63	090	270	090	270	272
62	102	258	078	282	283
61	113	247	067	293	306
60	122	238	058	302	338
59	129	231	051	309	376
58	135	225	045	315	420
57	140	220	040	320	468
56	144	216	036	324	518
55	147	213	033	327	570
54	150	210	030	330	623
53	152	208	028	332	677

From 64° Latitude

To Latitude	Northern Hemisphere		Southern Hemisphere		Distance (nm)
	East	West	East	West	
73	022	338	158	202	582
72	025	335	155	205	529
71	029	331	151	209	478
70	033	327	147	213	429
69	039	321	141	219	383
68	046	314	134	226	342
67	054	306	126	234	307
66	065	295	115	245	281
65	077	283	103	257	265
64	090	270	090	270	263
63	103	257	077	283	275
62	114	246	066	294	298
61	123	237	057	303	330
60	130	230	050	310	370
59	136	224	044	316	414
58	141	219	039	321	462
57	145	215	035	325	513
56	148	212	032	328	565
55	150	210	030	330	619
54	153	207	027	333	674

From 65° Latitude

To Latitude	Northern Hemisphere		Southern Hemisphere		Distance (nm)
	East	West	East	West	
74	021	339	159	201	578
73	024	336	156	204	524
72	028	332	152	208	473
71	032	328	148	212	423
70	037	323	143	217	377
69	044	316	136	224	335
68	053	307	127	233	299
67	064	296	116	244	272
66	076	284	104	256	256
65	270	090	270	270	254
64	103	257	077	283	265
63	114	246	066	294	289
62	124	236	056	304	322
61	131	229	049	311	363
60	137	223	043	317	408
59	142	218	038	322	456
58	146	214	034	326	507
57	149	211	031	329	559
56	151	209	029	331	614
55	153	207	027	333	669

About Me

I am an average pilot with average stick and rudder skills, but with an above average desire to learn and instruct. I spent twenty years in the United States Air Force as an aircraft commander, instructor pilot, evaluator pilot, and squadron commander. After retiring as a lieutenant colonel, I went on to fly for several private and commercial operators as an international captain, check airman, and chief pilot. My logbook includes the T-37B, T-38A, KC-135A, Boeing 707, Boeing 747, Challenger 604, the Gulfstream III, IV, V, G450, and VII, as well as several aircraft I've test flown for Aviation Week. My website, www.code7700.com attracts five million hits each month and my articles have appeared in several magazines, including Aviation Week. As you can see from this book, I am still writing, trying to get everything out of my head before it disappears.

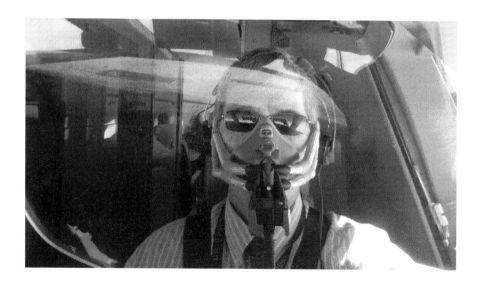

Made in United States
Orlando, FL
07 April 2025

60279732R00181